LITERARY MONOGRAPHS · Volume 2

Literary Monographs is appearing under the sponsorship of the Department of English, University of Wisconsin.

LITERARY
MONOGRAPHS
Volume 2

EDITED BY
Eric Rothstein
AND
Richard N. Ringler

THE UNIVERSITY OF WISCONSIN PRESS
Madison, Milwaukee, and London, 1969

Published by
The University of Wisconsin Press
Box 1379, Madison, Wisconsin 53701
The University of Wisconsin Press, Ltd.
27–29 Whitfield Street, London, W.1

Printed in the United States of America by
The Heffernan Press Inc., Worcester, Mass.

Standard Book Number 299-05410-1
Library of Congress Catalog
Card Number 66-25869

PREFACE

The Department of English of the University of Wisconsin continues with this volume a series of monographs in English and American literature. The series was inaugurated in 1967 to serve scholars whose work might take a form too lengthy for journals but too brief for a separate book.

For future volumes of *Literary Monographs* we invite works of high quality, scholarly or critical, that contribute to English or American literary studies. We welcome any promising contribution, from the United States or from abroad. We welcome not only conventional literary essays but also those involving experimental critical theories and methods whenever they are eloquent and persuasive. And we will be flexible enough to welcome monographs involving comparative literature or comparative aesthetics, so long as they significantly illuminate literature in English.

Eric Rothstein

Madison, Wisconsin
November 1968

NOTES ON SUBMISSIONS

Manuscripts should be from 15,000 to 35,000 words in length. They should be submitted, with return postage and self-addressed envelope enclosed, to

> The Editor
> *Literary Monographs*
> Department of English
> University of Wisconsin
> Madison, Wisconsin 53706

Manuscripts should follow the *MLA Style Sheet*, with a few exceptions or amplifications included in the specific instructions given below.

1. Paper should be 16-pound or 20-pound weight bond in normal quarto size; do not use highly glazed paper (sold under such trade names as "Corrasable"). To make satisfactory photocopying possible, the paper should be white and the typewriter ribbon black. Handwritten corrections may be made in pencil or washable ink; avoid ballpoint pen. Leave margins of 1 to 1½ inches on all sides.

2. Manuscripts should be double spaced throughout, including notes and all excerpts, prose or verse. Do not indent prose excerpts, but mark them with a pencil line along the left margin to the full length of the quotation and allow an extra line of space above and below.

3. Brief references should be inserted in the text (see *MLA Style Sheet*, Sec. 13*f*). In notes, first references should be cited in full. Succeeding references to books should use short titles rather than "*op. cit.*"; e.g., Taylor, *Problems*, p. 12. Short references to journal articles should use author's name, journal name, volume, and page; e.g., McKerrow, *RES*, XVI, 117.

As can be seen from this volume, *Literary Monographs* reserves the use of footnotes for information that is needed in order to follow the argument of the text or to understand a system of in-text citation. Endnotes supply documentation, or they may extend or parallel the text discussion. Contributors are requested to organize their manuscripts so that endnotes and footnotes are on separate pages, with separate numbering sequences.

CONTENTS

WINGLESS VICTORY:
MICHELANGELO, SHAKESPEARE,
AND THE "OLD MAN"

Lawrence J. Ross

The emblematic woodcut on the part-title page—an instance of the variously interpreted motif of wings-countered-by-a-weight commonplace in Renaissance imagery—was used as a printer's mark in England from 1563 (Ronald B. Mc-Kerrow, *Printers' & Publishers' Devices in England & Scotland, 1485–1640* [London, 1949], No. 142). It is reproduced here from the 1597 Quarto of *The Tragedie of King Richard the Second* (V. Simmes for A. Wise) by permission of the Huntington Library, San Marino, California.

Michelangelo's "Victory" and Shakespeare's *Henry IV* plays hardly leap into the mind as Renaissance works aptly associated or even likely to be brought into useful conjunction in a critical context. Yet in point of fact they do have in common an important feature, study of which not only has intrinsic interest but also enables their interpretation. At first, it may seem critically insignificant that an old man prominently figures in each of these works: these old men so obviously differ that resemblance between them would appear to end with their mere age. Under iconographic analysis, however, this elementary motif is revealed to be the bearer of a secondary, conventional significance, and these old men thereby prove to be versions of the same traditional image. Identification and study of this image have been neglected prerequisites of interpretation of the works themselves. That they of course can be only prerequisites, the patent disparity of the works will not let us forget. The critical problem is to determine how these very distinctive artists, working in different media and quite different circumstances, particularly adapted the image and made it their own.

The student of iconography has perhaps to be wary of even more pitfalls than are found in the paths of other sorts of historical criticism. Were it only because monolithic and unhistorical attitudes sometimes have been engendered by interest in traditional imagery, we might be cautioned to confront at the outset the inherent complexity of our inquiry. Here I would first emphasize a basic point. Having identified a traditional image, we dare not assume we may then invoke unimpaired the whole tradition which had earlier been its matrix. Iconographic formulas, even when they survive from age to changing age, alter in force. They undergo sometimes subtle, sometimes very radical, transformation according to general and individual context. Within the same period they may have very different valences, and indeed they may mean quite different things even in the same hands at different times within one career.

Such considerations have affected the purpose, methods, and limits of this study. My immediate object with each of the works considered will be to indicate how, under the pressure of an individual creative effort occurring in a specific postmedieval context, a traditional image has been transformed in the course of the artist's use of it. I shall be concerned to show how study of these transformations is important to historical criticism of both the particular works and the larger projects of which they were parts. However, the different transformations themselves and the representative tensions, characteristic of two aspects of the Renaissance, that become apparent in study of them comprise my overarching interests. These have determined the emphasis and limits of the criticism here attempted; and they explain the purpose of bringing together into one essay separate treatments of the disparate works. Studied together they are illustrative, as apart they could not be, of the characteristically various, and culturally revelatory, vicissitudes of inherited imagery in Renaissance artistic use; yet their very distinctiveness, with the critical obligations which that entails, is part of my point.

The reader should thus be disabused of possible expectations regarding its unity which such a cross-discipline study as this is bound to disappoint—by design. In particular, the reader may be tempted to make one assumption which I have not made. He may suppose that the study of Michelangelo's sculpture necessarily can be relevant to the whole only to the extent that it directly illuminates Shakespeare's dramatic practice. But to prove such a connection is not what I am trying to do. I am interested in a very different whole and therefore posit a different standard for the relevance of the parts. To expect such an argument will be to misconstrue my purposes which require that these works be accorded autonomous consideration. Actually, to some extent, and at some remove, study of the sculpture does shed some light on the plays. It will become apparent not only that these works share conventional images other than the central one emphasized, but also that they both are fundamentally dependent on aspects of the same widely diffused tradition. But it should be said im-

mediately that the illumination hopefully achieved by bringing extended treatment of them together has to do with something related
but different: the fact that they differently illustrate, in their transformations of the same image, consequences of the conflicted creative
situations produced by what C. R. Morey called "the collision of
mediæval Christianity with the Renaissance."[1] Those conflicted situations have humanistic interest in themselves, and they are crucial to
our understanding of the art that came out of them. On these terms,
indeed, the extraordinary complexity in representation characteristic
of these works becomes accountable. And so, in part, do their lasting
power and problematic fascination; for the Renaissance giants who
created them were led, by their exploration of the conflicts from which
their art in great measure springs, to radical contradictions in the
nature of human experience itself.

The motif to which I draw attention in these works—an old man—
was, as they themselves will compel us to recall, capable of development into a number of *topoi* turning on contrast of youth and age. In
the complex treatments of such a contrast in these works, however,
one conventional figurative conception of "the old man" appears to me
to be pivotal. It is found in the traditions of Christian theology. The
term "old man" is developed by St. Paul as an image of unregenerate
human nature in the sinful pattern of the fallen Adam, corrupt according to the deceitful lusts, unregenerated through grace, unjustified and
unredeemed through Christ. The *vetus homo,* which Paul elsewhere
calls "the body of sin," represents man's captive spiritual state, his
bondage to "the flesh" and its corrupt inclination;[2] he is opposed to
the New Man in the image of whom the Christian, by accepted grace,
is renewed in spirit and reborn to newness of life. The contrast traditionally imaged here, it might be stressed, is not between the body
and the soul, but between unregenerate and renewed or rejuvenated
spiritual states of man.[3] As a consequence of original sin all men are
considered to be in the image of the Old Man—or Old Adam; they
are sons resembling, in their *vita vetus in peccatis,* their father who
fell from the image of God;[4] and therefore they need to be reborn to
a new life as sons of their Father in heaven (Rom. viii.15–17) so that
they may be "made heirs according to the hope of eternal life" (Titus
iii.5–7).[5] By baptism the Christian is said to be buried with Christ,
to crucify the Old Man, to die to sin, and to be reborn in the image of
the New Man who "is renewed in knowledge, after the image of him

that created him" (Col. iii.10). The exemplar of this New Man, or Young Man (as he is sometimes called and later represented in art),[6] is the New Adam, Christ (Rom. xiii.14).[7] Thus Paul to the Romans (vi.3–6):

Know ye not, that so many of us as were baptized into Jesus Christ, were baptized into his death?

Therefore we are buried with him by baptism into death, that like as Christ was raised up from the dead by the glory of the Father, even so we also should walk in newness of life.

For if we have been planted together in the likeness of his death, we shall be also in the likeness of his resurrection.

Knowing this, that our old man is crucified with him, that the body of sin might be destroyed, that henceforth we should not serve sin.

As Christ was crucified in the flesh and buried to overthrow the Old Law, so ought the Old Man in everyman be crucified and buried, first in baptism, and then afterwards by service of God renewed in mortification and penance; for by such death to sin man attains to spiritual life, here reborn in spirit to freedom, as "a new creature" (Gal. vi.15) under the New Law. This is the burden of Christ's own message to Nicodemus: "Verily, verily I say unto thee, except a man be born again, he cannot see the kingdom of God." It will be recalled that the puzzled Nicodemus queries, "How can a man be reborn when he is old?" (John iii.3–4). The answer, for already baptized Christians, is developed in St. Paul's warning to the Ephesians to live according to that second nature received by them at baptism (Eph. iv.22–24):

. . . put off concerning the former conversation, the old man, which is corrupt according to the deceitful lusts:

And be renewed in the spirit of your mind:

And . . . put on that new man, which after God is created in righteousness, and true holiness.

This Old Man and his regenerate opposite represent, then, a central figurative embodiment of the Christian dual awareness of man—as fallen and imperfect being, as possible "partaker of the divine nature" (II Pet. i.4). And their history necessarily reflects the long and complex controversies about the constellation of doctrines—justification, sanctification, baptism, divine adoption—involved in them. Their appearances in art invariably, and variously, invoke their traditional connection with the idea of regeneration, a theme definitive of man's

relation to his own ideal spiritual potentialities, a theme necessarily
implicated in altering conceptions of man's place in the universal
order. For this reason this Old Man is worth studying for the reflection of cultural changes which his Renaissance transformations evidence. In the works to be considered here the image is in various
degrees and ways disengaged from its theological, and even its Christian, significance. Each of the works in its own way illustrates that
recasting of inherited medieval material characteristic of the Renaissance. In one case this is due in part to the creative interpenetration
of classic and Christian traditions; in the other, it appears to be due to
the disharmonies—the only tenuously reconcilable disharmonies—
existing between actual values and circumstances, and assumed traditional ideals. The traditional conception of the Old Man is altered as
the image is supposedly merged or actually thrown into conflict with
attitudes and ideas answering to different premises. The image thus
appears to us a focal point for ambivalences in Renaissance views of
man, and for the creative urge to their resolution. It remained a useful
expressive instrument because it yet retained for these Renaissance
artists a capacity to serve as a measure of man's reach and his actuality, as a means of assessing the authorities by which he might live,
and the imperfection from which he suffers.

II

The first of these works is the sculpture in marble by Michelangelo
known as the "Victory," or "Genius of Victory," in the Salone dei Cin-
quecento of the Palazzo Vecchio in Florence (Figs. 1 and 2). It
represents a nude tall young man with his left knee on the back of
a bound defeated adversary from whom he turns with a gesture instinct with energy; the vanquished is represented as an old man in
Roman-like armor, bowed down, it would seem, by a force greater
than the youth exerts, his face a dark study of tortured immobility.
A half century ago Carl Justi described this group as probably the
most puzzling of all of Michelangelo's works.[8] And in fact the
"Victory" is one of the very few major works of the artist about which
no document or other contemporary record distinctly comments.
Nevertheless, certain things can be asserted about it, the first being
that it was never intended to stand alone but was so designed as to
require a counterpart group. Its placement in the vast Gran Sala of

the Palazzo Vecchio in 1564 resulted in the commissioning of a pendant executed for the hall in 1567–1568 by Giovanni da Bologna. A
counterpart of the "Victory" at least visually, this is a political allegory
sometimes later called "Virtue Triumphant over Vice." Michelangelo
never executed his own pendant to his group, but it has been thought
that a free paraphrase of his design for it is probably to be seen in
another psychomachic group, Vincenzo Danti's "Honor Conquering
Deceit," in the Bargello (Fig. 3).[9] That Michelangelo's "Victory"
should require a pendant accords well with what remains the most
important piece of early evidence about it: Vasari's statement, in his
1568 life of Michelangelo, that the "Victory" was intended to have
formed part of the Tomb of Julius II.[10] Other indications corroborate
Vasari's statement. The oak leaves crowning the Victor's head are not
only a symbol of victory but a known emblem of the Della Rovere, the
Pope's family.[11] The forward curve of the block (Fig. 1) suggests,
moreover, that the statue was intended for a niche; and Victory
groups, to be placed in niches, are called for in more than one of
Michelangelo's designs for this monument, and for this one only.

Michelangelo's awesome repute at his death in 1564 was based not
only on his completed works but on the living memory of his great
projects. The most important of these had been the sepulchral monument for his patron, Pope Julius II, commissioned by that pontiff in
1505. Michelangelo continued to be involved in the creation of this
heroic tomb for the next four decades, during which time the work
was postponed and suspended but never entirely abandoned as the
artist was required to preoccupy himself with such major under-
takings as the ceiling of the Sistine Chapel, the façade of San Lorenzo,
the Medici Chapel, and "The Last Judgment." In the face of these
vast ventures the obligation to complete the tomb, not removed until
1545, became an oppressive nightmare to the artist so that in old age
he characteristically wrote: "I realize I lost all of my youth chained
to this tomb."[12] After innumerable vicissitudes, the tomb was finally
erected by Michelangelo himself, in 1542–1545, in San Pietro in Vincoli in Rome, in a reduced form which belied the ambition of the
original plans (Fig. 4). This final version, a redaction of his sixth
project for the tomb, represents a near-abandonment of the inspiration
which had informed the earlier more monumental projects. This was
due in part to his desperation to be free of the tomb, in part also to
the collapse, inevitable under the circumstances, of the artist's attempt

to bring a more heroic conception to fruition. The erected monument, a cenotaph rather than a tomb, is a lamentable compromise in which only three statues have been worked by Michelangelo's own hand, and two of these have been hastily done as replacements. The great "Moses" survives from an earlier project, though it has been displaced from the position for which it was originally carved. But a number of other statues created by Michelangelo for earlier rejected projects of the tomb found no place whatever in the monument finally erected. These are the two "Captives" (now in the Louvre), the four unfinished "Slaves" (now in the Accademia in Florence), and the "Victory" in the Palazzo Vecchio.

This means, in short, that really to understand Michelangelo's "Victory" group we must see it, as it has not invariably or entirely been seen, in its proper context, as an integral part of a larger monument which was never realized; we can evaluate it more truly only by comprehending how it was intended to fit in one of Michelangelo's earlier projects for the tomb. In deciding with which of the earlier projects the group was associated, we find the evidence for the statue's dating, though insufficient, of some importance. External evidence sets a date between 1519 (when the marble used was first available) and 1534 (when Michelangelo left his native Florence, where the work was found and undoubtedly had been carved). Stylistically, the slender figure of the victorious youth, with his small head, elongated but muscular body, and fine extremities, most resembles the "Giuliano" and the "Madonna" of the Medici Chapel, which were executed around 1531–1532. To get some idea of the nature of Michelangelo's ideas for the Tomb of Julius II around this time, it is essential that we consider, however cursorily, the most pertinent aspects of the rather complicated history of his conception to that point.*

The earliest projects of the Tomb of Julius II were quite as magnificently ambitious as Vasari claims. It would appear that the monu-

* In my slender account of the Tomb of Julius II, severely abbreviated and simplified for present purposes, I am heavily indebted to earlier studies, especially those of Tolnay, Panofsky, and Wilde (cited in nn. 9, 13, 15, and 29, below). Reference to their reconstructions of the different projects, although they are in many respects conjectural, at variance with one another, and individually open to question, nevertheless will clarify the present limited discussion and its own attempted contribution. For the convenience of the reader, I have illustrated, in Figs. 6–9, each of the major unrealized projects with one pictorial reconstruction selected from the work of these scholars. I also reproduce, in Fig. 5, the preliminary drawing for the 1513 contract in the copy attributed to Jacomo Rocchetti, which probably is a reliable guide regarding the lower story of the first projects.

ment according to the first project (1505) was to be an imposing freestanding structure in the form of a truncated stepped pyramid, whose various stages were to house "more than forty" statues in marble. The lower story of the exterior was to consist of a sequence of niches, each containing a Victory group, which were to be flanked by figures of Slaves (*prigioni*), tied to herms and standing on projecting pedestals. The corners of the platform above were to have four large statues: two figures personifying the Active Life and the Contemplative Life, a Moses, and (Vasari says) a St. Paul. A still higher platform was to be the base for two angels who were to carry a bier with the image of the Pope.[13]

This monument was to be placed in St. Peter's directly above the Confessio of the Prince of the Apostles, and thus conceivably was designed, as Tolnay has suggested, as a double commemoration: it was perhaps to have celebrated not merely the triumph of this particular Pope in death as well as life, but also the triumph of the Apostolic Church and the way of life inaugurated by it.[14] But already in this first projection of the work, this triumph has been simultaneously universalized in terms not in precise keeping with orthodox Christian dogma. In contrast with preceding Christian tombs, which show an abrupt division between terrestrial and celestial spheres, this monument has an emphasized transitional or intermediary zone, indicative of the Neoplatonic bias in the conception of the Pope's rise to apotheosis.[15] "There is a ladder," writes Pico della Mirandola, "extending from the lowest earth to the highest heaven, divided in a series of many steps . . . ."[16] The structure of the tomb in the first project is by now generally recognized to suggest in its levels the stages of purgation of the soul in its rise on the *scala platonica* toward pure contemplation of the Deity. The statues of the first platform, the intermediary zone, bear this out. For the Florentine Neoplatonists, Moses and St. Paul were the two exemplary figures of men in whom the soul, recovering from its descent into matter, has so mastered and purged its lower nature that the Mind—the superior part of the Higher Soul—can be freed to look up to the celestial sphere above it. It thereby wins a promise of redemption after death and makes possible, during this life, that devotion to *iustitia* and *religio*—the principles of action and contemplation, called "the two wings of the soul" by Cristoforo Landino—by which the soul is raised to higher spheres.[17]

By the time of the second project (1513), the plan to place the tomb in the new St. Peter's had been abandoned and with it the free-standing aspect of the monument and its (conjectured) double com-memorative purpose. The universal theme of the program thus could appear more distinctly. After the death of the Pope, his heirs (writes Michelangelo) "wished to increase the size of his Tomb, that is, to execute a larger work than the one I had first designed."[18] The monu-ment is now to be attached to a wall. The main innovation is the surmounting of the tomb with a high apse (*cappelletta*), projecting from the wall, which was to house (probably at the instance of the heirs) five huge statues of a Madonna and four saints. The static pyramid of the first design has thus been given a great ascending impetus, soaring with a final central accent to a now decidedly Chris-tian supercelestial level. However, while the highest level has now been made much more orthodox, other aspects of the project show that the Neoplatonic conception persists, no doubt on a Ficinian assumption of a consonance between Christian theology and Platonic doctrine. The intermediary zone not only remains but in fact has grown: six great seated figures are now planned. Moreover, although the lowest level remains unchanged in basic plan from the first project, we know from other evidence that, in Michelangelo's plans for their execution, the Slaves were already undergoing a development from mere trophies to symbolic figures, which would make the lower story more distinctly represent a terrestrial level of existence conceived in Neoplatonic terms. Since virtually nothing is known about the robed and winged female Victory figures still planned for the niches between the Slaves, this development of the Slave figures, to whose content the Victories would necessarily have been related, is our surest way of under-standing the growth of Michelangelo's thinking about the Victory groups.

Unfortunately, the interpretations of the Slaves which survive from Michelangelo's own lifetime tend to obscure this basic line of develop-ment. For they distract us with mutually contradictory notions which at best imperfectly represent delimited or tentative aspects of the artist's evolving idea. These interpretations were recorded some fifty years after the original conception of the tomb, in the lives of Michel-angelo by Condivi and Vasari. Condivi says the Slaves represented "the liberal arts as Painting, Sculpture, Architecture," and that they were fettered to show that, like the Pope, they were "prisoners of death, because they could never find such favor and nourishment as he gave them."[19] Vasari asserted that the Slaves symbolized the provinces subdued by the Pope to the true Church; in the second edition of his biography he undercuts his own authority by trying to conflate this interpretation with Condivi's.[20] There is perhaps (as Tolnay says) some remembrance of the 1505 St. Peter's project in the idea of conquest by the Church of those *ante lege*.[21] But, as stated, neither of these interpretations could apply to the 1505 project, for (as long ago observed) at that date Pope Julius had not yet subjugated any provinces or deserved fame as a patron of art. Moreover, at least sixteen and perhaps as many as twenty slaves were called for in that first design, and there simply would not have been enough liberal arts to go around. Edgar Wind remarks that "errors of description in Condivi are so frequent that . . . it is impossible to trust him on any detail."[22] Still, his testimony cannot be put aside, since this loyal and simple man did write with the benefit of Michelangelo's advice, and he does not elaborately fabricate.

In consequence, Professor Janson has proposed that Condivi's interpretation of the Slaves as personifications of the liberal arts may refer to the 1513 project, the first in which the number of Slaves was sufficiently reduced. And he finds possible evidence of such a plan's existence, and of its tentative nature, in the lightly sketched apes just discernible in the rough stone behind each of the two Louvre Slaves carved for the 1513 project (Figs. 10–12).[23] Now certainly it is true that the idea *ars simia naturæ,* normally applied to painting, could apply to other representational arts as well. One difficulty with this suggestion, however (already pointed out by Tolnay), is that slaves never were used to personify an art either before Michelangelo or, more significant, considering his huge influence, after him. A still more telling difficulty is that the delimited meaning for the statues which results when the apes are viewed as attributes of personified arts patently disagrees with the much broader and more profound expressive content of the Slave figures themselves. Fortunately, there are other possible interpretations of the apes—based on their ancient significance as symbols of slavery or of a lower level of existence—which better accord with the expressive scope of the statues.[24]

In the pursuit of the main line of Michelangelo's developing conception, we do much better, I think, to follow the evidence of his own designs. The Captives of the early projects are rather quiet and delicate, their forms undictated by any radical perturbation, as can be seen in the surviving visual evidence of the lower story of the designs (Figs. 5 and 13).[25] In six pen sketches of slaves preliminary to work on the 1513 project preserved at Oxford, these figures have already been markedly transformed, partly under the influence of the Laocoön, into defeated Titanic figures doomed to futile rebellion against their bonds (Fig. 14).[26] This conception reaches fruition in the two Louvre Slaves actually executed for the 1513 project (Figs. 10 and 11). Here the visible bands or fetters are merely the outward sign of an inner bondage, as Michelangelo evokes memories of earlier moralized fettered prisoners who had symbolized unregenerate human nature captive to sensual appetites. The two Louvre Slaves, succumbing and unavailingly rebellious, appear to represent immortal souls left devoid of freedom by their descent into matter. And the apes behind them, whose sketched forms are scarcely realized in the stone, whatever their origin in a tentative narrower program, are most consistently understood in relation to the Slaves if given the universal significance which Dr. Panofsky once suggested. They serve to help the figures symbolize the immortal soul suffering, in human nature, its capacity to be deprived of freedom by allowing the ascendancy of the animal and material nature it shares in common with the brutes. It may be supposed, then, that in the most continuous pattern of Michelangelo's thinking the corresponding Victories of the terrestrial zone were likely to have symbolized the attainment of such freedom as can be won by the enlightened Reason's control over the claims of man's Lower Soul.[27]

In 1516, in agreement with the Pope's heirs, the projected tomb began to be markedly reduced in size and scope.[28] But the new design represents a highly original development in which Michelangelo retained the dynamic organization of the 1513 project while suppressing its soaring movement. The apse is reduced and brought forward so that it is flush with the lower story. The upper story by its power and weight dominates the structure, and an increase in its height noted by Professor Wilde in a 1517 drawing indicates Michelangelo's intention to make this story the principal one.[29] There is now a much stricter division between the terrestrial and celestial zones, and the intermediary zone has been so conjoined with the sphere above it that it is virtually absorbed in it. It was perhaps partly in the spirit of this change (although clearly it would also have been in the interests of economy) that Michelangelo seems to have considered replacing the Victories in the front niches, possibly with Slaves (presumably the already completed Louvre figures), so that there would be six Slaves at the lower story front forming a consistent pedestal to the upper story.[30]

In 1525–1526 Michelangelo let it be known in letters that he was agreeable to third-party suggestions that he abandon all that had been done, and all that was most original in his designs, for a simple wall tomb in the Quattrocento fashion.[31] The Pope's heirs were by this time furious with the delays, frustrations, and perhaps also with this proposal—"and not without reason," as Michelangelo admitted in a letter.[32] After the lapse in negotiations due to the sack of Rome and the siege of Florence, the 1532 contract represents the compromise arrived at. The monument shrinks to a structure no longer three-sided and hardly projecting from the wall, yet presenting a frontal aspect similar to that planned in 1516. Michelangelo himself is to complete for the tomb six of the unfinished statues in his studios.[33] What these six statues were to be is not specified in the contract, and it is evident from a letter of Sebastiano del Piombo written before it that Michelangelo was free to choose, since the heirs did not know what unfinished statues existed.[34] This is important, for it is clear that the sculptor was already—even while the 1516 contract was still in force —engaged in a desperate effort to save the monumentality of the tomb, an effort which (it seems necessary to suppose) would have involved replacing the already completed architecture of the lower story (which the 1516 and 1532 contracts require to be used) to make room for four much larger Slaves and for Victory groups of corresponding size.

No document has been discovered to illuminate the details of this heroic plan; yet it appears that "it did not concern the general composition and the distribution of figures," which were still to be grouped in an ascending pyramidal form.[35] However, the accent of the tomb has now moved to its lower story. The component statues were to be placed in receding planes of depth; and if (as seems likely on the available evidence) the Virgin, Sibyl, and Prophet were now to be the seated figures above the lower story,[36] then the statues of the upper story were to be smaller than those of the lower as well as farther removed. The upper story, with its figures representing spiritual domination, seems distant and withdrawn, while its enormous

architectural weight is tensely counterbalanced by the new plastic
monumentality of the lower story. The keynote of this new emphasis
is struck by the astonishing new Slaves. These, in the confinement of
their violent power, vehemently express the soul's imprisonment in
the *carcer terreno*. Bands are still used as external symbols, and remind us that "the Neoplatonic expression for the principle which
binds the incorporeal soul to the material body" is *vinculum*.[37] But the
bondage now is of the essence of the figures: their very forms are
described by the expense of themselves to be free of the matter of
which they are made and from which they have barely emerged. The
Palazzo Vecchio "Victory" is of a size with these figures and was
probably (to judge on compositional grounds) to be placed between
the two Slaves here reproduced (Figs. 15 and 16). With its pendant,
it would have complemented the Slaves in symbolizing with them a
terrestrial zone of existence rather severely divided from the superior
translunary level of being above. Yet in relation to that level, the
stylistic and expressive difference of the Victor's form would have
been telling; his refined definition and relatively unencumbered energy clearly would have contrasted with the Slaves' trapped power
and crushing density.

What, then, is the significance of the "Victory"? Tolnay, noting that
the two heads are on one vertical axis, repeating almost the same
position, says we are confronted with a contrast between Youth and
Age which he interprets literally as the tragedy of youth's transient
and unmerited, because fated, outstripping of age bent under the
weight of years.[38] But the bound captive old man and the fetters
around the calves of the youth must be related to the fettered Slaves,
captives of matter. Moreover, age is a consequence of the suffering of
time, and in the Neoplatonic universe the only realm subject to time
is that including terrestrial human life, the realm of nature with its
transient union of form and matter.[39] Hence, in the Medici Chapel,
the statues of the Four Times of Day (paralleled in the Julius Tomb
by the Four Slaves) symbolize the mode, time, in which earthly existence is a realm of suffering. Man's attainment of freedom from this
subjection to time and mortality is the proper subject of the funerary
monument. But this freedom can be achieved only by his conformation to an order not subject to time. This comes about when the soul,
aspiring to its lost perfection, does its utmost to ascend to the trans-

lunary mode of being above it, by mastering its involvement with matter and by ordering itself in virtues in the likeness of the superior existence. Pico, in the Commentary on Benivieni's *Canzone d'Amore* which Michelangelo clearly knew, writes that viridity or permanence is one of the properties attending Ideal Beauty; in the ideal world, he says, no intelligible nature recedes from its being by growing old. And the ideal world communicates this property to sensible beings only so far as they partake of that unifying proportion which is the essence of such Beauty.[40] The corollary is evidenced in Michelangelo's poetry where what in the realm of time is other than eternal is said to "change its hair"—to grow gray (G 105).* Since for the Neo-platonist the body may be, within its limits, the outward expression of the soul, age and youth might be used to express the degree to which the soul has striven to shape itself in the likeness of the celestial existence. Michelangelo had, in fact, half-whimsically resorted to such an argument in defending himself to the naïve Condivi against critics who had said that he had made the Virgin of the "Pietà" in St. Peter's too young. He wryly argued that, apart from supernatural considera-tions, virtuous women retain youth longer than others, and the im-mortal youthfulness conferred on the figure had been intended (he said) to symbolize the perfect chastity of Mary.[41]

Michelangelo's concern in the Victory group would appear to be with that regeneration by which the soul, aspiring to Godhead, may be freed from the burden of life subject to time, passion, and matter. Such a conception evokes Pico's famous apostrophe to Adam: "Thou mayest by thy soul's decision be born again [*regenerari*] to the things above which are divine."[42] However, a victory implies a requisite struggle. From the nature of the already mentioned statues inspired by it, we can be sure that Michelangelo's group was capable, in the sixteenth century, of inviting interpretation basically in terms of the tradition of the *Psychomachia*, as representing a moral victory of vir-tue over evil. In a lecture on the "Victory" several years ago, Professor Wilde remarked that it has not been possible to particularize which

---

* My citations of Michelangelo's poems are accompanied by the numbers assigned to them in the Girardi edition: Michelangiolo Buonarroti, *Rime*, ed. Enzo Noè Girardi (Bari, 1960). Much of the artist's poetry is notoriously difficult to translate. With some diffidence, I offer my own renderings here, since available English translations of the poems unevenly represent concepts and imagery in them crucial to my argument.

The full texts of the more essential poems cited here will be found in an appen-dix, below.

personified Virtue and Vice Michelangelo intended.[43] But the identifying attributes are of course the youth and age themselves; and these make of the figures, not Virtue and Vice, but ideal characterizations of spiritual modes of the soul while earthbound in mortal life. For his purpose, Michelangelo has utilized the, for the Neoplatonists, readily adaptable Christian images of unregenerate and regenerate nature: the Old Man and the Young Man. In philosophy, a similar conception is found in Ficino, where a voluntary death to earthly things is the condition of that act of celestial love by which the purged soul becomes assimilated to God. There are passages in the *Opera* where Ficino articulates this in more strictly religious terms. In a discussion which he begins by paraphrasing St. Paul on the Old Man and the New, Ficino writes:

. . . we seek by ascending higher to be bound more closely to Christ who is on high, lest we perish internally. . . . Indeed, the animal and diabolic man, who was in us, already is dead through the Passion and Resurrection. Meanwhile we live in the spiritual man until the life of glory be revealed unto us, which now is hidden from us, and reserved in Christ with the Father.[44]

Nor did Michelangelo lack the authority of a representational tradition for such a Victory. In 1529 he revisited Venice, and it has been conjectured that two Byzantine reliefs of St. Demetrios and St. George on the façade of St. Mark's may have suggested the general composition of the statue of Giuliano in the Medici Chapel begun soon after.[45] The "Victory" probably is coeval with the "Giuliano," and Michelangelo may have drawn inspiration for it from the thirteenth-century mosaic of "The Descent into Limbo" also in St. Mark's (Fig. 17).[46] This represents Christ in His divine victory, making spiritual "captivity captive" (Eph. iv.8), as He leads the imploring souls from their close imprisonment. The Devil, beneath Christ's feet, is bound in chains; and he is represented (as sometimes in later depictions of the Temptation, another crucial conflict in which Christ proves the exemplary victor) as the anagoge of the Old Man. At this point we need remember that Christ, the New Man, was for the Florentine Neoplatonists, too, the *idea et exemplar virtutum*—and the ideal of the union of God and man.[47]

However, the New Man in Michelangelo's Victory group, depicted as he turns from the captive Old Man, is (whatever the traditions of Christ's youthful beauty) no recognizable Christ figure.[48] That the

Victor should be represented as a beautiful nude adolescent whose
face glows with an etherealized carnal beauty calls for some explanation. Not of course that the nudity, which Michelangelo in any case
artistically preferred over the draped form, in itself would have been
at this date in the slightest degree inappropriate for such a figure of
spiritual superiority—even apart from such established iconographic
values of nudity as symbolic of truth, simplicity, and innocence.[49]
Warrant for the acceptability, within Christian sculptural representation, of classical nudity as symbolic of virtue begins—whatever the
disturbing ambiguity of *that* statue's nudity—with Donatello's bronze
"David" (ca. 1430–1432), the first classically nude, life-sized free-
standing sculpture since late antiquity.[50] Moreover, evidence exists in
Michelangelo's own work for his consciousness of one powerful
rationale for the iconographic propriety of the motif. As Colin Eisler
recently has shown, the background of the Doni "Holy Family" *tondo*,
with its classical stadium and nude athletes—one of whom somewhat
recalls the master's heroic "David"—owes its existence to the Christian concept of the "athlete of virtue," which figuratively identified
ancient Greek athletic contests with the struggles for Christian virtue.[51] It seems not unreasonable to suppose that the nudity of the
artist's leaf-crowned Victor may draw, if less pointedly, upon the
same conception.

Nevertheless, the sensuous eloquence of the Victor's torso, his emphatic youth, and the pairing of the figure with that of an old man
in a work of this date have all seemed susceptible of another, decidedly less programmatic explanation—given the nature of Michelangelo's emotional attachments and the bent of much earlier criticism.
Some of the older writers thought they saw in the face of the Vanquished a resemblance to the artist, and by assuming that the Youth
was an idealized portrait of Tommaso Cavalieri, the handsome and
gifted young Roman nobleman for whom Michelangelo conceived a
profound Platonic passion, it was possible for them to arrive at an
erotic interpretation of the statue. Other, less literal interpretations
impelled by the Cavalieri relationship, which view the group "as a
kind of spiritual self-portrait with Platonic connotations,"[52] have appeared more defensible. The abject humility with which, in letters and
poems, the artist approached this beloved in whom he glimpsed the
splendor of the divine beauty, indeed the very image of himself as
love's bound captive to Cavalieri which concludes one of the poems

that is by now conventionally associated with the statue (G 98: "resto prigion d'un Cavalier armato")—all this has seemed to lend such biographical views some credibility. And no less a scholar than Erwin Panofsky has agreed in supposing that it would be possible (if the group was in fact executed as late as 1532–1534) to think that it reflects Michelangelo's passion for Cavalieri "in spite of the fact that it was destined for the Tomb of Julius II."[53]

In some sense it may indeed reflect Michelangelo's passion, even though it is likely that the work was begun (though I believe not finished) before Michelangelo even met Cavalieri. But to suppose its conceivable reflection of private emotion to mean a split in subject matter would be to underrate Michelangelo's capacity for creative synthesis, and to miss the critical point. That, actually, need not at all rest on any simplistic biographical supposition. Indeed, we can never be quite sure of the degree to which the statue may really represent a merging of personal reference and objective program. What we do know, however, is that the personal relationship set in motion for Michelangelo the man all his abstracting and idealizing powers.[54] And the Neoplatonic terms, the concepts and imagery, in which in poems and drawings he conceived of his love for Cavalieri, and which he so powerfully used as to make them appear his native vocabulary of address to experience, are relevant to our understanding of this statue because we have very good reason to suppose that the same symbolic mentality was brought to bear in its creation.

The importance to the "Victory" of Michelangelo's Neoplatonic ideas of love depends not on our biographical conjectures but on their obvious conceptual pertinence to a work concerned with the possibility of human conformation to an ideal order not subject to time and mortal imperfection. For Michelangelo as for Ficino, love is religious, and religion amatory.[55] And they merge plausibly and appropriately in his program for a funerary monument because the Neoplatonists viewed their theory of love "as the key to a philosophy of death." The basis is the idea, whose prevalence among the humanists comprising Michelangelo's formative intellectual milieu has lately been discussed by Edgar Wind, ". . . of Eros as a power that loosens or breaks the chains which bind the soul to the body."[56] Indeed, Pico writes that it is only by the amatory life that one ascends out of bondage to the terrene life, whose subjection to time is an image of its subjection to matter and thereby to Fate.[57] For Ficino,

of course, love is the circuit which defines the very world of his philosophy.

> This Divine Beauty creates in everything love, that is, desire for itself,
> because if God draws the world to Himself, and the world is drawn [from
> him] there is one continuous attraction, beginning with God, going to the
> world and ending at last in God, an attraction which returns to the same
> place whence it began as though in a kind of circle.[58]

The same conceptions compellingly manifest themselves in Michelangelo's *Rime*. The artist finds in life no clearer testimony of the
divine than the loveliness in which can be found that "beauty which
moves / And bears to heaven" (G 164).

> Nor elsewhere of his grace does God more show
> Himself to me than in some mortal-lovely veil;[59]
> And that I love alone that in it is His shadow.   (G 106)

What his soul—that "half of me" which longingly aspires to "wing
back" to the heaven whence it came (G 168)—views in the adored
face is not the *cosa mortale*, but rather the beauty his *intelletto* per-
ceives shadowed there which can transform and raise him through his
love of it.

> These eyes of mine no mortal thing beheld
> When in your fair ones I found entire peace;
> But one within, where each ill must displease,
> Who by love compels my soul like to himself.   (G 105)

Hence, the message sent him on behalf of Love bids: "Love on! more
ardent burn! for mortals own / No other wings on earth to go to
heaven" (G 39).

> Love wakens, Love stirs us, Love plumes our wing;
> Nor from noble flight impedes vain furor;
> It is like the first step to her creator
> The soul ascends and mounts, for him still yearning.   (G 260)

It is love alone that, sculptor-like, must break away the *soverchio* which
encloses his soul that by itself would lack the force and will to free itself (G 152).

The poems to Cavalieri develop this complex of familiar Neoplatonic themes in seizing upon them as the appropriate description of
the relationship. In a single poetic fragment, the sculptor distills in a

pair of lines the essential argument explored in the whole group of poems to his friend: "Blessed the soul where time fleets no more; / Through you it has been brought to look on God" (G 37).

> For every loveliness regarded here
> Past other things by those who wisely see
> Recalls that merciful spring whence all things are;
>   Nor earnest else, nor other fruit they find
> Of heaven on earth: Who loves thee faithfully
> Ascends to God, and death itself makes kind.   (G 83)

To achieve such wise seeing of the *accorti*, moreover, to attain such virtuous and perfecting love, a purgation of the soul is required which corresponds to that putting off of the Old Man to which the Christian is enjoined. For Michelangelo, "that love in which virtue dwells can never hold / Firm hope of a thing that grows less" (G 106), that changes, ages. The Florentine Neoplatonists remind us of the doctrine which Michelangelo takes for granted. The more perfect lovers, according to Pico, "are those that, remembering a more perfect Beauty that their souls saw of old, before they were fettered to the body, are kindled with an incredible desire of rebeholding that Beauty; and to the end that they may obtain this purpose, they sever themselves as much as they can from the body, in such a fashion that the soul returneth to her pristine dignity." Only then can one be "in that love which is the image of celestial love," from which state alone can he attain to further grades of perfection "until at last . . . uniting his soul entirely with the understanding, . . . utterly purged from all the dross and stains of the earthly body, he is transformed" and can fly up "even to the intelligible heaven."[60]

As Lorenzo de' Medici succinctly explains, the beginning of the *amorosa vita* proceeds from death because one cannot arrive at that perfection which is in love without first dying to more imperfect things.[61] Michelangelo writes to Cavalieri, probably in 1532,

> That in your beautiful face I yearn, and learn,
> Mere human wit can scarce appreciate:
> He who would know it well has first to die.   (G 60)

Two deaths are poetically fused here. More generally in the poems, the purgative dying is only a requisite and prefiguration of that final death through which alone the schooling and the kindling can be completed, and the lovers find their true fulfilment.

> I say what dies cannot appease
> A living man's desire; nor ought we expect
> The eternal of time, where all grow gray.
>   Unbridled will is sense, not love:
> That kills the soul; our love but here perfects
> Us friends, but more, through death, in heaven.   (G 105)

That Michelangelo should perhaps in a sense have cast some part of himself in the role of the vanquished Old Man whose gaze is toward the earth should not surprise us. On the one hand, this corresponds to the anguished awareness of his own material captivity, indeed, to the intense consciousness of sin which vehemently erupts at intervals in the *Rime*.

> Living for sin, for myself dying I live;
> Surely my life belongs to sin, not me.
> My good from heaven comes, from me my ill,
> From my loosed will: a free will have I none.
>   Slave my freedom, mortal my god becomes.
> O hapless state!
> To what wretchedness, what living was I born!   (G 32)

In such outbursts we can discern one basis of that humility and grotesque irony which led the artist, in painting "The Last Judgment," to give St. Bartholomew's flayed skin (suggestive of the flesh) the form of a hound which holds in its mouth the contorted image of Michelangelo's face suspended over Hell. As Wind explains, this "Marsyas-like self-portrait is a prayer for redemption, that through the agony of death the ugliness of the outward man might be thrown off and the inward man resurrected pure . . . ."[62]

The bound Old Man, moreover, accords not only with this sense of sin, but also, in his contrast to the beautiful young Victor, with the charged self-abasement typical of such idealizing love as Michelangelo's. In such love, the lover not only helplessly submits, as he must, to seeking his blessedness in his captivity (G 98); he would also transcend his unworthy and imperfect self by losing his identity in the ideality perceived in the beloved. The basic idea, of course, is the familiar commonplace of Neoplatonic love theory. As readers of Castiglione will recall, true lovers pray to love to consume "all mortal ugliness" in their souls, "so that, being wholly separated from the body, they may unite with divine beauty . . . and that we, being outside ourselves, may, like true lovers, be able to become one with the beloved, and, rising above the earth, be admitted to the banquet of angels."[63]

This idea, of amorous dependence for such *ascensio* on identity with the beloved, occurs in Michelangelo's love poetry, not as a conceit or pose, but as a profound emotional conviction: "In me death, in thee my life" (G 37). It is most stunningly expressed in those verses addressed to Cavalieri:

> With your fair eyes I see a gentle light
> That with my blind ones I can never see.
> Upon your feet I bear a weight on me
> Which with my lame ones is never borne aright.
>   Wingless, upon your wings I mount my flight
> Heavenward moved by your genius constantly.   (G 89)

In the light of this conception, realized with such imaginative intensity in the poetry, the figure of the Young Man seems not only to body forth that beauty through love of which the soul may ascend, but to image that state of the soul, contrasting with the captive Old Man, when it would by such love "become one with the beloved." The analogy in the sculptor's poetic creation is to be found in his fervent vision of "a chaste love" that could make his soul—according to one despondent poem, a soul "plucked and shaved of its plumes" (G 168)—surmount the imperfection of its earth-bound state: ". . . one soul is in two bodies made eternal, / Upraising both to heaven on equal wings" (G 59).

What is surprising and I think indicative is that these wings should not have been given to the Victor. The original female Victories, we recall, were to have been winged figures. A transitional sketch (Fig. 18), apparently based on a Michelangelo original, shows a male winged Victory.[64] The wings are perhaps the most constantly iterated image of the poems to Cavalieri which celebrate that Love which "fits the soul with wings and bids her win / Her flight aloft nor e'er to earth decline."[65] And we know that in 1532 Michelangelo presented to Cavalieri a drawing of Ganymede (Fig. 19), symbolizing the mystic rapture of the *furor amatorius*, in which the eagle and the passive nude youth seem to form one single rising winged creature.[66] "Wingless, upon your wings I mount my flight / Heavenward . . ."[67] In connection with the theme of regeneration in the "Victory," moreover, one recalls the conventionally associated line in Psalm ciii (Vulgate: cii.5): "Your youth is renewed like the eagle."[68] And also the passage in Exodus (xix.4), traditionally allegorized to refer to the soul's *ascensio a Dio,* in which the Lord declares: "I bare you on eagle's wings and brought you in to my self."[69] Another drawing for Cavalieri was understood by its owner to be the complement of the "Ganymede," however, and this represents the torture of Tityus bound in Hades and symbolizes the enslavement and debasement of the soul tortured with sensual love.[70]

The "Ganymede" and "Tityus" represent polarities of vision whose pull creates much of the characteristic tension in Michelangelo's poetry and in his "Victory." Their contradictory energy is generated by the basic paradox for the Christian Neoplatonist, that the world as *sombra di Dio* through which he must ascend to the realization of the divinity in his nature is also the place of exile of which he is by nature a part. In fallen man, the power to pass through sensible things to the divine has been so enfeebled that the very vehicle of his potential enlightenment and freedom proves itself his dark prison. Thus, one whole profound aspect of Michelangelo's creative impetus is epitomized in this glowing poetic fragment:

> Nor can I now perceive in that which dies
> Your light eternal without great desire.   (G 34, variant)

But he might also have written these answering lines by Benivieni:

> Our mind, led astray,
> Well desires the true sun, but clasps the shade.[71]

The evidence is the unforgettable voice of his anguished spiritual need breaking through his congealing doubt:

> Rend thou the veil, O Lord! break down that wall
> Which with its hardness holds back
> The sun of your light in the darkened world.   (G 87)[72]

There is really no question, then, from the iconographic point of view, why the Victor is wingless. It is for the same reason he has one foot on the ground, and fetters still associated with his lower extremities;[73] it is for the same reason that the rising spiral movement which animates him is counterbalanced and arrested: the limited separation from the Old Man and his world, from the desire of things which die, which is achieved here in the *prigion oscura.*[74] "Heavy and mortal, wingless yet," writes Michelangelo in a later poem, "One ill follows a little angel's flight" (G 166). The significance of this lack (or, sometimes in the *Rime*, loss) of wings is of course already suggested in the *Phaedrus* (246); it is implicit in the Christian image of the virtuous wings of the soul found in Patristic writings, as well as in Landino's definition of them as *iustitia* and *religio*.[75] And the figurative idea is developed by Pico (who refers to it also in the *Oratio*) in this relevant passage which refers directly to the verses in Colossians concerning the Old Man and the New:

Let us therefore fly from the world, which is confirmed in evil; let us soar to the Father in whom are the peace that unifies, the true light, and the greatest happiness. But what will give us wings to soar? The love of the things that are above. What will take them from us? The lust for the things below, to follow which is to lose unity, truth, and goodness. For we are not one and integrated if we do not link together with a bond of virtue our senses, which incline to the earth, and our reason, which tends to heavenly things; this is rather to have two principles ruling in us in turn, so that, while today we follow God by the law of the spirit, and tomorrow Baal by the law of the flesh, our inner realm is divided and as it were laid waste.[76]

Such a split authority in man is reflected in Michelangelo's statue of the victorious Young Man, checked in his turn from that captive Old One who yet gazes upon "the things below."[77] It is similarly paralleled in Ficino's conception of the problematic situation of man's soul, and in a manner which helps us still more distinctly to understand the sculptor's two-figured group, not as a simple contrast of Old Man and New ("Primus homo de terra, terrenus; secundus homo de cœlo, cœlestis"), but as a unified essential image of the striving soul's terrestrial state.[78] Indeed, for Ficino, too, "the Soul, like the double-faced Janus, seems to have a double face" because it "looks at both the corporeal and the incorporeal."[79]

The rational Soul . . . is placed on the borderline between eternity and time, since it possesses an intermediary nature between eternal things and temporal things; and because it is intermediary, it possesses rational forces and actions ascending toward the eternal Beings and it also possesses other forces and activities descending toward the temporal Beings.[80]

In keeping with this intermediary position, the Soul by natural instinct both "ascends . . . to the higher things and descends to the lower things." And although the Soul, while ascending, "does not leave the lower things, and while . . . descending, . . . does not abandon the higher ones,"[81] the tendency of terrestrial experience—with its habituations, preoccupations, troubles—is divisive. "When one nature, containing two dissimilar active forces is directed too much to the act of one force, it almost stops the act of the other."[82] Hence the impossibility, amidst the corporeal ills and burdens and temptations of earthly life, of long continuance of the Mind (*mens*) in its proper activity, contemplation of the realm of ideas; for it is deflected from this aspiring purpose and forced to look down instead of up by the need to illuminate the Reason (*ratio*) in its effort to govern the baser parts of man's nature. Moreover, this necessary involvement with the body may imperil the Soul, through dedication to the outside world, with the unhappiness of the external and imperfect life. "Just as all tranquility and virtue result from the love of divine things, so from the love of mortal things come all trouble and wickedness."[83] It is proper, and indeed morally neutral, that "because of love for the animated body, which is its work and instrument, the Soul itself stoops willingly towards it from its own state."[84] But through too great a love of the body, and through too ready an habitual inclination of the *ratio* towards it, the Soul "vitiates itself."[85] "Thus alas" (writes Ficino "Concerning the Mind"), "outside the sublime fatherland, we unhappy people are confined to the lowest places, where nothing presents itself which is not exceedingly difficult, where nothing happens which is not lamentable."[86]

Michelangelo's "Victory" is thus a tragic image of the earth-bound striving of the Soul that would victoriously free itself to rise to the fulfilment of the divinity in its nature. It already hints of his so-called "conversion," and looks forward to his interest in religious opinions emphasizing grace.[87] It represents such a victory as gives a measure of mortal distance from that perfect rebirth man would attain to, such a victory as (Neoplatonic optimism set aside) makes more poignantly apprehensible that "the immortal soul is always miserable in its mortal body."[88]

III

William Shakespeare must have come by the idea of the Old Man through the extreme emphasis on religious instruction characteristic of the Elizabethan Petty and Grammar Schools.[89] But it was a stock and remained a frequent subject matter of the vast sermon literature of his time; and it was otherwise part of his literary tradition: no less a writer than Chaucer had made use of the image in "The Pardoner's

Tale."[90] Moreover, a pictorial tradition—one that would still be vital
for Rubens—kept the image vivid: it is evidenced in England by
such a work as the finely painted stained glass window of the Temptation of Christ in King's College Chapel, Cambridge, in which the
Tempter is represented as an old man (Fig. 20).[91] To that end another tradition, even more important to Shakespeare the dramatist,
appears to have contributed. There is evidence that the devil was
sometimes portrayed as old in English mystery plays of such subjects
as the Temptation of Man in the Garden of Eden. A late Inventory
of the Grocers' Guild at Norwich (1565) has the item, "A Cote w^t
hosen & tayle for ye serpente, stayned, w^t a w^t [white] heare"—that
is, a white wig.[92]

Tudor interludes carry on the idea: Christ in John Bale's *The
Temptation of Our Lord* (1538) is "a yonge man"; Satan (as in the
King's College Chapel window, and here, certainly, with a Reformation polemical point) is an old hermit.[93] In the tradition of the
morality play, moreover, from the early Tudor examples down to instances in Shakespeare's own day, we find a long series of Vice characters, such as Sensualitie in Henry Medwall's *Nature* (ca. 1495?),
Hypocrisy in *Lusty Juventus* (1550?), Inclination in *The Triall of
Treasure* (1567), who are given the declared or exhibited attribute
of old age.[94] These keep a stage motif alive without, however, in all
cases preserving intact the specific vitality of the traditional image.
For there would appear to be almost as little active reference to the
theological Old Man in some of these figures as there is in those commonplace names, "Old Nick" and the "Old One," which suggest the
primeval quality of the devil and the inveteracy of his evil.

But Shakespeare, for his part, already shows, in a complicated joke
in *The Comedy of Errors*, a very complete awareness of the concepts
and imagery associated with the theological Old Man.[95] In *Richard II*,
we hear the Duchess of York greet her son, just pardoned of treason,
"Come my old son. I pray God make thee new" (v.iii.146).[96] And in
five later plays—*1 Henry IV*, *2 Henry IV*, *As You Like It*, *Othello*,
and *King Lear*—he actually brought a version of this symbolic Old
Man on stage. In the first of these, the two *Henry IV* plays (to which
I will limit the present discussion), he integrated the stage figure of
the aged Vice with the concept of the Old Man and put the revitalized
image to work at the symbolic level of his drama. The traditional image
is considerably transformed in the process, and study of this trans-

formation provides a valuable perspective on the plays and the interpretative problems they have raised.

The possibility that the Old Man might be one ingredient in that
amazingly rich and vital amalgam of traditions, Sir John Falstaff, has
not gone unregarded.[97] It already has been briefly noticed in a suggestive and humane essay on Prince Hal by J. A. Bryant, Jr., but in
terms which demand, I think, that the whole question be more fully,
and more critically, examined.[98] In a recent paper, Jonas Barish remarks that these plays, and especially the rejection of Falstaff at the
end of *2 Henry IV,* tend to make us reveal ourselves as either moralists or sentimentalists. And he interestingly argues that, although
either of these extreme views "certainly oversimplifies," the latter is
the truer, and that the pattern of Shakespeare's other plays, especially
the comedies, supports those who join Bradley in finding "the rejection
scene an affront, Hal a preaching humbug, and the whole episode a
distasteful illustration of the incompatibility of kingship with kindness." Barish cites Bryant's essay because he considers it "one of the
best rejoinders" to the moralistic critics "from a point of view explicitly Christian and theological."[99] Here one must object that the
point of view is inconsistently applied—and at precisely the juncture
where Barish wishes to depend upon it—with insufficient reference to
the usage of the motif centrally at issue in traditions of representation,
and without adequate critical examination of Shakespeare's actual
handling of it. For Bryant ceases to see Falstaff as the Old Man
(which Hal must cast off "in the sense that he must recognize and
attempt to correct the ancient penchant for sin within himself as well
as in those about him") as soon as he would have us see Hal lessened
by an "unfortunate impulse to condemn the whole man" Falstaff
"rather than struggle through the difficult course of trying to redeem
what is basically good in him."[100] As will become apparent, I can
accept neither of these formulations as grounded in just description of
the way in which the Old Man figure is used in the *Henry IV* plays.
But the real point, I think, is that this inconsistent view may reflect an
unexamined complexity in Shakespeare's handling of the image which
is fundamental to our understanding of these plays.

The apparent subject of the two *Henry IV* plays is the triumph of
the House of Lancaster through the growth and reformation of a
prince who so combined the public and private virtues that he became

England's ideal king, Henry V. In the chronicles and in the popular
imagination, Henry's youth had already become legendary according
to the pattern of the wild-young-man-reformed.[101] Traditionally, he
was the prodigal madcap prince who by a sudden and even miraculous conversion became a perfect monarch.[102] Shakespeare interprets
the legend in a pair of plays which are partly parallel in structure,
which share an overarching action, and which yet must be considered
distinctive unities. This dramatic diptych, as we might somewhat eva-
sively term it, develops the theme of the education and responsibility
of the prince.[103] The large form of the plays is basically affected by
this concern with Hal's coming of age, and in this sense Shakespeare
remained true to the prodigal myth. It is by now a critical commonplace that he adapted, in the skeletons of these two histories, the pattern of the morality as it had developed in the interlude. The basic
characters of a Prodigal Play make their appearance: the Tempter,
the Younker, or Young Man, and the Father who has property to be-
queath; and so does its basic progression; the easy irresponsibility of
tavern vice and reveling must give way at the end to the edifying
repentance at which the tutor and feeder of the Youth's riots is rejected.[104]

In Shakespeare's plays, however, such an action is shifted to a new
secular plane. In the chronicles before Holinshed, the reformation of
Prince Hal had generally been treated explicitly as a theological question of spiritual repentance and amendment of life: "Thys man before
the deth of hys father, applyed hym vnto all vyce & insolency & drew
vnto hym all riottours & wildly dysposed persones. But after he was
admytted to ye rule of the lande anon & sodaynly he became a new
man, & tourned all that rage & wyldnes into sobernes & wyse sadnes,
& the vyce into constant vertue."[105] In Shakespeare's plays this reformation has been secularized as a matter of political ideals and necessities.
In *1 Henry IV*, we are invited to view in morality fashion the choice
Hal must make; but we find it a choice between, on the one hand,
Vanity and Idleness with his tempting companion at the Boar's Head
Tavern, and, on the other, chivalric honor and political responsibility
with the King in defense of the realm. The threat to the kingdom is
twofold: rebellion of the peers from their proper place in the "natural"
political order, and rebellion of the Prince of Wales from his princely
nature and station. By proving himself capable of loyal and high
chivalric deeds at Shrewsbury, Hal removes both of these threats in

one and the same action. The unreformed Hal of the play is thus not precisely guilty as a sinner, but, in his own words, as "a truant . . . to chivalry" (v.i.94); his father's complaint is not that he is immoral, but that he has "lost [his] princely privilege / With vile participation," that he has "grafted" himself to vain "inordinate and low desires" which should not "hold their level with [his] princely heart" (iii.ii.86–87, 11–17).

In so secularizing the morality action, moreover, Shakespeare has it performed in the more complex perspectives guaranteed by his own compelling interests. One is his concern with political and psychological realities; another is his search for the more comprehensive unities which the popular drama's mixture of serious and comic tones might of their natures be made to afford. In accord with this latter purpose he has cast in what should be the Vice's role an incarnation of a different sort of conventional inverter of established order, the holiday Lord of Misrule. And he has given him a wit which bodies forth the essence and scope of wit: a wit which ranges from skepticism about the human nature sacrificed by any inevitably limited decorum, to a levity which outruns and thereby clarifies the limits which our sense of social obligation acknowledges proper; from mockery of ideal notions which assume that human nature and actuality are what they are not, to a cynicism which finds nothing sacred. The consequences of this characterization, for the action of 1 Henry IV, is that we regard Hal's truancy from his princely role in the light of "holiday"; and from that vantage, his life of license itself is explored as actually requisite to his growth in awareness about what the ultimate order of his life and reign must comprehend. What this means is epitomized when Hal finally stands above the prostrate Hotspur and Falstaff in a stage emblem of victory derived from the moral tradition.[106] The absolute psychomachic opposition has been sophisticated. We do not see Hotspur and Falstaff simply as defeated virtual symbolic personifications of Vainglory and Vanity. They appear, instead, attractive incarnations of aberrant, destructively limited versions of public and private impulse and value, whose properly viable life Hal has subsumed in his own being.

The far-reaching implications of Falstaff as Misrule have already been ably examined. In a recent study, C. L. Barber has brilliantly displayed the light which can be thrown on Henry IV by viewing Shakespeare's dramatic art as the transformation into Saturnalian comedy of analogous patterns of ritual release and clarification to be found in folk festival.[107] Yet even as we avail ourselves of this illumination, we perceive further degrees of understanding demanded by the plays themselves. For Shakespeare's perspective is even more complex than Barber's vantage allows us to see. I suggest that one reason for this is that the playwright, in building upon a more primitive dramatic form like the morality, characteristically assimilates and exploits, rather than abandons, its values.

This reflection is compelled by Shakespeare's pervasive use of religious ideas and imagery in these plays. The idea of a spiritual conflict over the soul of the representative hero was so native to the conventional morality structure Shakespeare so qualifyingly employs, that it was yet natural for him to use the religious terms pertaining to rebellion from "nature," to repentance, and to regeneration to describe Hal's secular reformation *by analogy*. Hence, at various points, Falstaff is specifically associated not only with the Riot of the interlude, but with the Vice and even (as in his exit with Hotspur on his back) the Devil of the morality.[108] Hence too the repeated wordplay about the "grace" which Hal will lack when he is king—a motif that continually evokes the ideal view of king as regenerate man.

Fal. And I prithee, sweet wag, when thou art king, as, God save thy Grace—Majesty I should say, for grace thou wilt have none—
Prince. What, none?
Fal. No, by my troth; not so much as will serve to be prologue to an egg and butter.

(*1 Henry IV*, I.ii.17–23)

In keeping with this are the repeated references to religious repentance. Most of these are comically placed in the mouth of the old reprobate, but it is apparent, from his complaints that Hal's evil company has corrupted *him*, that they obliquely apply largely to the seemingly careless Prince.[109]

Fal. O, thou hast damnable iteration, and art indeed able to corrupt a saint. Thou hast done much harm upon me, Hal—God forgive thee for it! Before I knew thee, Hal, I knew nothing; and now am I, if a man should speak truly, little better than one of the wicked. I must give over this life, and I will give it over! By the Lord, an I do not, I am a villain! I'll be damn'd for never a king's son in Christendom.
Prince. Where shall we take a purse tomorrow, Jack?
Fal. Zounds, where thou wilt, lad! I'll make one. An I do not, call me a villain and baffle me.

Prince. I see a good amendment of life in thee—from praying to purse-taking.

Fal. Why, Hal, 'tis my vocation, Hal. 'Tis no sin for a man to labour in his vocation.

                                                    (*1 Henry IV*, i.ii.101–117)

What gives such burlesque its essential comic force is that Falstaff from the start has been projected as, first among so many things, a powerful embodiment, both traditional and archetypal, of belly-authority winkingly posing as rule. He thus serves to remind us of the ideal decorum he inverts, and at the same time functions as a virtual symbolic personification, abstracting analogous misrule evidenced in the world of the play and supposed in Hal. It is in relation to both these aspects that he enters the picture in his symbolic role as Old Man—as what Hal at one point names "That villanous abominable misleader of youth, Falstaff, that old white-bearded Satan" (ii.iv.508–509). Falstaff's belly is reminiscent of earlier personifications of Gluttony;[110] and it also helps to make him an incarnation of holiday misrule and cheer—of fat Shrove-Tuesday, "that wadling, stradling, bursten-gutted Carnifex of all Christendome, . . . Protector of the Pancakes . . . ."[111] At the same time it is made punningly symbolic of the theological Flesh itself: "Thou seest" (he says) "I have more flesh than another man, and therefore more frailty" (iii.iii.188–189).[112] His age and gray hair (which Shakespeare, in contrast to his sources, seems to have bestowed on the Prince's companion) are similar.[113] At specific points we are invited to view the misrule he embodies through the image of unregeneracy, the Old Man.

Thus, for example, the elaborate, and traditional, irony of Falstaff's repeated comic claims of a place among those "in the vaward . . . of youth" (*1 Henry IV*, i.ii.199). These invariably concern rationalization of the anarchic, and they have been seen as illustrations of his wit of inversion as an expression of the theme of disorder in the plays. But the specific traditions involved help us particularize further. One is the theme, widespread in allegorical literature generally and in the moral interludes especially, of the self-revelation of Vices when they pretend to be Virtues. Another is the theme of mock or inverted *renovatio*.[114] An old man ought to be spiritually "young." The very attempt of a foolish or perverse old man to be youthful (in the "lusts of youth") may therefore serve ironically to underscore, not only his unrealistic aged folly, but also, through inversion of the "youth" he really needs, the pejorative symbolic implication of age. Literary opportunities for the expression of this complexity were widely afforded by the perennial popularity of the *senex amans,* of which Falstaff, Doll on knee, is a late grotesque (and with a typical Shakespearean complexity, also pathetic) version: "Is it not strange, that desire should so many years outlive performance? . . . I am old, I am old" (*2 Henry IV,* ii.iv.263–276). But the most telling climax of this theme occurs when Falstaff attempts to establish his claim at a confrontation with his symbolic antagonist, the Lord Chief Justice. The old man's argument has just been, "You that are old consider not the capacities of us that are young." The elderly Justice protests:

> *Just.* Do you set down your name in the scroll of youth, that are written down old with all the characters of age? Have you not a moist eye, a dry hand, a yellow cheek, a white beard, a decreasing leg, an increasing belly? Is not your voice broken, your wind short, your chin double, your wit single, and every part about you blasted with antiquity? And will you yet call yourself young? Fie, fie, fie, Sir John!
>
> *Fal.* My lord, I was born about three of the clock in the afternoon, with a white head and something a round belly. For my voice, I have lost it with halloaing, and singing of anthems. To approve my youth further, I will not. The truth is, I am only old in judgment and understanding; and he that will caper with me for a thousand marks, let him lend me the money and have at him.
>
> (*2 Henry IV,* i.ii.201–217)

Falstaff's irresistible and incongruous vitality provides only part of the fun here, as the "great fool" (his label in their next encounter, ii.i.208) contrasts himself with the old Lord Chief Justice, whose own age of course is the attribute long manifested by Prudence and Good Counsel.[115] As the prologue to the anonymous *Life of Sir John Oldcastle* makes clear, Falstaff is to be seen against the convention of the "aged Councellor to youthfull sinne."[116] His anthem-singing would parade him as spiritually "young" (see, e.g., Eph. v.17–19) in spite of his age; but the very age he admits comically undercuts his pretension. In contemporary discussions, it is a commonplace that the "vnregenerate part of our Nature," the Old Man, "is perfectly born";[117] and that he wills corruptly precisely because (as Henry Bullinger wrote) his "judgment and understanding"—his powers to "discern . . . what to receive or what to refuse"—being not yet regenerate, not yet "young," are only "a blind guide."[118]

Of course, it is especially in *2 Henry IV* that we find Shakespeare's emphasis upon the symbolic value of Falstaff's age to be insistent. Thus the deeper comic point of even so innocent-appearing a passage as that in which Hal asks Bardolph and Sir John's page of their master's whereabouts:

> *Prince.* Where sups he? Doth the old boar feed in the old frank?
> *Bard.* At the old place, my lord, in Eastcheap.
> *Prince.* What company?
> *Page.* Ephesians, my lord, of the old church.
> *Prince.* Sup any women with him?
> *Page.* None, my lord, but old Mistress Quickly and Mistress Doll Tear-sheet.
> *Prince.* What pagan may that be?
>
> (*2 Henry IV*, II.ii.159–168)

As Bryant has noted, the primary meaning of "the old church" here—enforced by the iteration of "old" in the passage—is the body of the unregenerate.[119]

This aspect of Falstaff's dramatic identity affects the pattern of the plays at their center, which is Prince Hal. In the troublesome soliloquy near the start of *1 Henry IV*, in which he assures the audience that his participation in a vain life is but an appearance, he compares himself to the sun that allows itself to be obscured:

> Yet herein will I imitate the sun,
> Who doth permit the base contagious clouds
> To smother up his beauty from the world,
> That, when he please again to be himself,
> Being wanted, he may be more wond'red at
> By breaking through the foul and ugly mists
> Of vapours that did seem to strangle him.   (I.ii.221–227)

In the image of the sun we easily detect a royal emblem. At a deeper level of suggestion, we should also see a conventional religious figure which nicely accords with Hal's announced determination, echoing Ephesians v.16, to redeem the time:[120]

> I'll so offend to make offence a skill,
> Redeeming time when men think least I will.   (I.ii.240–241)

"The old man" (wrote John Bradford) "so mightily prevaileth against the new in the children of God, that the Spirit and seed of God seemeth to be utterly taken from them" so that they appear to be "plain reprobates"; "where yet notwithstanding the truth is otherwise, the Spirit and seed of God at the length appearing again, and dispelling away the clouds which cover 'the Sun' of God's seed from shining, as the clouds in the air do the corporal sun . . . ."[121]

Thus, one might be tempted to say of the entire plays that Shakespeare so colors the action by the morality scheme as to give it a suggested symbolic depth or extension. This extension would result from the fact that we are asked to view the protagonist's progress toward the crown of England through the familiar image of the progress of the struggling Christian toward possession of the Crown of Life, hampered (as in our engraving, Fig. 21) but not held back by the World, Flesh, Devil, and the Old Man.[122] The summary restatement of Hal's reformation at the start of *Henry V*, which is based on the Baptismal Service in the Book of Common Prayer,[123] might be placed in partial evidence in support of such a view:

> *Cant.* The breath no sooner left his father's body
> But that his wildness, mortified in him,
> Seem'd to die too. Yea, at that very moment
> Consideration like an angel came
> And whipp'd th' offending Adam out of him,
> Leaving his body as a paradise
> T'envelope and contain celestial spirits.   (i.i.25–31)

For the Elizabethans, surely, some part of the significance of Falstaff's comic resurrection after seeming to be dead at Hal's feet (*1 Henry IV*, v.iv.111) must have consisted in the doctrine that the Old Man does not remain completely mortified in this life, and the battle between spirit and flesh must continue until the Crown of Life is achieved.

Clearly, however, any such sustained allegoric interpretation of the action cannot be entirely convincing. The validity of the required symbolic values would have to depend on a complete faith in the literal force of the analogies involved; and in point of fact those analogies continually break down. The bishops, from whose discussion of Hal's conversion I have just quoted, actually spend most of their eulogy of the young king describing his worldly learning and statecraft. Hal's soliloquy, in which he deliberately imitates the sun, shows he is truly his father's son, and that he identifies his values with those requisite in the political world in which he will have to move. It inevitably represents him (though not unsympathetically) as John Danby's "sheep in wolf's clothing," as the Machiavel of good ends who has a fine sense of political timing.[124] A symptom of what challenges an allegorist point of view may be found in the grand descrip-

tion of the Prince and his comrades before the battle of Shrewsbury
—"All furnish'd, all in arms; / All plum'd like estridges that with the
wind / Bated like eagles having lately bath'd" (*1 Henry IV*, IV.i.97–99)
—and in the ensuing picture of the armor-clad Hal leaping on his
horse:

> I saw young Harry with his beaver on,
> His cushes on his thighs, gallantly arm'd,
> Rise from the ground like feather'd Mercury,
> And vaulted with such ease into his seat
> As if an angel dropp'd down from the clouds
> To turn and wind a fiery Pegasus
> And witch the world with noble horsemanship.
>
> (IV.i.104–110)

The image of the eagle is reminiscent of and in fact appears to be
partly derived from the passage in *The Faerie Queene* (I.xii.24) in
which the Red Cross Knight rises regenerated like an eagle from his
bath in the Well of Life to continue his battle with the Dragon.[125] A
figure of spiritual regeneration and combat has been mustered to
glorify a vision of *sprezzatura* in the performance of a refurbished
chivalric ideal.

The image of the Old Man can in fact successfully, and richly,
operate throughout most of such an action only when it is used with
a loose metaphorical or referential force, because the ideality of the
actually displayed political world to which Hal might be regenerated
is itself distinctly limited. For, to think of Falstaff in terms of the Old
Man is to place what passes for decorum against a moral measure it
cannot be made to fit. As long as Shakespeare compels recognition of
this, our awareness of the ironies engendered by the reference to
spiritual values need not be closed off; nor need Hal's. We can watch
this awareness at work in that passage in the plays which most
blatantly identifies the fat knight with the Old Man. When, in preparing for his interview with his father, Hal plays the King—as he must
inevitably do indeed—Falstaff plays Hal, and we are presented with
a preparative version of the young Prince's rejection of his own ir-
responsible self in the image of Falstaff. Hal's broad religious coloring
paints the Falstaff to be rejected as a scapegoat effigy of spiritual
unregeneracy. And we note that even Old Jack's inflationary self-nam-
ing "in behalf of that Falstaff" amusingly plays into the hands of this
design.

Prince. The complaints I hear of thee are grievous.

Fal. 'Sblood, my lord, they are false! Nay, I'll tickle ye for a young prince, i' faith.

Prince. Swearest thou, ungracious boy? Henceforth ne'er look on me. Thou art violently carried away from grace. There is a devil haunts thee in the likeness of an old fat man; a tun of man is thy companion. Why dost thou converse with that trunk of humours, that bolting hutch of beastliness, that swol'n parcel of dropsies, that huge bombard of sack, that stuff'd cloakbag of guts, that roasted Manningtree ox with the pudding in his belly, that reverend vice, that grey iniquity, that father ruffian, that vanity in years? . . .

Fal. I would your Grace would take me with you. Whom means your grace?

Prince. That villanous abominable misleader of youth, Falstaff, that old white-bearded Satan.

Fal. My lord, the man I know.

Prince. I know thou dost.

Fal. But to say I know more harm in him than in myself were to say more than I know. That he is old (the more the pity) his white hairs do witness it; but that he is (saving your reverence) a whoremaster, that I utterly deny. If sack and sugar be a fault, God help the wicked! If to be old and merry be a sin, then many an old host that I know is damn'd. If to be fat be to be hated, then Pharoah's lean kine are to be loved. No, my good lord, banish Peto, banish Bardolph, banish Poins; but for sweet Jack Falstaff, kind Jack Falstaff, true Jack Falstaff, valiant Jack Falstaff, and therefore more valiant being, as he is, old Jack Falstaff, banish not him thy Harry's company, banish not him thy Harry's company. Banish plump Jack, and banish all the world!

Prince. I do, I will.

(*1 Henry IV*, II.iv.496–500, 506–528)

In this passage, Hal's religious stance is so self-consciously exaggerated as comically to discount the assertions it makes possible; it therefore also qualifies the specific moral superiority it appears to aggrandize. This does not make the "I do, I will" less determined, less finally minatory—any more than the consciousness which prevents one from being a prig commits one to radical irreverence. But it does advertise an awareness that such extreme claims for authority as those implied may be vulnerable. In this sense Hal's speech is analogous to that of Falstaff, who (as usual) turns the indictment by turning it to laughter. Falstaff's defense is witty in part because it acknowledges in advance the deflation it cannot avoid by the very means used to lay claim to admirable and noble identity: euphemism, bathos, incantatory self-award of all-very-fine qualities, inveigling of tolerance for the disreputable through special pleading analogy, inadmissible sentiment, baldly sophistical syllogism. We can glimpse a real preparation for Hal in all this. To pretend may be to learn to avoid the delusive pitfalls of idealizing pretense in reality; to play-act can be a way of learning how to make acts adequate to the reality where they are performed and identity is tested. The expansion of consciousness here is like that afforded Hal when Falstaff defends his cowardice at Gadshill by burlesquing the subject's instinctive awe before the magical power of legitimate and sacred majesty (*1 Henry IV*, ii.iv.295 ff.).[126]

The ironic context established by controlled reference to a spiritual scale of value is especially useful in calling into question the high world of chivalric contest and power politics. Amusingly, this can best be accomplished by means of the character uncommitted to the code, the unregenerate Old Man himself. Frequently, Falstaff exculpates himself by questioning the humane inclusiveness or completeness of the chivalric ideals and by touching on the layered guilt attaching to the political struggle for power. Thus, he "damnably" misuses the King's right to impress soldiers to make himself money, but can then disengage himself from comment on the wretches, left to serve under him, who could not afford to buy their release from service. His response to Hal's awed, "I did never see such pitiful rascals," is an indictment of the inhuman indifferences of Authority: "Tut, tut!" he answers, "good enough to toss; food for powder, food for powder. They'll fill a pit as well as better. Tush, man, mortal men, mortal men" (*1 Henry IV*, iv.ii.71–73).

Here as elsewhere Falstaff tries to make commodity of the fact (which he thereby emphasizes) that, as Misrule, he analogizes disorder in his world more often than he contrasts with a convincingly established decorum. Indeed, Hal's father, who as king must stand for the order being defended in the plays, himself is very far from being immune to doubts about the ideality of his authority. As Monsieur Remorse, Falstaff, thinks of slimming, drying out, and repentance, we recall the parallel with the King, who dreams of a penitent (and politic) crusade to the Holy Land, and who also does not let his postponed repentance get in the way of his vocation. For Henry IV, whatever his genuine patriotic stature, came "By . . . by-paths and indirect crook'd ways" (*2 Henry IV*, iv.v.185–186) to a usurper's throne built on a murder; and his shaky title, which Hal is to inherit, stands under a curse and is the pragmatic cause of the disorder in his realm. At

Shrewsbury, Falstaff is not the only one who counterfeits to survive. The character who calls himself "the very king" "hath many marching in his coats" counterfeiting "the person of a king" in the field where his kingship and its order are being challenged (1 *Henry IV*, v.iii.21–25, iv.25–36).[127]

Barber would have it that the relation between comic and serious in this play is "not one of mocking echo"—that, for example, "it is not true that Falstaff's impudence about Hal's grace undercuts Bolingbroke's majesty."[128] Perhaps it would be more accurate to say that they are kept sufficiently separate to make their own uninvalidated claims, but are never allowed to exist in the total impression without reservations which balance and place those claims. But the ironic echoes surely are there. The robbery at Gadshill distinctly parallels the rebellion, but beyond that—for these robbers also are to rob a robber of the king's exchequer—Bolingbroke's usurpation as well. Later, in the tavern-scene play extempore, when Hal plays himself and Falstaff plays King Henry, the old man performs the part as a travesty of the regal nature. He takes as his "state" (or throne) a tavern chair, and as his scepter—which "shows the force of temporal power, / The attribute to awe and majesty / Wherein doth sit the dread and fear of kings" (*Merchant of Venice*, iv.i.190–192)—a dagger; and he places on his head, instead of a regal crown, a cushion—the traditional symbol of idleness and lechery which the personification of the Flesh similarly sports in our emblematic engraving from Jan David's *Veridicus Christianus* (Fig. 22).[129] Hal interprets the figure by reversing the imaginative process and prophetically undercutting Falstaff's pretension.

Fal. . . . This chair shall be my state, this dagger my scepter, and this cushion my crown.
Prince. Thy state is taken for a joined stool, thy golden scepter for a leaden dagger, and thy precious rich crown for a pitiful bald crown.
(1 Henry IV, ii.iv.415–420)[130]

Clearly, this performance as Misrule, which lasts until the Prince questions his decorum and deposes him, does not simply burlesque what the state dominated by Falstaff would be like.

It is the role of Misrule mockingly to pose as Rule, but the effect can be unqualified Saturnalian comedy only when the legitimacy of true rule is basically unquestioned. Nevertheless, it is true, at least in 1 *Henry IV*, that the inverter of decorum plays out his role in relation not only to a questionable order but to a decorum in the process of definition. The burlesque, the comic parallels, in this play never operate so as finally to deny a movement, bearing Hal forward, toward a balanced and complex awareness at once realistic and humane.

But the harsher world of *2 Henry IV* is quite another matter. In that second play, the England which Hal is to inherit is a more distinctly disordered, diseased, and corrupt one. It is a world divided between appetitive camps, presided over by a sick and dying king whose authority is justified on the ground of the nearly desperate need of order, but who can claim only that sanction for the order it would impose. "Rank diseases" grow "near the heart" of the body of Henry's kingdom (III.i.38–40), and rebels can suppose his failing "power, like to a fangless lion / May offer, but not hold" (IV.i.218–219). In *1 Henry IV*, Falstaff may complain comically that "the *poor* abuses of the time want countenance" (I.ii.174–175, my italics); in *2 Henry IV* (as the referential Old Man in a cast noticeably replete with aged figures),[131] he self-consciously sets himself up in the business his anarchic world is engaged in: turning "diseases to commodity" (I.ii.278). In a word, it is a world of which a sourer Falstaff, himself more heavily burdened with age, disease, vice, and vicious opportunism (precisely to undercut his comic immunity), pronounces the keynote: "If the young dace be a bait for the old pike, I see no reason in the law of nature but I may snap at him. Let time shape, and there an end" (*2 Henry IV*, III. ii.355–358).

King Henry hopes that "the soil of the achievement" will go with him into the grave so that the crown will descend to Hal "in a more fairer sort"; his "reign hath been but as a scene / Acting" the argument of civil strife, and his hopeful prediction is that his death now "Changes the mood" (IV.v.190–201). Prince Hal, it would appear, however, is committed to maintaining his "right . . . possession" in the delimited world of political success or failure in which his father moved (IV.v.221–225); and it is surely no minor irony that he is enabled to come to a throne momentarily secure from rebellion because of his sober brother's despicable but highly politic treachery to the rebels in Gaultree Forest.

There is an indicative importance in the fact that we are asked to see that action in the light of the conception of the Old Man. The crosscut to the Gaultree scenes is from Falstaff's bravura monologue on old Justice Shallow's fanciful memories of the "wildness of his youth,"

and on his financial plans to devour this "young dace" (III.ii.324 ff.).
"Lord, Lord, how subject we old men are to this vice of lying!" is his
remark, and it is one that cannot help but recall the exhortation St.
Paul found implicit in the command to "put off . . . the old man":
"Wherefore putting away lying, speak every man truth with his neigh-
bour" (Eph. iv.22–25). Falstaff's observations cast ironic shadows on
the Gaultree sequence immediately following. The Archbishop of
York ("whose beard the silver hand of peace hath touch'd") now
enters with the disaffected "noble lords" at the head of the rebel
force. Rebellion thus comes (as Westmoreland says) not "like itself,
. . . / Led on by bloody youth," but mendaciously "dress'd" in their
"fair honours" (IV.i.32–41). Yet, as the encounter at Gaultree turns
out, it is a young man who plays the part of the "old pike" and with
the duplicity of his "princely word" does the snapping. That Prince
John should conclude by crediting God with such a happy victory
only fulfils a prepared sardonic point. Derek Traversi has sensitively
remarked in this play the "bitter contrast between aged dissolution
and the controlled frigidity so unnaturally ascribed to youth."[132] But
with the concept of the Old Man, Shakespeare, depicting a world
where men are not "members one of another" (Eph. iv.25), provides
a view in which we see the aged and youthful figures in one perspective.

All this regulates the effect of what Shakespeare finally tries to do
with the image of the Old Man in 2 *Henry IV*. That Hal will undergo
a final "reformation" at the end of the play is conventionally expected
by the audience, is indeed so much a foregone conclusion that it can
be performed almost as a ritual. The ritual proves nothing less than
the investment of the Prince as ideal king. To accomplish this, Shakespeare shows Hal disappointing the fearful expectation of the court
that his rule will mean the overthrow of order and justice, the substitution of vanity and riot and uncurbed license for "royal state" (IV.
v.120–138). In an extraordinary passage, the dramatist attempts to
disengage Hal from both the dead politician Henry IV (himself an
almost sacrificial guilt-bearer now), and also the Prince's own former
"unregeneracy":

> And, Princes all, believe me, I beseech you:
> My father is gone wild into his grave;
> For in his tomb lie my affections,
> And with his spirit sadly I survive.

> To mock the expectation of the world,
> To frustrate prophecies, and to rase out
> Rotten opinion, who hath writ me down
> After my seeming. The tide of blood in me
> Hath proudly flow'd in vanity till now.
> Now it doth turn and ebb back to the sea,
> Where it shall mingle with the state of floods
> And flow henceforth in formal majesty.   (v.ii.122–133)

Hal indeed has just placed himself under the tutelage of the symbol of good government on all the corresponding planes of the theoretic Elizabethan universe by taking (as the New Man should) a new father. He figuratively has made himself son by adoption of the Lord Chief Justice, who here must virtually stand for nothing less than the concept of *Justitia:* "You shall be as a father to my youth" (v.ii 118).[133] In his next scene, crowned, Hal is ready to enact the rejection of the Old Man.

Falstaff, hearing of the old king's death, has confidently spurred from Gloucestershire to Westminster, aggrandizement personified, crying, "Let us take any man's horses; the laws of England are at my commandment. Blessed are they that have been my friend, and woe to my Lord Chief Justice!" (v.iii.142–145).

Now stained with travel, he stands with his rout awaiting the crowned and robed young King* as the solemn procession returns from the Abbey:

> *Fal.* God save thy Grace, King Hal, my royal Hal!
> *Pist.* The heavens thee guard and keep, most royal imp
> of fame!
> *Fal.* God save thee, my sweet boy!
> *King.* My Lord Chief Justice, speak to that vain man.
> *Just.* Have you your wits? Know you what 'tis you speak?
> *Fal.* My king! my Jove! I speak to thee, my heart!
> *King.* I know thee not, old man. Fall to thy prayers.
> How ill white hairs become a fool and jester!
> I have long dreamt of such a kind of man,

---

* Hal's change of costume for this scene still has an on-stage force easily underestimated in reading; it is likely, considering the context, to have been more than a literal one in the Elizabethan theater. "It was a common phrase that one actor played many parts, and that he changed his stage-personality with his dress. And since so many of the moral interludes are concerned with changes of heart (either falls to wickedness or conversions to virtue) it is appropriate that changes of dress should signify them; for the reformed speaker has become, theologically speaking, a new man."—T. W. Craik, *The Tudor Interlude* (Leicester, 1958), p. 73.

> So surfeit swell'd, so old, and so profane;
> But being awak'd, I do despise my dream.
> Make less thy body, hence, and more thy grace;
> Leave gormandizing. Know the grave doth gape
> For thee thrice wider than for other men.
> Reply not to me with a fool-born jest.
> Presume not that I am the thing I was;
> For God doth know (so shall the world perceive)
> That I have turned away my former self;
> So will I those that kept me company. (v.v.44–63)

The Elizabethans, who knew their bibles, would have recognized that the words "I know thee not" echo the very ones which (according to the parable, Luke xiii.25–27) Christ will say to those claiming admittance to heaven from the master of the house on the score of having enjoyed his acquaintance on earth.[134] Hal thus does much more than represent himself as a "new creature" who has turned away his "former self": he plays the royal analogue of the New Man Himself, and with a vengeance, rejecting the personified mode of being of the "workers of iniquitie." And for this reason it is perfectly consistent symbolically for the Lord Chief Justice to return in a moment and order Falstaff and company to be put in the Fleet. It is not merely a long-standard disposition of the Vice which recurs here;[135] the victorious New Man makes "captivity captive" in more than one sense.

The dramatic validity of this episode—which of course is one of the most disputed in all of the Shakespearean canon—must depend upon the way we respond to the assertiveness of Hal's rhetoric, wherein his likeness to the New Man is now assumed to be virtually an identity. The terms in which the new King "sets himself apart from the stock of Adam"[136] are scarcely figurative. The mode has changed indeed, and therefore we must not expect that the "ambivalence" characteristic of much of the earlier action continues to be realized in the same kind or degree, or that ironic viewpoints, which we would prefer Shakespeare not to have suppressed, will constitute the real burden of Henry V.[137] We are asked here to see in Hal the perfection a king ought to be according to royal Christology: there is no flesh but Falstaff to rebel against what Hal's grace says. But this is only one way the passage asks to be read. If we are unconvinced, it is because Hal supposes he can confirm his grace by labeling and rejecting Falstaff's belly and white hair. If we look with jaundiced eye upon the speech as political announcement, it is because, in voicing the Establishment's view of his relation with Falstaff, the new king conveniently rewrites what has been a more complex history. If we are disappointed, it is surely, as Barish says, because a self-sufficiency and success are claimed for Hal which put out of court our hope for a comic fulfilment for him, and for the action, wherein dream, holiday, and even awareness of folly enrich with humane fullness a commitment to responsibility.[138] An ideal purgation is proclaimed, and it must seem a displacement of comedy, not by "history," but by history posing as morality.

To be discontent with the rejection need not mean either to sentimentalize Falstaff or to be insensitive to the powerful sanction of the traditions that Hal invokes. The problem is not the rejection of an anarchic Falstaff or even, as such, the chill and shrunken withdrawal into a constricted viewpoint as Hal limits his identity to the impressive but dehumanized public figure. I should say that the difficulty manifests itself primarily as an artistic one. The dramatic preparation which has justified the rejection has also led us to expect the appearance of a youthful figure who will fulfil the promise of health to replace the diseased senility that has distempered the state. The difficulty is that this preparation, as *dramatic* rhetoric, asks us to see such a figure in this Hal, which is to say, to look at his speech as true report and not another of the false reports—the rumors—which the prologue has led us to find everywhere in the world of the play. The expected reformation and the cutting down of Falstaff to fit it give the stage to Hal's rhetoric in a manner which leaves but uncertain ground for ironic judgment upon it. To be sure, our misgivings are not mitigated but rather reinforced by John of Lancaster's unappealing approbation of the new king's "fair proceeding" toward his former companions. And I am by no means saying that all of Shakespeare could be in or with the moralizing Hal: only that less of that multiple viewpoint he had earlier insisted upon is operative here. Shakespeare allows himself to have appeared to have returned, without the qualification which we have learned to expect, to an official Tudor view of the sanctity of the state, and to an ideal view of the king as regenerate man, and to have done so by ignoring the actual political world, the England of power and appetite, which he had earlier created. That is why the ending strikes us as factitious or problematic resolution which seems to blur the more complex commitments implicit in his own material.

The *Henry IV* plays, as Danby has seen, represent a Shakespeare in transition;[139] and there are later plays which suggest that Shakespeare may himself have grown dissatisfied with this use of the Old Man. It is the year 1598: we are almost at the threshold of the tragedies of idealist figures who become culpable as they enter the sphere of action; nearly at the threshold, too (I should say), of Shakespeare's disenchantment with the possibility of bringing political realities and spiritual regeneration into one sphere. His later uses of the Old Man assume a spiritual order which never becomes easily identified with the actualities of authority or the finitude of power. And his next king who glimpses for us what regeneration might mean, and what it might cost, is King Lear.

IV

Michelangelo's "Victory" group and Shakespeare's *Henry IV* plays are separated by difference in medium, by more than a half century in time, and by cultural milieux in some senses worlds apart. Furthermore, they are truly unique works, created by towering figures whose art challenges an identity not entirely suiting the categories applicable to that of many of their contemporaries as well as that of preceding and later artists. (Indeed, in Michelangelo's mature sculpture, it has been shown analytically that the principles of artistic organization differ in kind from those definitive of High Renaissance, Manneristic, and Baroque statuary.[140]) This uniqueness and the gulf between them make only a very special kind of comparative study of these works appropriate or meaningful. They share, in a genetic sense, a fundamental tradition and certain specific images it provided. But what they significantly have in common is the capacity to show the critical importance of the vicissitudes of inherited matter in the Renaissance. They do not so much directly illuminate one another as complement each other in illustrating what great artists could make of the contradictions with the still-living medieval past brought about by their postmedieval culture.

Such contradictions, amounting to divergent perspectives on experience, manifest themselves in these artists' uses of an earlier image under the unstable aegis of doctrines which allowed the radical problems involved to achieve formidable expression if not complete resolution. An essential clue is found in their transformation of still usable psychomachic oppositions. These had allowed medieval man to repre-

sent divisions in his soul in terms of the definitive possibilities for his
nature which a compellingly polarizing religious faith warranted. For
these Renaissance artists, however, the issues involved could no longer
seem so simple. Among the greater late Elizabethan dramatists, for
example, where the morality play conflicts survive, they often have
become more internal and psychological in their realization,[141] and
not seldom they are conditioned by skeptical ambivalence. It is a
marked feature of both our works that the compositional effort—to
make a true organic unity out of what may be considered in each a
double-figured subject—itself becomes the reflection of a tensional
interplay, rather than a pure antagonism, perceived in what the
figures are capable of signifying. Michelangelo's figure of the Vanquished does not merely serve as a kind of "living plinth" to afford
stability for the charged spiral movement animating the Victor's
violently turned body;[142] it participates in the powerful *contrapposto*
which inhibits and qualifies the energy the Victor embodies.

The group as a whole thus appears an epitome of the sculptures
that strike us as peculiarly Michelangelesque: those where, in Panofsky's words,[143] "the terrific contortions and muscular tensions never
seem to result in effective action," where there is neither "consum-
mate repose" nor "achieved action," where the "forms express a mute
and deadly struggle of forces forever interlocked with each other."
Dr. Panofsky has taken the actual Tomb of Julius II completed in
1545 as a symbol of "the failure of Neoplatonism to achieve a lasting
harmony between the divergent tendencies in post-mediaeval culture."
In the "Victory," made for Michelangelo's heroic attempt to preserve
his most deeply developed conception of the tomb, there can be little
doubt that Neoplatonism, which framed the sublimation of his personal experience of those divergent tendencies, intellectually guided
its fusion with an objective sculptural program. But the unity and
power of the "Victory" are made from the profoundly and representa-
tively met fact of the unachieved harmony itself.

Such unity out of discord could not finally sustain itself as principle
for his work. The "powerful, inhibited figures" of his most characteristic creations, which "reflect the disparity between Christian emotion
and the antique ideal, between free human will and the will of
God,"[144] are displaced in the religious sculptures to which his last
years were devoted. This is nowhere more poignantly clear than in

the Gothicism of his very latest work, the uncompleted "Rondanini Pietà," where we can yet see that a classically impelled ideal image of the human body was literally hacked away in favor of a hauntingly bare and bereft image in stone of a vision of the incorporeal.

If there is anything in Shakespeare's *Henry IV* plays that corresponds to the design of interlocked struggle in the "Victory," it is the pervasive tendency to mutual qualification by parody and irony. But this tendency has been superimposed upon a morality pattern finally reasserted with constricting effect to conclude near-ritually something that the ironies have been telling us may be inherently inconclusive. In these plays, what is engaged but not ultimately dealt with is the gulf between the "King's two bodies" already exposed in *Richard II*.[145] It will later be coolly explored, along with the conflicts and continuities between public and private moralities, in a context liberated from inhibitions induced by either jingoistic or Christian expectations: the problematic Rome of Caesar, Brutus, and Antony. What is touched on, but only prematurely solved, is a problem with which Hamlet will have to come to sacrificial terms: the distance of authority, within the individual as within the state, from the ideal sanctions which should inform it if human nature, suffering its radical limitations, is to be "in action . . . like an angel" instead of the "quintessence of dust" relishing "of the old stock" which its actions reveal it to be. The questions disorder can ask about assumed order will most comprehensively be raised in *King Lear,* and answered in terms which offer a perspective upon King Hal's achieved sufficiencies. A still later tragedy will renew, in a very different context, a conflict basic in the *Henry IV* plays by dramatizing the delimited success of Octavius Caesar, "A minister of [Fortune's] will," the frigid economies of whose impetus must displace but can never afford the dream that Cleopatra dreamt.[146] It is, finally (and seemingly, inevitably, given the coherence of an artistic career of the order of Shakespeare's), only in the tragicomically ideal world of *The Tempest*, with its deliberate fictitiousness multivalent in the audience's response, that we find a vision of the possible regeneration of reason, and the reconciliation of the oppugnant forces in man's nature, which might assure his achievement of authority, community, and identity. That the fictive Duke of Milan's power to accomplish this is theurgic, and that his accomplishment is for the carefully limited if profoundly resonant late Shakespearean tragicomic theater, is a testimony to the inherent questions—demanding exploration through Shakespeare's art, compelling its unfolding—which could not be dismissed by King Hal's coronation.

"Vetus homo." Detail from a title-page border engraved by [Jo]hn Payne. From John Downame, *The Christian Warfare*, 4th ed. (London, 1634). Courtesy of the Princeton Theological Seminary.

Acknowledgments

The basic substance of this study originally was presented in a lecture before the Philological Association of The Johns Hopkins University in 1958, and I am grateful to my colleagues then and since for stimulation and criticism which aided its development. I have tried, in text and notes, to indicate my very considerable indebtedness to earlier scholarship and criticism. However, as students of his admirable work will appreciate, my debt to Dr. Panofsky's seminal studies is of an order deserving special acknowledgment here.

I should like to express my gratitude for other kinds of aid: to the Folger Shakespeare Library for a summer fellowship, and to the Dean's Faculty Research Committee of Washington University for a grant-in-aid, which facilitated revision and preparation for publication of this among other writings; to the staffs of the Folger and the Library of Congress, where much of the research was done, for their unfailing kindness and help; and to my Italianist friends, Dr. Louise George Clubb and Dr. Maria Rita Rohr, for trying to rein Pegasus in my translations of Michelangelo's *Rime*.

APPENDIX

Because of the importance for interpretation of Michelangelo's sculpture which I ascribe to his *Rime*, and because of the value of the full poetic context for appreciation of the parts translated in the course of this study, the full texts of the more essential poems are given here, taken from the Enzo Noè Girardi edition (Bari, 1960), which is the best corpus of the *Rime* and in which they are arranged in a carefully determined chronological order.

32

Vivo al peccato, a me morendo vivo;
vita già mia non son, ma del peccato:
mie ben dal ciel, mie mal da me m'è dato,
dal mie sciolto voler, di ch'io son privo.
    Serva mie libertà, mortal mie divo
a me s'è fatto. O infelice stato!
a che miseria, a che viver son nato!

34

| La *casa mie d'* |[1] amor non è *el* cor mio,
ch'amor di quel ch'io t'amo è senza core;
dou'è cosa mortal, piena d'errore,
esser non può g[i]à ma', né pensier rio.
    Amor nel dipartir l'alma da dDio
me fe' san ochio e te luc' e splendore;

[1] La uita del mie

né può non riuederlo in quel che muore [2]
di te, per nostro mal, mie gran desio.

Chome dal foco el caldo, esser diuiso
non può dal bell'etterno ogni mie stima,
ch'exalta, ond'ella uien, chi più 'l somiglia.

Tu ch'*ài* negli ochi tutto 'l paradiso,
per ritornar là dou'i' t'ama' prima,
ricorro ardendo sott'alle tuo ciglia.

37

In me la morte, in te la vita mia;
tu distingui e concedi e parti el tempo;
quante vuo', breve e lungo è 'l viver mio.

Felice son nella tuo cortesia.
Beata l'alma, ove non corre tempo,
per te s'è fatta a contemplare Dio.

39

Del fiero colpo e del pungente strale
la medicina era passarmi 'l core;
ma questo è propio sol del mie signore,
crescer la vita dove cresce 'l male.
E se 'l primo suo colpo fu mortale,
seco un messo di par venne d'Amore
che mi disse:—Ama, anz'ardi; ché chi muore
non ha da gire al ciel nel mondo altr'ale.

I' son colui che ne' prim'anni tuoi
gli occhi tuo infermi volsi alla beltate
che dalla terra al ciel vivo conduce.—

49

Amor, la tuo beltà non è mortale:
nessun volto fra noi è che pareggi
l'immagine del cor, che 'nfiammi e reggi
con altro foco e muoui con altr'ale.

[2] *a)* né *posso or non uederlo* in quel che muore
   b) né può *qui non amarlo* in quel che muore
   c) né *posso or non ueder dentr'a chi* muore
     tuo luce ecterna senza gran desio

59

S'un casto amor, s'una pietà superna,
s'una fortuna infra dua amanti equale,
s'un'aspra sorte all'un dell'altro cale,
s'un spirto, s'un voler duo cor governa;

s'un'anima in duo corpi è fatta etterna,
ambo levando al cielo e con pari ale;
s'Amor d'un colpo e d'un dorato strale
le viscer di duo petti arda e discerna;

s'amar l'un l'altro e nessun se medesmo,
d'un gusto e d'un diletto, a tal mercede
c'a un fin voglia l'uno e l'altro porre:

se mille e mille, non sarien centesmo
a tal nodo d'amore, a tanta fede;
e sol l'isdegno il può rompere e sciorre.

60

Tu sa' ch'i' so, signor mie, che tu sai
ch'i vengo per goderti più da presso,
e sai ch'i' so che tu sa' ch'i' son desso:
a che più indugio a salutarci omai?

Se vera è la speranza che mi dai,
se vero è 'l gran desio che m'è concesso,
rompasi il mur fra l'uno e l'altra messo,
ché doppia forza hann' i celati guai.

S'i' amo sol di te, signor mie caro,
quel che di te più ami, non ti sdegni,
ché l'un dell'altro spirto s'innamora.

Quel che nel tuo bel volto bramo e 'mparo
e mal compres' è dagli umani ingegni,
chi 'l vuol saper convien che prima mora.

83

Veggio nel tuo bel viso, signor mio,
quel che narrar mal puossi in questa vita:
l'anima, della carne ancor vestita,
con esso è già più volte ascesa a Dio.

E se 'l vulgo malvagio, isciocco e rio,
di quel che sente, altrui segna e addita,
non è l'intensa voglia men gradita,
l'amor, la fede e l'onesto desio.

A quel pietoso fonte, onde siàn tutti,
s'assembra ogni beltà che qua si vede
più c'altra cosa alle persone accorte;
   né altro saggio abbiàn né altri frutti
del cielo in terra; e chi v'ama con fede
trascende a Dio e fa dolce la morte.

87

Vorrei voler, Signor, quel ch'io non voglio:
tra 'l foco e 'l cor di ghiaccia un vel s'asconde
che 'l foco ammorza, onde non corrisponde
la penna all'opre, e fa bugiardo 'l foglio.
   I' t'amo con la lingua, e poi mi doglio
c'amor non giunge al cor; né so ben onde
apra l'uscio alla grazia che s'infonde
nel cor, che scacci ogni spietato orgoglio.
   Squarcia 'l vel tu, Signor, rompi quel muro
che con la suo durezza ne ritarda
il sol della tuo luce, al mondo spenta!
   Manda 'l preditto lume a noi venturo,
alla tuo bella sposa, acciò ch'io arda
il cor senz'alcun dubbio, e te sol senta.

89

Veggio co' be' vostr'occhi un dolce lume
che co' mie ciechi già veder non posso;
porto co' vostri piedi un pondo addosso,
che de' mie zoppi non è già costume.
   Volo con le vostr'ale senza piume;
col vostro ingegno al ciel sempre son mosso;
dal vostro arbitrio son pallido e rosso,
freddo al sol, caldo alle più fredde brume.
   Nel voler vostro è sol la voglia mia,
i miei pensier nel vostro cor si fanno,
nel vostro fiato son le mie parole.
   Come luna da sé sol par ch'io sia,
ché gli occhi nostri in ciel veder non sanno
se non quel tanto che n'accende il sole.

98

A che più debb'i' omai l'intensa voglia
sfogar con pianti o con parole meste,
se di tal sorte 'l ciel, che l'alma veste,
tard' o per tempo alcun mai non ne spoglia?
　　A che 'l cor lass' a più languir m'invoglia,
s'altri pur dee morir? Dunche per queste
luci l'ore del fin fian men moleste;
c'ogni altro ben val men c'ogni mia doglia.
　　Però se 'l colpo ch'io ne rub' e 'nvolo
schifar non posso, almen, s'è destinato,
chi entrerà 'nfra la dolcezza e 'l duolo?
　　Se vint' e preso i' debb'esser beato,
maraviglia non è se nudo e solo
resto prigion d'un cavalier armato.

105

Non vider gli occhi miei cosa mortale
allor che ne' bei vostri intera pace
trovai, ma dentro, ov'ogni mal dispiace,
chi d'amor l'alma a sé simil m'assale;
　　e se creata a Dio non fusse equale,
altro che 'l bel di fuor, c'agli occhi piace,
più non vorria; ma perch'è sì fallace,
trascende nella forma universale.
　　Io dico c'a chi vive quel che muore
quetar non può disir; né par s'aspetti
l'eterno al tempo, ove altri cangia il pelo.
　　Voglia sfrenata el senso è, non amore,
che l'alma uccide; e 'l nostro fa perfetti
gli amici qui, ma più per morte in cielo.

106

Per ritornar là donde venne fora,
l'immortal forma al tuo carcer terreno
venne com'angel di pietà sì pieno,
che sana ogn'intelletto e 'l mondo onora.

Questo sol m'arde e questo m'innamora,
non pur di fuora il tuo volto sereno:
c'amor non già di cosa che vien meno
tien ferma speme, in cui virtù dimora.

Né altro avvien di cose altere e nuove
in cui si preme la natura, e 'l cielo
è c' a' lor parti largo s'apparecchia;
    né Dio, suo grazia, mi si mostra altrove
più che 'n alcun leggiadro e mortal velo;
e quel sol amo perch'in lui si specchia.

152

Sì come per levar, donna, si pone
in pietra alpestra e dura
una viva figura,
che là più cresce u' più la pietra scema;
tal alcun'opre buone,
per l'alma che pur trema,
cela il superchio della propria carne
co' l'inculta sua cruda e dura scorza.
Tu pur dalle mie streme
parti puo' sol levarne,
ch'in me non è di me voler né forza.

164

Per fido esemplo alla mia vocazione
nel parto mi fu data la bellezza,
che d'ambo l'arti m'è lucerna e specchio.
S'altro si pensa, è falsa opinione.
Questo sol l'occhio porta a quella altezza
c'a pingere e scolpir qui m'apparecchio.
    S'e' giudizi temerari e sciocchi
al senso tiran la beltà, che muove
e porta al cielo ogni intelletto sano,
dal mortale al divin non vanno gli occhi
infermi, e fermi sempre pur là d'ove
ascender senza grazia è pensier vano.

166

Ben posson gli occhi mie presso e lontano
veder dov'apparisce il tuo bel volto;
ma dove loro, ai pie', donna, è ben tolto
portar le braccia e l'una e l'altra mano.
   L'anima, l'intelletto intero e sano
per gli occhi ascende più libero e sciolto
a l'alta tuo beltà; ma l'ardor molto
non dà tal previlegio al corp' umano
   grave e mortal, sì che mal segue poi,
senz'ali ancor, d'un'angioletta il volo,
e 'l veder sol pur se ne gloria e loda.
   Deh, se tu puo' nel ciel quante tra noi,
fa' del mie corpo tutto un occhio solo;
né fie poi parte in me che non ti goda.

168

Perché 'l mezzo di me che dal ciel viene
a quel con gran desir ritorna e vola,
restando in una sola
di beltà donna, e ghiaccio ardendo in lei,
in duo parte mi tiene
contrarie sì, che l'una all'altra invola
il ben che non diviso aver devrei.
Ma se già ma' costei
cangia 'l suo stile, e c'a l'un mezzo manchi
il ciel, quel mentre c'a le' grato sia,
e' mie sì sparsi e stanchi
pensier fien tutti in quella donna mia;
e se 'lor che m'è pia,
l'alma il ciel caccia, almen quel tempo spero
non più mezz'esser, ma suo tutto intero.

197

La carne terra, e qui l'ossa mie, prive
de' lor begli occhi e del leggiadro aspetto,
fan fede a quel ch'i' fu' grazia e diletto
in che carcer quaggiù l'anima vive.

260

Non è sempre di colpa aspra e mortale
d'una immensa bellezza un fero ardore,
se poi sì lascia liquefatto il core,
che 'n breve il penetri un divino strale.

Amore isveglia e desta e 'mpenna l'ale,
né l'alto vol preschive al van furore;
qual primo grado c'al suo creatore,
di quel non sazia, l'alma ascende e sale.

L'amor di quel ch'i' parlo in alto aspira;
donna è dissimil troppo; e mal conviensi
arder di quella al cor saggio e verile.

L'un tira al cielo, e l'altro in terra tira;
nell'alma l'un, l'altr'abita ne' sensi,
e l'arco tira a cose basse e vile.

264

Come portato ho già più tempo in seno
l'immagin, donna, del tuo volto impressa,
or che morte s'appressa,
con previlegio Amor ne stampi l'alma,
che del carcer terreno
felice sie 'l dipor suo grieve salma.
Per procella o per calma
con tal segno sicura,
sie come croce contro a' suo avversari;
e donde in ciel ti rubò la natura,
ritorni, norma agli angeli alti e chiari,
c'a rinnovar s'impari
là sù pel mondo un spirto in carne involto,
che dopo te gli resti il tuo bel volto.

Figure 1. Michelangelo, "Victory" (*side view*). Palazzo Vecchio, Florence. Photo by Alinari, Florence.

Figure 2. Michelangelo, "Victory" (*front view*). Photo by Alinari, Florence.

Figure 3. Vincenzo Danti, "Honor Conquering Deceit." Bargello, Florence. Photo by Alinari, Florence.

Figure 4. Michelangelo, "The Tomb of Pope Julius II." San Pietro in Vincoli, Rome. Photo by Alinari, Florence.

Figure 5. Attributed to Jacomo Rocchetti. Copy after the preparatory drawing for the 1513 contract for the Tomb of Julius II. Kupferstichkabinett (No. 15305), Berlin. Reproduced by permission.

Figure 6. Approximate reconstruction of the 1505 project for the Tomb of Julius II (*front elevation*). After Erwin Panofsky, *Tomb Sculpture,* ed. H. W. Janson (New York, n.d.), Fig. 418. Reproduced by permission.

Figure 7. Approximate reconstruction of the 1513 project for the Tomb of Julius II (*front elevation*). After Panofsky, *Tomb Sculpture,* Fig. 420. Reproduced by permission.

Figure 8. Approximate reconstruction of the 1516 project for the Tomb of Julius II (*front elevation*). After Johannes Wilde, *Michelangelo's "Victory,"* The Thirty-sixth Charlton Lecture (Oxford, 1954), Fig. 2. Reproduced by permission.

Figure 9. Approximate reconstruction of the 1532 project for the Tomb of Julius II (*front elevation*). After Charles de Tolnay, *Michelangelo. IV: The Tomb of Julius II* (Princeton, 1954), Fig. 206. Reproduced by permission.

Figure 10. Michelangelo, "The 'Dying' Slave." Louvre, Paris. Reproduced by permission of the Service de Documentation Photographique des Musées Nationaux, Versailles.

Figure 11. Michelangelo, "The 'Rebellious' Slave." Louvre, Paris. Reproduced by permission of the Service de Documentation Photographique des Musées Nationaux, Versailles.

Figure 12. Detail from "The 'Dying' Slave": the ape. Photo by La Photothèque Giraudon, Paris.

Figure 13. Attributed to Aristotile da Sangallo. Drawings after the wax figures of the model of the Julius Tomb, version of 1505(?). Uffizi (No. 14750F), Florence. Reproduced by permission of the Soprintendenza alle Gallerie, Florence.

Figure 14. Michelangelo. Six sketches for the Slaves of the Julius Tomb (with studies for the Sistine Ceiling: putto of the Libyca and her right hand). Ashmolean Museum, Oxford. Reproduced by permission.

Figure 15. Michelangelo, "The 'Atlas' Boboli Slave." Accademia delle Belle Arti, Florence. Photo by Alinari, Florence.

Figure 16. Michelangelo, "The 'Young' Boboli Slave." Accademia delle
Belle Arti, Florence. Photo by Alinari, Florence.

Figure 17. "The Descent into Limbo" (mosaic, thirteenth century). St. Mark, Venice. Photo by Alinari, Florence.

Figure 18. "A Genius of Victory." Drawing after a Michelangelo original. Casa Buonarroti (No. 51F), Florence. Reproduced by permission of the Soprintendenza alle Gallerie, Florence.

Figure 19. "The Rape of Ganymede." Chalk drawing after Michelangelo original. Royal Collection, Windsor. Reproduced by permission of Her Majesty the Queen of England.

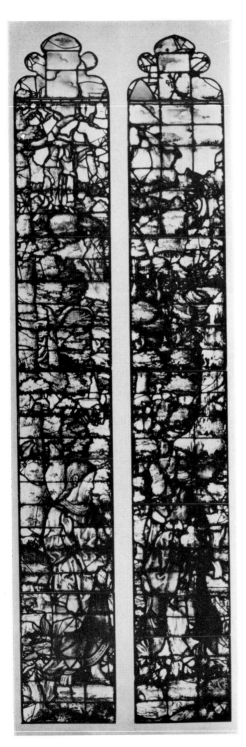

Figure 20. "The Temptation of Christ" (stained glass, between 1532 and 1536). King's College Chapel (Window 7, lower right), Cambridge. Photo by Ramsey and Muspratt, Cambridge.

Figure 21. The Christian Soldier-Pilgrim hampered by the World, Flesh, Devil, and the Old Man. Bottom panel of title-page border engraved by [Jo]hn Payne. From John Downame, *The Christian Warfare,* 4th ed., London, 1634. Courtesy of the Princeton Theological Seminary.

Quæ nos infeſto circumſtant agmine peſtes?
Mundus ouans:Sathanaſq; furens:Caroq;intimus hoſtis.

Die dvy vianden fel,voekb ſynſe; die vnd quellen?
De voeevelt:t Vleekh rebel: en den Vrinxe der Hellen.

Quel ennemy tache/Sans treue et relache/Sur nous trionfer?
La Chair fretillarde/Le Monde,et la darde/Du Prince d'enfer.

Figure 22. "Tres conivrati Animæ hostes." Engraved emblem, No. 38, from Jan David, *Veridicus Christianus*, Antwerp, 1601. Reproduced by permission of the Folger Shakespeare Library.

THE RARER ACTION:
HAMLET'S MOUSETRAP

Herbert Randolph Coursen, Jr.

$\mathcal{T}$*he Tempest* is Shakespeare's final look at the problem he explored so profoundly in *Hamlet*—the question of revenge. *The Tempest* offers, in fact, a point of view on *Hamlet*. One could say, as William Empson does of the two plots of *Wuthering Heights*, that *Hamlet* and *The Tempest* tell "the same story twice with the two possible endings."[1]

Prospero attempts to put Alonzo and the other conspirators through a penitential experience, to evoke within each a "heart's sorrow" leading towards redemption—"a clear life ensuing" (III.iii.81–82).* The banquet spread before the sinners disappears, a Communion Feast deferred until the sinner has, in the words of the 1559 version of *The Book of Common Prayer*, "openly declared himself to have truly repented and amended his former naughty life."[2]

Immediately after the table is removed, Alonzo repents:

> O, it is monstrous, monstrous!
> Methought the billows spoke and told me of it;
> The winds did sing it to me, and the thunder,
> That deep and dreadful organ-pipe, pronounc'd
> The name of Prosper; it did bass my trespass.
> Therefore my son i' th' ooze is bedded, and
> I'll seek him deeper than e'er plummet sounded
> And with him there lie mudded. (III.iii.95–102)

Here "heart's sorrow" is expressed as a precondition not for salvation but for suicide. Alonzo's reason *will* be obliterated—it will, in Prospero's metaphor, lie "foul and muddy" (v.i.82). But Alonzo, like Lear, will awaken on the far side of annihilation. His repentance

---

* Quotations accord with *The Complete Plays and Poems*, ed. William A. Neilson and Charles Hill (Cambridge, Mass., 1942).

speech contradicts his impulse towards suicide by implying the essential rhythm of *The Tempest*—the transition from storm ("billows," "wind," "thunder") to harmony ("sing," "organ-pipe," "bass").[3]

Prospero's redemption involves the same movement, from "mutinous winds" to "heavenly music" (v.i.42 and 52). The redemption of Prospero shows us clearly the alternative Hamlet ignored when he created and then destroyed his own potentially redemptive drama, the play-within-the-play. As Francis Fergusson says, Prospero "has a ripeness and a clarity and a power which Hamlet lacks, but for that very reason he helps one to see what Hamlet, with his play, was trying to do."[4] The harmonious results of Prospero's drama provide a dimension against which to place the disaster of Hamlet's incomplete play.

The climax of Prospero's production and of *The Tempest* comes once each of his enemies "Lies at [his] mercy" (IV.i.264). It may be, as Kenneth Muir suggests, that "when he has his enemies in his power Prospero has to overcome again the natural desire towards vengeance."[5] It is tempting to believe that Prospero has struggled all along with his inclination to revenge, that his outbursts have been signs of inner conflict. In the absence of much solid evidence for this view, however, it is safer to assume that Prospero finally experiences the truth of what until now has been an intellectual conception. His decision is perhaps better described as a choice between judging and not judging. On returning from Prospero's spellbound enemies, Ariel poses a crucial question:

> *Ariel.* . . . the good old Lord, Gonzalo,
> His tears run down his beard like winter's drops
> From eaves of reeds. Your charm so strongly works 'em,
> That if you beheld them, your affections
> Would become tender.
>   *Prospero.*   Dost thou think so, spirit?
>   *Ariel.* Mine would, sir, were I human.   (v.i.15–20)

Are you human, Ariel asks, or have you removed yourself so far into your godlike role that you have lost the ability for compassion? Ariel hints that thus far Prospero's affections have been far from tender. Ariel's is another of the analogues of compassion presented to Prospero —Miranda's for those on the ship and later for Ferdinand, Ferdinand's for his father, Alonzo's for Ferdinand, Gonzalo's for his companions, and now Ariel's. At last, Prospero's humanity emerges from the godlike façade:

> Hast thou, which art but air, a touch, a feeling
> Of their afflictions, and shall not myself,
> One of their kind, that relish all as sharply
> Passion as they, be kindlier mov'd than thou art?   (v.i.21–24)

Prospero, in the words of David Horowitz, "is moved to mercy by the image of himself, suffering in their agony."[6] Having himself achieved compassion, he reasserts the principle of control, applying it at last to himself as he had earlier applied it to Miranda, Ferdinand, Ariel, and, more harshly, to Caliban:

> Yet with my nobler reason 'gainst my fury
> Do I take part. The rarer action is
> In virtue than in vengeance. They being penitent,
> The sole drift of my purpose doth extend
> Not a frown further. Go, release them, Ariel.
> My charms I'll break, their senses I'll restore,
> And they shall be themselves.   (v.i.26–32)

In breaking his charms, he becomes himself. Prospero the god has accomplished all he can and the need for the role is over. He frees himself, achieving the harmony he hopes to have encouraged in his enemies. He throws over the magic which " 'twixt the green sea and the azur'd vault / Set roaring war" (v.i.43–44) in favor of "heavenly music" (v.i.52), the last outward manifestation of his potent art. He had been like the Christ who stilled the "great tempest in the sea, so that the ship was covered with waves" (Matt. viii.24);* and when he said, "not so much perdition as an hair / Betid to any creature in the vessel" (1.ii.30–31), he echoed the Apostle Paul, who had said "There shall not an haire fall from the head of any of you" to a group of frightened men on a tempest-tossed boat (Acts xxvii.34).[7] Prospero is most Christ-like, however, as he descends from the remote reaches of godhead to rejoin humanity as healer and man of compassion:

> A solemn air and the best comforter
> To an unsettled fancy cure thy brains,
> Now useless, boil'd within thy skull! . . .
> Holy Gonzalo, honourable man,

---

* Prospero is, in the Old Testament sense, "a type of Christ." His defeat of Setebos is analogous to Samson's of Dagon (in Judges)—a contest, in Miltonic terms, to determine "whose god is God"—and to Elijah's victory over Baal (I Kings). In Milton, Christ chases away the pagan gods in "On the Morning of Christ's Nativity," defeats the rebel angels in *Paradise Lost,* and vanquishes Satan in *Paradise Regained.*

> Mine eyes, ev'n sociable to the shew of thine,
> Fall fellowly drops.   (v.i.26–64)

As Theodore Spencer says, "Prospero is purged, but his purgation is exactly opposite to the purgation of Alonzo: Alonzo sinks *below* reason before returning to it; before Prospero returns to the rational human level he has lived for a time *above* it. The important thing to notice is his return."[8] The "fellowly drops" shed by Prospero for "Holy Gonzalo" are reminiscent of Cordelia's tears, "holy water" (iv.iii.32), which she hopes will prove restorative:

> . . . All blest secrets,
> All you unpublish'd virtues of the earth,
> Spring with my tears! Be aidant and remediate
> In the good man's distress!   (iv.iv.15–18)

While the situations are similar, the primary restoration occurring with Prospero's tears is his own.

Significantly, Prospero does not provide the rationale behind his production until Act v. (Ariel, of course, has done so earlier.) Prospero's explanation coincides with his return to humanity from the remote and lofty plane he had inhabited. His feelings catch up with his understanding. Appropriately, we are invited to identify with him at this "sociable" moment. As he finally takes us into his confidence, we experience his return to humanity. The moment represents a perfect coalescence of a character's awareness of himself and the spectator's awareness of the character.

Prospero recognizes that the quality of redemption is not strained. Were he to continue playing God he might destroy whatever his play has accomplished *within* its participants.[9] Instead, he surrenders his role and frees himself from the bondage of his own will, becoming a humble exemplification of the theme of his play, of *The Tempest*, and of The Sermon on the Mount (which Prospero's Epilogue paraphrases), forgiving others as a precondition to his own suit for grace. He recognizes the potential irony of his position, and in surrendering one of his roles he eliminates the ironic possibilities inherent in the dichotomy between man and god. Instead of judging, he forgives.

Hamlet, like Prospero, is a dramatist and impresario, producer of a play in which a guilty king will be forced to react to the mirror-like image of his guilt. But Hamlet subordinates his role as playwright-producer to his role as revenger. It is a tragic subordination. Hamlet discovers the way out of tragedy, the means of harmonizing his role and his nature. His error in judgment lies in his not recognizing what he might have accomplished with his play-within-the-play. Prospero shows us. He allows his redemptive drama to work unhindered inside the guilty Alonzo and it redeems the king—as it redeems Prospero.

This essay, which is divided into five sections, will suggest that Hamlet's play falls crucially short of the potentiality Hamlet himself ascribes to it. It evokes in Claudius a sorrowful heart, but because Hamlet interrupts it it cannot complete in Claudius or Hamlet the movement towards clarity of life. A vehicle for redemption becomes instead a device for torture (Section I). Hamlet, the single character capable of cleansing Denmark of its corruption, merely adds to it (Section II). Section III will suggest that the breakdown of Hamlet's play is central to one of the recurring motifs of the larger play—the failure of ritual. That all rituals fail in Denmark raises the question of Hamlet's responsibility for the disasters which follow the breakup of the play. Had he alternatives or is he merely the victim of a deeply flawed universe? Section IV will attempt to show that the conflict which Hamlet resolves so negatively during his play is reiterated throughout Act I, and that the question of revenge is examined both in the Player's speech and in the career of Laertes. Section V will suggest that the Hamlet of Act v is not redeemed but has continued to fall since the moment when he shattered the promise of his play. The examination of the Hamlet of Act v will raise a final question—if this is the meaning of Hamlet, what is the meaning of *Hamlet?*

I

The play-within-the-play performs several functions. It captures the conscience of its producer as well as, in a later scene, that of the king. Thematically, it captures profoundly the larger play's concern with truth and illusion. Structurally, it is undoubtedly the climax of the drama surrounding it. After the smaller play is over, the events of *Hamlet* follow inexorably.

Most critics see Hamlet's play as a success. "His only deliberately chosen act, his only real *success* in the course of the tragedy, is dramatic: the play within the play," says Leslie Fiedler.[10] "The presentation of the play is Hamlet's attack; it succeeds; it convicts Claudius' regime," says Francis Fergusson.[11] Dover Wilson calls the play and

Hamlet's management of it "a marvellously successful performance of histrionic art."[12] H. D. F. Kitto states that "with the climax of the Gonzago-play, so relentlessly stage-managed by Hamlet, the King's guilt breaks through his guard. Hamlet challenged him, and has caught his conscience."[13] Andrew J. Green describes the climax of Hamlet's play: "The realities of play and play within have coalesced; and Hamlet gives one last fierce, triumphant wrench to the screw. And Claudius gives way."[14] The play, then, designed to torture and expose Claudius, is a triumph. But is it?

Hamlet provides the rationale behind his play—as certain other Shakespearean manipulators do not*—thus helping us to recognize the crucial inconsistency between his plans and their execution. Hamlet's conception of *The Murder of Gonzago* suggests that torture is not its ultimate aim:

> . . . I have heard
> That guilty creatures sitting at a play
> Have by the very cunning of the scene
> Been struck so to the soul that presently
> They have proclaim'd their malefactions;
> For murder, though it have no tongue, will speak
> With most miraculous organ.†   (II.ii.617–623)

Here, Hamlet adumbrates a play whereby Claudius's *soul* will be worked so as to force him to public confession—"presently" (meaning "at once") to "proclaim" (the word suggests a public declaration) his "malefactions," not merely reveal his guilt to an intently watching Hamlet. Hamlet has designed a play which will torture Claudius with guilt, but which will give that guilt release, as in a religious sacrament designed to deal with the soul. The play is constructed so as to enforce upon Claudius what Robert Hunter calls "the first and last parts of repentance . . . 'contrition of the heart' and 'an amendment of life.' "[15] The sacramental possibilities are emphasized by Hamlet's use of "miraculous" and, later in this soliloquy, "conscience." But, as Fergusson says, "if [Hamlet] stumbles on the theater as a means of realizing

---

* Prince Hal provides the rationale behind his sojourn in Eastcheap, but Henry V does not impart to the audience his plan for manipulating England into the French war. Henry V becomes for us a more remote, withdrawn figure than was Prince Hal; we are appropriately "distanced" from the king. Vincentio offers conflicting reasons for absenting himself, forcing us, I believe, to suspect his motives.
† Cf. Alonzo's "deep and dreadful organ-pipe."

his vision . . . , he does not clearly understand what he has accomplished."[16] Rather than develop his own suggestions, Hamlet reduces his conception of the play to the level of a duel between himself and Claudius:

> . . . I'll observe his looks.
> I'll tent him to the quick; if he but blench,
> I know my course.   (ii.ii.625–627)

His play will suffer at its climactic moment from just such a reduction. Hamlet's personal feelings will cancel the higher vision he himself has defined.

That Hamlet does not clearly understand the potential of his creation is suggested again in his instructions to Horatio immediately prior to the play. He speaks of Claudius's "occulted guilt" unkenneling itself (iii.ii.85–86), leaping forth like an animal from a hiding place. The strength of the metaphor suggests more than a mere private revelation. Then, however, Hamlet reverts to a belief that the play will provide not public exposure but mere facial expressions meaningful to those anticipating them:

> For I mine eyes will rivet to his face,
> And after we will both our judgements join
> To censure of his seeming.   (iii.ii.85–86)

Apparently, Hamlet believes that Claudius may escape detection by the uninformed. If so, his play will be a disaster; if not, if the play can force Claudius publicly to proclaim his malefactions, it will be a triumph.[17] But although he has expressed the latter possibility, Hamlet views the play primarily as a prelude to further action ("if he but blench, / I know my course"), not as a vehicle relieving him of the *necessity* for further action, a possible solution to his dilemma. We should enter the Play Scene aware of the two ways in which it may develop. The play-within is like the ghost, who may be a "spirit of health or goblin damn'd," who may bring "airs from heaven or blasts from hell," whose intentions may be "wicked or charitable" (i.iv.40, 41, 42). Events following the play prove that the meaning of the ghost *is* determined by the play—but not as Hamlet thinks it is.

Has Shakespeare shown Claudius's character to be susceptible to open confession? A hardened criminal, an Iago, Iachimo, or Edmund, for example, might be expected to sit through the performance osten-

sibly unmoved.* Shortly before the play, however, Claudius reveals a
conscience to be caught. Polonius speaks of "devotion's visage / And
pious action" with which "we do sugar o'er / The devil himself" (III.i.
47–49). These sententiae draw a tortured aside from Claudius:

> How smart a lash that speech doth give my conscience.
> The harlot's cheek, beautied with plast'ring art,
> Is not more ugly to the thing that helps it
> Than is my deed to my most painted word.
> O heavy burden!   (III.i.50–54)

As Harold Goddard says, "The character of Claudius fits the situation
[of Hamlet's play] as if explicitly created for it . . . a man conscious
of his sin and longing to be rid of it—a fit subject of the redemptive
power of art."[18] To claim that a play cannot have this effect on a
guilty creature is to deny not only Hamlet's own words but the ritual
sources and ritual power of drama, of which Shakespeare has already
shown such an awareness in the comedies. It is to ignore what Shakespeare is soon to do with Macbeth in the Banquet Scene,[19] where a
ghostly pantomime evokes virtual confession of regicide from the sin-
haunted king.

If Claudius is fit for redemption, what of Hamlet? Is he capable
of an attitude which might permit his play to redeem rather than
torture? He exhibits such an attitude on the arrival of the players.
When news of their approach reaches him, he shows, according to
Rosencrantz, "a kind of joy / To hear of it" (III.i.18). He greets them
graciously: "You're welcome, masters, welcome all. I am glad to see
thee well. Welcome, good friends" (II.ii.440–441).

He asks Polonius to "see the players well bestow'd" (II.ii.546), and
when the counsellor replies that he "will use them according to their
desert" (II.ii.552), Hamlet exclaims:

> God's bodykins, man, better. Use every man after his desert and who
> should scape whipping? Use them after your own honour and dignity. The
> less they deserve, the more merit is in your bounty. Take them in.
>   (II.ii.553–557)

---

* *The Tempest*'s Antonio is a good example. His final comment, about Caliban's
marketability, places him in the company of Shakespeare's other calculator-villains.
He chooses, as Auden has him say in *The Sea and the Mirror,* to remain "myself,
alone." As Frank Kermode says of Antonio's refusal to repent, "A world without
Antonio is a world without freedom."—Introduction to *The Tempest* (Cambridge,
Mass., 1958), p. lxii. Alonzo, not Antonio, is the "Claudius" of *The Tempest*.

"God's bodykins"—the wafers of the Communion Service. And while the phrase was a common expletive, not to be construed in its full religious context, the words which follow are precisely in the spirit of the sacrament of forgiveness. At this moment, Hamlet has risen above the cynicism and despair which have characterized him thus far. His melancholy drops like a robe from his shoulders; we glimpse him as he might have been had not events in Denmark thwarted his creative drives. Suddenly, he is an artist: "You could for a need, study a speech of some dozen or sixteen lines which I would set down and insert in't, could you not?" (ii.ii.566–568). "Aye, my lord" (ii.ii.569), replies the First Player. Hamlet tells him to follow Polonius, "and look you, mock him not" (ii.ii.571). The man Hamlet has mocked so mercilessly becomes subject to Hamlet's charity. For a moment, free of negation, he follows his own advice about using men better than they deserve. He loses himself in the coming of the players, and, in losing himself, finds himself. He also finds a potential solution to his chief external problem—that of Claudius and revenge.

The transformation of Hamlet, however, is brief. The echo of a former Hamlet, patron of actors and the arts, amateur performer and playwright, is overwhelmed by the realities of Elsinore. Between his plans for the play and its performance comes the bitter scene with Ophelia with its scathing misogyny. "Love," exclaims Claudius, "his affections do not that way tend!" (iii.i.170). The charity which quickened in Hamlet as the players arrived surrenders to hatred. Bitterness characterizes his performance at the play. He pursues the theme of woman's frailty: "What should a man do but be merry? For, look you, how cheerfully my mother looks, and my father died within's two hours" (iii.ii.133–135).

> *Hamlet.* Is this a prologue, or the posy of a ring?
> *Ophelia.* 'Tis brief my lord.
> *Hamlet.* As woman's love.
>
> (iii.ii.162–164)

The point of Hamlet's "posy of a ring" becomes clear when we remember Gratiano's ring, "whose posy was . . . 'Love me, and leave me not'" (*The Merchant of Venice*, v.i.148–150).

So obsessed is Hamlet with infidelity—his mother's and what he may consider to be Ophelia's—that he seems to forget that Claudius is his object. He turns to his mother:

> *Hamlet.* Madam, how like you this play?
> *Gertrude.* The lady protests too much, methinks.
> *Hamlet.* O, but she'll keep her word.
>
> (III.ii.239–241)

Claudius interrupts the colloquy: "Have you heard the argument? Is there no offense in't?" (II.ii.242–243). Claudius thinks perhaps (or pretends to think, depending on his recognition of the dumb show) that the play thrusts at his hasty marriage to Gertrude. Hamlet must demur, lest Claudius seize a pretext for halting the performance: "No, no, they do but jest, poison in jest, no offense i' th' world" (III.ii.244–245.) This merely arouses further suspicion: "What do you call the play?" (III.ii.246). Hamlet calls it "The Mouse-trap," and suggests that he now conceives of it not as evoking a confession from Claudius or even as forcing him to reveal himself to two sets of informed eyes. Hamlet sees the play as a rack on which to torture Claudius: " 'Tis a knavish piece of work, but what o' that? Your Majesty, and we that have free souls, it touches us not. Let the gall'd jade wince, our withers are unwrung" (III.ii.250–253).

Hamlet's own soul is becoming less free as the performance continues. He identifies Lucianus as "nephew to the king" (III.ii.254), a slip containing a naked threat to Claudius and revealing Hamlet's increasing personal involvement in the drama being enacted before the court. As the play becomes more real for him, Hamlet abandons the role he has defined for himself, that of spectator of a play and of careful observer of Claudius's face as the king's crime is reflected back at him from the stage. Hamlet becomes a participant in the play, as Ophelia suggests: "You are a good chorus, my lord" (III.ii.255). But Hamlet's choric comment was about a *king*, not, as in *The Murder of Gonzago*, a duke. Hamlet's movement towards the play is a movement towards personal bitterness. He is losing his artistic objectivity. The play-within must pause, while he vents more cynicism about love and marriage:

> *Hamlet.* I could interpret between you and your love if I could see the puppets dallying.
> *Ophelia.* You are keen, my lord, you are keen.
> *Hamlet.* It would cost you a groaning to take off my edge.
> *Ophelia.* Still better, and worse.
> *Hamlet.* So you mistake husbands.   (III.ii.256–262)

As Weston Babcock says of this colloquy: "He has spat out his bitterness on his mother and Claudius; now he flares at the girl who, he
thinks, has betrayed him. The bait Hamlet had inserted in the trap
for the King has caught himself."[20] As Madariaga says, "Shakespeare
turns the tables of the experiment. It is the tester who is most tested
of all."[21]

Having interrupted his play, Hamlet commands it to continue:

> Begin, murderer; pox, leave thy damnable faces and begin.
> Come, "the croaking raven doth bellow for revenge." (III.ii.263–264)

Since the crime of Lucianus is not motivated by revenge, Hamlet reveals here either that he is anxious for the murder to be perpetrated
so that revenge can follow, or, more probably, that he views the
staging of the murder as a revenge on Claudius. Hamlet is forgetting
in his rising excitement and deepening bitterness that his play was
to represent "something like the murder of my father." It becomes instead, as his "nephew . . . king" slip and his use of "revenge" suggest,
the murder of Claudius. The scene before him—quite apart from its
effects on Claudius—becomes a fulfillment of Hamlet's desire for revenge. As Miss Prosser says, "[Hamlet's] hatred of Claudius is so intense that he is led subconsciously to identify himself with the
murderer."[22] Hamlet's psychic participation in the smaller drama reveals what he has become in the larger drama—a man bellowing for
vengeance. Even Hamlet's lesser vision of his play—that it might
reveal to him Claudius's guilt—surrenders for the moment before
Hamlet's inability to separate art from life. Hamlet, not Claudius,
breaks down before the play. We approach the play-within expecting
to observe with Hamlet the guilt of Claudius, hoping perhaps that
Claudius will break down publicly. Instead, we find the prince, with
whom we have so strongly associated, writhing in the agony of his
own hatred.

Alfred Harbage summarizes what follows: "As the act of poisoning
occurs, Claudius rises, crying for lights and rushing out, with all but
Hamlet and Horatio following."[23] Summaries must be simplified, but
this omits the crucial fact that Hamlet, not Claudius, interrupts the
play for the final time. At the moment of the poisoning, Hamlet leaps
up and blurts out much of the rest of the story: "He poisons him i'
th' garden for 's estate. His name's Gonzago, the story is extant, and

writ in choice Italian. You shall see anon how the murderer gets the love of Gonzago's wife" (III.ii.272–275).

The play interrupted again (by what could, after all, be construed as Hamlet's lunacy),[24] "The King rises" (III.ii.276). Hamlet cries, "What, frighted with false fire?" (III.ii.277). Gertrude asks Claudius how he fares, and Polonius commands unnecessarily, "Give o'er the play" (III.ii.279). Claudius flees, crying, "Give me some light. Away!" (III.ii.280). That is all he says, regardless of what agony may have played across his countenance. The indelible impression is that something in Hamlet—not in Claudius—forced the play's premature closing. Hamlet was unable to maintain his role as spectator—like the character in *Great Expectations* who leaps onstage to rescue Desdemona from Mr. Wopsle, or like Partridge in *Tom Jones* who cannot control his fear of the ghost during a performance of *Hamlet*. There, however, the interruption was comic. Here, it is tragic.

Hamlet demonstrates in the Play Scene the lack of that control he advocated to the players and admired in Horatio: "Give me that man / That is not passion's slave" (III.ii.77).* Hamlet was not that man. He did precisely what he had instructed the clowns *not* to do:

> . . . let those that play your clowns speak no more than is set down for them; for there be of them that will themselves laugh to set on some quantity of barren spectators to laugh too, though in the mean time some necessary question of the play be then to be considered. That's villainous . . . .
> (III.ii.42–47)

By speaking more than was set down for him, Hamlet interrupts the consideration of the necessary question of both *The Murder of Gonzago* and *Hamlet*. Overcome by a compulsion born of excitement, bitterness, and hatred, the man betrays the artist. Just as he should step back and say, Now, let it work, he leaps forward to mar what might have been his masterpiece. The desire to inflict pain overwhelms the possibilities of redemption, Hamlet's as well as Claudius's. As Goddard says, "In so far as he regards *The Murder of Gonzago* as [a work of dramatic art] and is willing to let it have its own way with the King, he is doing what his soul calls on him to do. But in so far as he regards it as a trap, an engine for torturing a victim, for catching not the King's conscience but the King himself, the play is nothing but a contrivance for murder on the mental plane."[25] The play reveals not

---

* Cf. Prospero's "that relish all as sharply / Passion as they . . ."

the king's guilt—that is not shown explicitly until his soliloquy—but Hamlet's desire to twist the wheel of the rack his play becomes. He has fallen from that moment when he could advocate charity even for Polonius. And, as Hamlet falls, his play falls short of the great possibilities he had once ascribed to it.

II

The events immediately following the play suggest both what it might have been and what it becomes. After the play breaks up, Hamlet excitedly compares Claudius and himself to animals:

> . . . let the stricken deer go weep,
> The hart ungalled play . . . .   (iii.ii.282–283)

He has not caught a conscience, he has wounded an animal. While he sees himself as a "hart ungalled," his performance at the play suggests that his heart was hardly ungalled and that his words to Claudius then applied as well to himself (the plural pronouns support the suggestion): "Your Majesty, and we that have free souls, it touches us not. Let the gall'd jade wince, our withers are unwrung" (iii.ii.251–253). Tillyard says that "Hamlet is painfully aware of the baffling human predicament between the angels and the beasts, between the glory of having been made in God's image and the incrimination of being descended from fallen Adam."[26] The choice between these possibilities is made in the Play Scene. Hamlet translates the play's higher potential into a bestial and fallen version which wounds an animal and traps himself as well.

Hamlet calls his play "false fire," which Kittredge defines as "the harmless discharge of a gun loaded with powder only."[27] Thus Hamlet himself describes the ineffectuality of his play. "False fire" is part of what Roger L. Cox calls "the dominant metaphor" of Hamlet— "the use of weapons," particularly weapons which "miss the mark"— as, of course, Hamlet's play has done.[28] For Claudius, however, the play has taken on the deepest of meanings. As Fiedler says of the play, it has been "a plot configuration with an archetypal meaning quite independent of any individual's conscious exploitation of it."[29] If Hamlet did not recognize the fullest implications of his play, Claudius does, clearly, if too late. The drama of his guilt enacted before him— a mere fragment of a play—drives him to his knees in an attempt at prayer. The question of what the full performance might have

accomplished is answered by a confession which is private, hence
mere self-torture. The private man, ruthlessly aware of his guilt, is
helpless to free himself of it. Hamlet's play might have forced
Claudius to do what he realizes is inevitable anyway, to reveal himself regardless of whatever protective façades he has erected between
his guilt and this world:

> In the corrupted currents of this world,
> Offence's gilded hand may shove by justice,
> And oft 'tis seen the wicked prize itself
> Buys out the law. But 'tis not so above;
> There is no shuffling, there the action lies
> In his true nature, and we ourselves compell'd
> Even to the teeth and forehead of our faults
> To give in evidence.   (III.iii.57–64)

Hamlet's play was conceived to produce precisely the effect Claudius
describes—to strike so to the soul that the malefactor would be compelled to proclaim his crimes.

While the king attempts to pray, Hamlet accepts the ghost's word
"for a thousand pound" (III.ii.297). Henceforth he never questions it.
His reaction to the play is hardly that of Claudius:

> 'Tis now the very witching time of night,
> When churchyards yawn and hell itself breathes out
> Contagion to this world. Now could I drink hot blood,
> And do such bitter business as the day
> Would quake to look on.   (III.ii.406–410)

Even as the ghost is accepted, one must wonder whether it *did* bring
"blasts from hell." The Communion suggestion of "God's bodykins"
had devolved to the vampiric overtones of "hot blood."* The hellish
implications of the speech are underscored a moment later, as Hamlet
discovers the kneeling king:

> Now might I do it pat, now he is praying;
> And now I'll do't—And so he goes to heaven,
> And so am I reveng'd. That would be scann'd.
> A villain kills my father, and for that
> I, his sole son, do this same villain send
> To heaven.

---

* Miss Prosser says of Hamlet's "hot blood" that "to the Elibabethan audience,
the statement would inevitably have suggested one of the most degenerate prac-
tices of the Black Mass . . . . Shakespeare's audience almost certainly found
Hamlet's thirst for blood a terrifying indication of his state of mind."—*Hamlet
and Revenge*, pp. 181–182.

> Oh, this is hire and salary, not revenge . . .
> Up, sword, and know thou a more horrid hent.
> When he is drunk asleep, or in his rage,
> Or in th' incestuous pleasure of his bed,
> At gaming, swearing, or about some act
> That has no relish of salvation in't,—
> Then trip him, that his heels may kick at heaven,
> And that his soul may be as damn'd and black
> As hell, whereto it goes. (iii.iii.73–95)

Dr. Johnson calls these words "too horrible to be read or to be uttered."[30] They are so horrible, in fact, that critics from Coleridge on have viewed them as a rationalization of Hamlet's *real* reason for sparing Claudius. "The determination to allow the guilty King to escape at such a moment," says Coleridge, "is only part of the indecision and irresoluteness of the hero."[31] While the utter calculation of the speech suggests no mental conflict in Hamlet (as opposed, for example, to the fragmented first soliloquy), one might ask what soliloquy or aside in all of Shakespeare does not represent what its speaker believes to be the truth? To argue otherwise is hopelessly to complicate Shakespeare's use of the convention. Hamlet believes what he says; his words are the logical consequence of the desire for vengeance which overwhelmed him during the Play Scene. His deepest motivation, in fact, may be revealed as he puts up his sword. The full performance of *The Murder of Gonzago* would have cost Claudius his life, but it might have saved him his soul. But revenge is not revenge, says Hamlet, unless the victim goes to hell.

Claudius himself defines accurately not only his own, but Hamlet's dilemma:

> My stronger guilt defeats my strong intent,
> And, like a man to double business bound,
> I stand in pause where I shall first begin,
> And both neglect. (iii.iii.40–44)

Hamlet and Claudius are caught in the same trap. Hamlet too is bound to double business—to exact temporal vengeance and to ensure Claudius's eternal damnation. Revenge is not merely "an eye for an eye" but "a soul for a soul"—" 'Tis heavy," Hamlet believes, with his father (iii.iii.84). Here, Hamlet's desire to send Claudius's soul to hell defeats his wish for revenge in this world—a stronger guilt defeating a strong intent.

After this pause, Hamlet arrives at Gertrude's closet and runs Polonius through. Hamlet's farewell to Polonius contains reminders of his own behavior at the play:

> Thou wretched, rash, intruding fool, farewell!
> I took thee for thy better. Take thy fortune.
> Thou find'st to be too busy is some danger.   (III.iv.31–33)

Soon Hamlet demands of Gertrude, "What devil was't / That thus hath cozen'd you at hoodman-blind?" (III.iv.76–77). What devil prompted Hamlet to thrust through the arras? Surely the action represents some grisly game of blindman's buff. Hamlet's castigation of Gertrude throws back an image of his own loss of control:

> . . . Rebellious hell
> If thou canst mutine in a matron's bones,
> To flaming youth let virtue be as wax
> And melt in her own fire. Proclaim no shame
> When the compulsive ardour gives the charge . . .
>   (III.iv.82–86)

Gertrude's pleas of "No more!" (III.iv.101) are ineffectual. Only the ghost interrupts Hamlet's bitter lecture. While the ghost comes "to whet [Hamlet's] almost blunted purpose," his effect on Hamlet is ambiguous:

> . . . Look you how pale he glares!
> His form and cause conjoin'd, preaching to stones,
> Would make them capable.—Do not look upon me,
> Lest with this piteous action you convert
> My stern effects; then what I have to do
> Will want true colour, tears perchance for blood.
>   (III.iv.125–130)

He becomes a Hamlet who might substitute pity for vengeance, tears for blood. But it is too late for that. Hamlet's play is over, its promise forever unrealizable, and, as part of the fatal rhythm emanating from the interrupted drama, the body of Polonius grows cold at Hamlet's feet. That the ghost who prompted vengeance and who comes here to whet Hamlet's purpose should now, in Hamlet's eyes, be an agent of its mitigation is perhaps the supreme irony in this intensely ironic scene.

The ghost departs and Hamlet reads his mother another of his lectures on self-control:

> . . . Refrain tonight,
> And that shall lend a kind of easiness
> To the next abstinence; the next more easy;
> For use almost can change the stamp of nature,
> And either master the devil or throw him out,
> With wondrous potency.   (III.iv.165–170)

As he points Gertrude in one direction, Hamlet embarks on another.
Use can almost change the stamp of nature. He closes the scene with
this curious mingling of harshness towards his victim and tenderness
towards his mother:

> I'll lug the guts into the neighbor room.
> Mother, good-night. Indeed this counsellor
> Is now most still, most secret, and most grave,
> Who was in life a foolish prating knave.—
> Come, sir, to draw toward an end with you.—
> Good-night, mother.   (III.iv.212–217)

Again, Hamlet seems to be about the devil's business.

At certain moments in Shakespeare's plays, his characters are in control of the alternatives they face—or at least seem to be. Shakespeare
makes it seem that events are the products of a character's decision—
whether Brutus's decision to kill Caesar or Richard's to seize the Lan-
castrian estates or Antony's to return to Cleopatra after marrying
Octavia—even though we know that Holingshed or North has already
provided Shakespeare with an unalterable framework of events. The
imitation of decision turns the framework into drama. After their de-
cisions, the characters become fragments in a flow of larger forces:
Macbeth's murder of Duncan elicits the moral imperative of his damnation and the political necessity of his temporal defeat. As Hamlet's
play begins, he controls the forces of appearance and reality which
have thus far been confusing him (in the persons of Gertrude,
Ophelia, the ghost). When he limits his play to the only realities he
sees there, bitterness and hatred, he loses control again. Immediately
he is the victim of appearances again—in believing the kneeling
Claudius to be praying and in blindly stabbing Polonius. To argue
that the sparing of Claudius or the killing of Polonius is the climax of
Hamlet is to deny that these events or events like them are inevitable
once Hamlet surrenders to hatred and once Claudius's guilt achieves
no effective release.

Fredson Bowers suggests that heaven has placed Hamlet "in a position of a minister for whom public justice would be arranged at heaven's own pleasure."[32] Bowers does little with the Mousetrap Scene, calling the Closet Scene the climax of *Hamlet*. Yet the mousetrap fits precisely the conditions he sets for Hamlet's ministerial function: "If Hamlet hopes to right the wrong done him and his father, he must contrive a public vengeance which will demonstrate him to be a minister of heaven's justice."[33] Bowers' definition of a play's climax is "that scene in the play in which an action occurs which tips the scales for or against the fate of the protagonist in terms of the future action."[34] The Play Scene, then, becomes the climax of the play. By the time Hamlet is deceived into sparing Claudius or killing Polonius, his chance to be a minister has passed. He becomes again the victim of the very forces of appearance and reality he had so recently controlled.[35]

In a later article, Bowers argues against the play-within as climax: "We may inquire what is the significant issue of this scene, what the fateful decision that thereupon makes the tragic catastrophe inevitable? Might not the identical scene serve as the climax for a denouement in which Hamlet succeeds in a well-planned revenge and ascends the throne of Denmark?"[36] Precisely.

Helen Gardner would suggest that speculation about the possibility of Claudius's confession is irrelevant, since, as she skillfully shows, Shakespeare is committed to the pattern of revenge drama.[37] Again, however, Shakespeare does not make us feel that his character is subjected to a preconceived pattern. In fact, the drama *Hamlet* emerges from the interaction of the revenge thesis and the character of Hamlet.

It is easy to say, as Traversi does, that "there is . . . no question of the rightness or otherwise of revenge," that revenge is simply a "given" we must accept.[38] Shakespeare, however, often explores what for other dramatists would be initial premises. M. R. Ridley is correct when he says that "Shakespeare had not yet contrived a harmony between plot and character. Hamlet is not the right character for that particular plot."[39] Indeed, Hamlet is not fitted for the role of revenger, and the play depicts the struggle between the demands of the revenge code and Hamlet's nature. The struggle culminates at that central moment when the lives and souls of virtually all the characters balance on an artist's ability to understand what he has created. *Hamlet* follows the pattern of the revenge play, but Shakespeare makes Hamlet responsible for the imposition of that pattern on the other characters. To see

Hamlet in relation to its genre is a useful corrective to studies which ignore generic considerations. Generic studies, however, tend to reduce *Hamlet* to the level of *The Revenger's Tragedy*. One reason why *Hamlet* will continue to fascinate us even after the differences between Tourneur's revenge plays have blurred in our minds is suggested by J. C. Maxwell: "In *Hamlet,* just because the central moral question about revenge is not overtly raised, and is, indeed, kept from the full recognition of the hero, it can be built into the central fabric of the play. . . . Yet that sense of incongruity between central figure and background remains, and this is best attributed . . . to the decision to leave the framework of a revenge play standing, while raising the moral problem of revenge only by implication and by that very fact giving it a more universal significance than it had had before on the English stage."[40] We must be aware of *Hamlet's* genre, but we must be aware also that *Hamlet* is an *incomparable* revenge play, made so partially by the conflict between the nature of the task and the nature of the man selected to fulfill it.

III

Lest it be claimed that Hamlet's play has been emphasized out of proportion to its significance in terms of the larger play, the incomplete *Murder of Gonzago* should be placed in the context of one of the most pervasive patterns of *Hamlet,* that of the corrupted ritual. From the beginning to the end of *Hamlet,* rituals are undermined or interrupted.

Even so simple a ritual as the changing of the guards does not go smoothly at Elsinore:

> Francisco [*at his post. Enter to him*] Bernardo.
> *Bernardo.* Who's there?
> *Francisco.* Nay, answer me. Stand, and unfold yourself.
>
> (I.i.1–2)

Not the sentry but the intruder issues the challenge—the guards are nervous. Another ceremony qualified by suspicious associations is the marriage of Claudius and Gertrude, linked to the memory of a recent funeral:

> . . . our sometime sister, now our queen,
> Th' imperial jointress of this warlike state,
> Have we, as 'twere with a defeated joy,—

> With one auspicious and one dropping eye,
> With mirth in funeral and with dirge in marriage,
> In equal scale weighing delight and dole,—
> Taken to wife.   (i.ii.8–14)

> Thrift, thrift, Horatio! The funeral bak'd meats
> Did coldly furnish forth the marriage tables.   (i.ii.180–181)

The linkage of death and marriage reaches almost to the end of the play, as a heartbroken Gertrude scatters flowers on Ophelia's grave:

> Sweets to the sweet; farewell!
> I hop'd thou shouldst have been my Hamlet's wife.
> I thought thy bride-bed to have deck'd, sweet maid,
> And not t' have strew'd thy grave.   (v.i.266–269)

Ophelia's career exemplifies the perversion of ritual suffered by Denmark. Polonius early instructs her not to believe Hamlet's protestations of love, which she says have been accompanied "With almost all the holy vows of heaven" (i.iii.114). Her father's retort defines the force which will prevail over Ophelia. She will realize the fulfillment of no "holy vows," but will be figuratively prostituted by the corruption surrounding her:

> Do not believe his vows; for they are brokers,
> Not of that dye which their investments show,
> But mere implorators of unholy suits,
> Breathing like sanctified and pious bawds,
> The better to beguile.   (i.iii.127–131)

Polonius anticipates only seduction, and commands Ophelia to reject the prince. Thus one of the world's promising beginnings is thwarted. Later, Ophelia becomes a pawn in Polonius's plot to discover the source of Hamlet's madness. The old man hands her a prayer book, "that show of such an exercise may colour / Your loneliness." The girl who would have believed Hamlet's vows becomes an actress playing Piety. Hamlet accepts her appearance at first—. . . "in thy orisons / Be all my sins rememb'red" (iii.i.88–89) — but soon senses her fraudulence. Bitterly he offers her a choice between escape from this world to a convent or contamination by this world, as in a brothel ("nunnery," as Dover Wilson points out, means both). Before the play, the girl who yearned to believe Hamlet's "holy vows" is the target of his cynical view of marriage—"So you mistake husbands" (iii.ii.262).

Ophelia's deception contributes to Hamlet's cynicism in the Play Scene and thus to his failure to hold to his original vision of his play.

Ophelia goes to both nunneries in her madness. She mingles religious snatches with bawdy songs. The prayer "God be at your table" (IV.v.44) is interrupted by the theme of lost virtue:

> "Then up he rose and donned his clothes,
>   And dupp'd the chamber door;
> Let in the maid, that out a maid
>   Never departed more."   (IV.v.52–55)

"God 'a' mercy on his soul," she sings of her father, "And of all Christian souls, I pray God" (IV.v.199–200). Soon her funeral train approaches. She ends up *between* the two nunneries; while she is buried in sanctified ground by order of the king, her death was dubious and she is interred with "maimed rites" (V.i.242), in spite of Laertes' objection "What ceremony else?" (V.i.245). Laertes has already complained bitterly about the lack of "trophy, sword . . . hatchment . . . noble rite . . . formal ostentation" (IV.v.214–215) over the bones of Polonius, who was buried "In hugger-mugger" (IV.v.84). Ophelia's truncated ceremony is further disrupted by the brawl which rages between Hamlet and Laertes in her very grave.

In this world, the normal and necessary ceremonies of society—the rites of passage—are maimed or unobserved. Marriage carries lingering memories of a funeral, last rites are denied (in the cases of Rosencrantz and Guildenstern—and of old Hamlet, of course), funerals are obscene, attempts at prayer abortive. Sporting events like the duel are deathtraps. Even the drinking of a toast becomes a poisoning of oneself, as Gertrude discovers. Into this pattern of negation fits Hamlet's play, which might have risen to ritual significance, but which breaks up in confusion.* The play, like the careers of Ophelia and of Hamlet (as recounted by Ophelia in III.i.158–168) begins auspiciously but ends by refuting its potential.

Underlying the breakdown of ritual in *Hamlet* is the fact that in murdering the former king Claudius suspends the rules of society. As a regicide, he cannot reinstate them. Denmark is cut off by the crime from the vital forces which endow social actions with relevance. The deepest implications of the crime are suggested by Hamlet, who sees

---

* A student of mine, Charles N. Head, points out that it is a further reversal of ritual for an *audience* to rush out leaving the actors on stage.

the world as "an unweeded garden / That grows to seed" (i.ii.135).
The image of a corrupted Eden might be merely that of a young man
recently initiated into the world's imperfections and looking back
across his adolescence to the happy garden of his youth. The ghost,
however, employs even more explicit evocations of Eden:

> It's given out that, sleeping in my orchard,
> A serpent stung me; so the whole ear of Denmark
> Is by a forged process of my death
> Rankly abus'd; but know, thou noble youth,
> The serpent that did sting thy father's life
> Now wears his crown.   (i.v.35–40)

The real process of old Hamlet's death—the pouring of poison into the
ear—is equivalent to the serpent's action in Eden. Claudius's crime is
equated with man's first disobedience, the act which created the
breach between man and God—the separation Denmark suffers. Claudius himself compares his crime to the first murder, that of Abel by
Cain:

> O my offense is rank, it smells to heaven:
> It hath the primal eldest curse upon't,
> A brother's murder.   (iii.iii.36–38)

Not only has Claudius destroyed the harmony of a perfect world, he
has been the first to commit crime in a fallen world. The fundamental
nature of his crime could hardly be made more emphatic.

Denmark, then, is corrupted, plague-ridden like the Thebes of
Oedipus, as critics from Caroline Spurgeon to Francis Fergusson have
indicated. Ignorance of the king's crime produces no immunity from
its effects. Francisco, the soldier who sees kings only from the ranks,
is "sick at heart" (i.i.9). Those who shiver through the first night's
cold are aware of the disease in the air: "This bodes some strange
eruption to our state" (i.i.68). The hidden "impostume" (iv.iv.27) kills
all who adhere to Claudius. Polonius dies in his service. Rosencrantz
and Guildenstern present what they believe to be the king's commandment and find, to their brief bewilderment, that the warrant is for
their deaths. In a sense, the commission *is* that of Claudius; his fol-
lowers are doomed. Rosencrantz himself unwittingly defines the effect
of the murder of a king, one which dooms him and his twin, Guildenstern:

> . . . The cease of majesty
> Dies not alone, but like a gulf, doth draw
> What's near it with it.   (iii.iii.15–17)

Gertrude loves her son but has married this king, and when Hamlet presents her with the alternative of clinging to one king or another her heart is "cleft . . . in twain" (III.iv.156). She dies by drinking poisoned wine prepared by Claudius for Hamlet. Laertes falls in with the king's plot and is killed in its execution. Claudius himself is "justly serv'd . . . [with] poison temp'red by himself" (v.ii.338–339). Since he serves himself, he too must die.

While such an account of the source of Denmark's disease is accurate to a point, it tends to absolve Hamlet of any responsibility in the spreading of the contagion. He, after all, kills Polonius, and sends Rosencrantz and Guildenstern to their deaths, "not shriving time allow'd" (v.ii.47). It is difficult to agree, however, with G. Wilson Knight and Derek Traversi[41] that Hamlet is the source of the disease. This view, as John Holloway says, claims "that Shakespeare meant his play to depict the harm a society may incur from the disillusion of a man suffering from the familiar Jacobean disease of melancholy; and threw in regicide, usurpation, and incest in the royal line to enliven the middle distance."[42] Knight and Traversi raise, however, the valid question of Hamlet's responsibility for the deadly events which engulf Denmark. Granted that the contagion begins with Claudius's crime, to what extent is Hamlet responsible for its spread? Granted the way in which ritual is perverted in Denmark, could Hamlet's play have been the great exception?

It is partly true that Hamlet's intervention in the play shows that he is corrupted by the atmosphere surrounding him. He is infected with disgust and deep doubts—"that the sun doth move" (II.ii.116), for example.[43] Hamlet's interruption of his play can be termed symptomatic of a malaise for which he is not wholly responsible. But Hamlet is the only one in his world who has demonstrated the potential for redeeming it—significantly in the scene with the players. And in the soliloquy preceding his play, he uses the words "soul," "conscience," and, perhaps most significantly, "miraculous." If he is a tragic hero, rather than a victim, he falls. His fall results from his inability to retain his highest vision of his artistic creation—another way of saying that he fails to achieve his own potential greatness. He is unable as the play develops to surrender to forces larger than his own personality, forces he himself has defined and set in motion. Instead, he becomes the victim of other forces, the negation which has begun to work in Denmark before his play. His interruption of the play makes the victory of these forces inevitable. Tragedy, of course, involves the conflict of a hero *with* these forces, but it is important to note that Hamlet had a chance to dispel them with a redemptive drama, but actually promoted them by destroying that drama. Like any true tragic hero, Hamlet is primarily responsible for what happens to him and to the lesser characters inhabiting his world. If his fall comes at the moment he sees his play as a means of torturing Claudius, and if he does identify himself with Lucianus, then his fall is endowed with the mythic significance of Claudius's. "He poisons him i' the garden for 's estate" (III.ii.272). Hamlet becomes another poisoner, spitting his hatred into Claudius's ear, when he might have restored the un-weeded garden to health.[44] In one sense Hamlet *does* restore Denmark to health, but at an appalling cost. He achieves Denmark's restoration only through its obliteration.

If Hamlet is not capable of reinstating health in Denmark in a positive way, we should have to regard him as a passive spectator to his own destruction, no tragic hero, but a diminished being, who, as D. G. James says, "inhabits a middle region where philosophy and passion, judgment and honour, reason and blood, annul each other and leave him, for all essential purposes, helpless and angry, passive and violent."[45] This characterization is true of every Hamlet except the one who creates a play, a potential solution in art not available in life. The play, as Fiedler says, is "his only deliberately chosen act."[46] Arthur Sewell, however, suggests of Hamlet that "the puzzle and the explanation both lie in our common predicament; that action is imperative for man; but that all action whatsoever involves man in evil."[47] Helen Gardner says something similar: "How can man secure justice except by committing injustice, and how can he act without outraging the very conscience which demands that he should act?"[48] What they say is true, of course, of individual action, but not of Hamlet's play. Once it begins, it becomes a power independent of its creator. Hamlet releases forces which might relieve him of the necessity for further action, forces calculated to activate Claudius's guilt and his penitential imperative. Hamlet cancels what might have been a transcending of the dilemma defined by Sewell and Miss Gardner. Had he allowed the charitable Hamlet of the Player's Scene to remain alive, he might also have recognized the great possibilities of his play. Negation intervenes, however, and he becomes a guilty creature sitting at a play, proclaiming his malefactions—either to torture Clau-

dius, or worse, to send his soul to hell. After the play, the Knight-
Traversi thesis pertains.

Hamlet, then, is as much a victim of himself as of the corrupt world
of his play. This is as it must be if he is a tragic hero. The tragic hero
is invariably his own worst enemy, no matter how much he and his
apologists attempt to externalize his conflict. Perhaps modern criticism
has pushed too far in the direction of Aristotle's "imitation of an
action" and too far away from his "error in judgment." Are the two—
one pointing to theme and design, the other to character—irreconcilable? Obviously not. Hamlet encompasses the themes of the larger
play—of promise perverted and of appearance and reality—as he fails
to recognize and thus destroys the promise of the play he presents
for Claudius.

IV

Harold Rosenberg says that "The Central Intuition of Greek Tragedy . . . is, there is one unique fact that each individual anxiously
struggles to conceal from himself, and this is the very fact that is the
root of his identity."[49] This is also the central intuition of *Hamlet*. As
Edith Sitwell says, "*Hamlet* is a hunting story—that of a man who is
hunting his own soul, or the truth of his own soul, and who never
finds it."[50] The failure of Hamlet's play suggests that the spiritual
tragedy of Hamlet results from his inability to recognize that for him
conventional revenge is unthinkable.

Many critics see Hamlet as a victim of irresolution. This claim, even
if true, isolates a symptom rather than a cause. Beneath any single
explanation of Hamlet's character, whether it be procrastination or
the rashness Professor Grebanier proposes,[51] must lie a conflict. The
conflict culminating in Hamlet's devising a play, then breaking it up,
is seen often in Shakespeare: the struggle between a man's better
nature and his worst, between self-control and savagery (as later in
Othello), between conscience and ambition (as later in Macbeth).
Among other things, Hamlet is a profound morality play, where good
and evil angels struggle within a character. The story of Ophelia, with
its tension between "holy vows" and "unholy suits," piety and prosti-
tution, is a variation in a minor key of Hamlet's spiritual tragedy. An
examination of Act I, of the Player's speech, and of Laertes' career will
suggest that the play gives the spectator a different education in re-

venge than it provides Hamlet. Such an examination will show what
Hamlet chooses when he interrupts his production.

Act I traces the evolution of conflict within Hamlet, a conflict he
constantly expresses but does not recognize. In the opening scene,
frightened voices float at us from the battlements, voices talking of a
ghost and of sickness in the state, "ancestral voices prophesying war."
The sole release from this atmosphere is a speech by Marcellus:

> Some say that ever 'gainst that season comes
> Wherein our Saviour's birth is celebrated,
> The bird of dawning singeth all night long:
> And then, they say, no spirit can walk abroad;
> The nights are wholesome; then no planets strike,
> No fairy takes, nor witch hath power to charm,
> So hallow'd and so gracious is the time.   (I.i.157–163)

David Daiches claims that this speech "sings out to suggest a benefi-
cent spirit ruling over all these things."[52] This seems a hopelessly
optimistic reading. That a ghost *has* appeared suggests that the times
are neither hallowed nor gracious. The season in which the ghost appears *contrasts* with that in which "our Saviour" was born. The ghost,
then, may bring into the world qualities opposite to those of Christ.

Suddenly we are in the bright throne room of Denmark. One figure
seems to have carried some of the first scene's darkness into the re-
splendent court. We identify him as Hamlet. Almost with his first
words, he tells Claudius that he is "Too much i' th' sun" (I.ii.67), suggesting that he dislikes being called Claudius's son, and seethes at
being Gertrude's son.[53] The words suggest also that Hamlet may still
be controlled by his father, a domination which hardly needs to be
reasserted by the ghost; Hamlet sees his father in his mind's eye even
before Horatio informs him of the sightings on the parapets. In describing his continued mourning for his father, Hamlet has talked of
"that within which passeth show" (I.ii.85). One of the deep forces
working within him may be the control his father still exercises over
him. The idea is woven through Act I.

In a prophetic speech to Ophelia, Laertes says:

> . . . you must fear
> His greatness weigh'd, his will is not his own;
> For he himself is subject to his birth
> . . . on his choice depends
> The sanity and health of the whole state.   (I.iii.16–21)

"Subject to his birth" means primarily that Hamlet is heir apparent. It also suggests, however, subjection to the dead king. As Hamlet waits in the night for the ghost to come again, he talks of "some vicious mole of nature" in certain men, "As in their birth," which ultimately destroys them, which "Doth all the noble substance often dout / To his own scandal" (i.iv.24–38). Later, as he demands that his companions swear to secrecy on his sword, Hamlet hears the ghost echo the command from below and shouts, "Well said, old mole!" (i.vi.162). "Vicious mole of nature"—a blemish; "old mole"—an animal which works in the ground. Perhaps it works inside Hamlet too, in precisely the terms he has defined in the speech about the "vicious mole" which immediately precedes the arrival of the ghost.

Marcellus's speech about the gracious and hallowed time suggests God, and forces threatening God. The conflict is repeated as Hamlet faces the shape of his father:

> Be thou a spirit of health or goblin damn'd,
> Bring with thee airs from heaven or blasts from hell,
> Be thy intents wicked or charitable . . .   (i.iv.40–42)

The two possibilities concentrated in the image of the father—angelic and diabolic—are translated almost immediately to the son. "Haste me to know't," cries Hamlet,

> . . . that I, with wings as swift
> As meditation or the thoughts of love
> May sweep to my revenge.   (i.v.29–31)

Meditation swift? And who would select "the thoughts of love" as a prelude to revenge? Only a man at whom opposite motivations had begun to tug. The conflicting potentialities of the ghost—"intents wicked or charitable"—are becoming the terms of Hamlet's conflict, as he suggests a moment later when he shouts, "O you host of heaven! O earth! What else? / And shall I couple hell?" (i.v.92–93). What does Hamlet mean when he informs the others, "Look you, I'll go pray" (i.v.132)? Is "pray" a pun on "prey"?* Horatio has just called to Hamlet with the falconer's summons, and later Hamlet will talk of feeding Claudius's remains to all the carrion birds of the region (ii.ii.606–608). More immediately, he draws his sword, and, with the

---

* Cf. *1 Henry IV* (ii.i.87–91): ". . . they pray continually to their saint, the commonwealth; or rather, not pray to her, but prey on her, for they ride up and down on her and make her their boots."

ghost seconding him from the cellarage, forces his friends to swear on it. The sword, like the word "pray," embodies the alternatives which emerge so insistently in Act I.* It represents revenge, of course, and suggests perhaps the ominous words from Matthew xxvi.52 about perishing with the sword. As Hamlet uses it here, however, it represents the opposite of death; the hilt and handle represent the cross, symbol of salvation. Like the ghost, the sword symbolizes both wickedness and charity.

Hamlet's choice, then, is between heaven and hell, love and revenge, prayer and preying, the cross and the sword, "our Saviour" and the devil. That he does not see clearly the terms of his decision is due in part to the influence his father still asserts over him. The conflict is captured most profoundly in the discrepancy between what his play might have done and what it does. As the play breaks up, the decision is made and the spirit that Hamlet has seen becomes the devil. As Santayana says, "So Hamlet's whole entanglement with the Ghost and with the crude morality of revenge . . . fails to bring his own soul to a right utterance, and this stifling of his better potential is no small part of the tragedy."[54]

A subtle commentary on the question of Hamlet and revenge is offered by the Player's speech, which shows the spectator one thing and Hamlet another. Hamlet begins it with a misquotation:

> "The rugged Pyrrhus like th' Hyrcanian beast"
> —It is not so. It begins with Pyrrhus:—
> "The rugged Pyrrhus, he whose sable arms . . ."
>
> (II.ii.472–474)

Pyrrhus, as Arthur Johnston says, "unites in his person the avenger of Paris' double crime of lust and murder of Pyrrhus' father, as Hamlet is the avenger of Claudius' double crime."[55] The parallel is unmistakable, and, significantly, Hamlet's slip at the beginning of the speech likens Pyrrhus to a ravenous tiger, the beast the revenger must become. Both Pyrrhus and Hamlet are clothed in black. At the play, Hamlet links himself with the sable-armed Pyrrhus: "Nay then, let the devil wear black, for I'll have a suit of sables" (III.ii.137–138). By then, Hamlet and Pyrrhus are becoming the same person, and Hamlet is merging with Lucianus's "thoughts black" (III.ii.266).

---

* Cf. *The Spanish Tragedy* (II.i.91–93): "But if I prove thee prejur'd and unjust / This very sword whereon thou took'st thine oath / Shall be the worker of thy tragedy."

Hamlet stops his recitation at the point where Pyrrhus seeks Priam:

> . . . "Roasted in wrath and fire,
> And thus o'er-sized with coagulate gore,
> With eyes like carbuncles, the hellish Pyrrhus
> Old grandsire Priam seeks."
> So, proceed you.   (ii.ii.483–487)

He loves the speech, yet while he can express the motivation for the killing of Priam he does not continue to the portion paralleling what Pyrrhus does and what Hamlet feels he must do. (As Miss Prosser says, "If Pyrrhus has any counterpart in the play at all, it must be Hamlet."[56]) Hamlet's halt may result, then, from his perception that revenge is depicted in the Pyrrhus episode as a devilish activity. Pyrrhus is "hellish" and Troy is wrapped in a "tyrannous and damned light" (ii.ii.482). As Pyrrhus is about to kill the prostrate Priam, he pauses:

> "So, as a painted tyrant, Pyrrhus stood
> And, like a neutral to his will and matter,
> Did nothing."   (ii.ii.502–504)

His pause anticipates Hamlet's, standing over the kneeling Claudius, when Hamlet himself defines the hellish nature of his revenge. (Pyrrhus's momentary neutrality also defines the dilemma of Claudius at that later moment—the painted tyrant trapped between will and matter.) Finally, as Hamlet lashes through the arras, after sparing Claudius, ". . . so, after Pyrrhus' pause, / Aroused vengeance sets him new a-work" (ii.ii.509–510). He slays the defenseless old man. As Johnston says, "What is significant about the episode chosen to mirror the act that Hamlet is called to do is the reversal of emotional sympathy; the deed is one of terror, its perpetrator inhuman and brutalized. 'Roasted in wrath and fire' the 'hellish Pyrrhus' is damned."[57]

While the parallel between Pyrrhus and Hamlet seems clear, and while his stopping his recitation suggests that intuitively he grasps it, Hamlet chooses to develop a correspondence between himself and the Player, a parallel which, as Johnston says, is "less immediately obvious" but which serves as "a spur to his own dulled sense of duty."[58] Yet the Player's speech has a strangely therapeutic effect on Hamlet in spite of its ominous content. The "dream of passion" (ii.ii.578), as he calls the rendition, seems to relieve Hamlet of a conscious burden, as dreams often do; he seems to release the problem vicariously through Pyrrhus. After the speech comes Hamlet's most charitable moment, and the speech motivates that potential instrument of redemption, Hamlet's play. Had Hamlet drawn the parallel between Pyrrhus and himself and rejected the role of hellish revenger, he might have seen his play's possibilities more clearly. Instead, his plans for the play are preceded by a cry for vengeance, the cry which interrupts the play itself.

The Laertes story represents a final exploration and rejection of the revenge thesis. Ophelia's career is an adumbration of Hamlet's conflict; her brother is a parallel revenger, as Hamlet admits: ". . . by the image of my cause I see / The portraiture of his" (v.ii.77–78). As Dover Wilson says, "All that [Laertes] says and does is a reflection upon Hamlet."[59] Their characters are dissimilar, of course; Hamlet's fits of resolve and recklessness alternate with other moods, while calmness seldom visits the determined Laertes. The son of Polonius, however, does express Hamlet's conflict, although for Laertes it seems no conflict at all:

> How came he dead? I'll not be juggl'd with.
> To hell, allegiance! Vows, to the blackest devil!
> Conscience and grace to the profoundest pit!
> I dare damnation. To this point I stand,
> That both the worlds I give to negligence,
> Let come what comes; only I'll be reveng'd
> Most thoroughly for my father.   (iv.v.130–136)

Conscience and grace against damnation and the devil—a violent rephrasing of Hamlet's problem. And again, revenge is equated with damnation. If Hamlet wants Claudius's heels to kick at heaven, Laertes is as extreme. "What would you undertake," asks Claudius, "To show yourself your father's son in deed / More than in words?" (iv.vii.125–127). "To cut his throat i' th' church," snarls Laertes (iv.vii. 128). Again, the sword and the cross, but this time the church offers no refuge from the sword, as Claudius's reply suggests: "No place, indeed, should murder sanctuarize. / Revenge should have no bounds" (iv.vii.129–130). Hamlet's desire for revenge is so boundless that prayer forestalls murder only because the victim's soul must go to hell. When Hamlet appears at Ophelia's funeral, Laertes shouts, "The devil take thy soul!" (v.i.282). Hamlet tells him, "Thou pray'st not well" (v.i. 283). What is Laertes' prayer, however, but a concise version of Hamlet's wish for Claudius's soul? The Laertes story demonstrates again, as Hamlet does when he has the kneeling Claudius at his mercy and as Pyrrhus does as he smites the fallen Priam, what revenge is, stripped of all rationalization. Even the unreflective Laertes penetrates to an awareness of his sin: "And yet, 'tis almost 'gainst my conscience" (v.ii.307), he says before thrusting the unbated and envenomed sword at Hamlet. Hamlet expresses this insight but, like Laertes, does not explore it completely enough to save himself: "Thus conscience does make cowards of us all . . ." (iii.i.83). The unfortunate equation between conscience and cowardice suggests again the basis of Hamlet's spiritual tragedy.

V

Act v is a pivot on which any interpretation of Hamlet or *Hamlet* must turn. We have either the cleansing of a state or its destruction, either the regeneration of Hamlet or his continued fall.

Many critics see a redeemed Hamlet in Act v. Karl Polanyi says that "in the end our beloved hero retrieves some of life's fulfillment."[60] Irving Ribner suggests that "by submission to the will of God, Hamlet attains the victory."[61] "In Act i," says S. F. Johnson, "he was a student prince; in Act v he is the ordained minister of providence."[62] These views stem primarily from Hamlet's philosophical statements to Horatio, particularly this:

Not a whit; we defy augury. There's a special providence in the fall of a sparrow. If it be now, 'tis not to come; if it be not to come, it will be now; if it be not now, yet it will come; the readiness is all. Since no man has aught of what he leaves, what is't to leave betimes? Let be.

(v.ii.230–235)

C. S. Lewis calls this "the precise moment" at which Hamlet finds his way again.[63] Others call it an awareness of "the world's order,"[64] "a clear apprehension of the truth,"[65] and "a glimpse of himself as a fragment of a mighty pattern."[66] Hamlet has now ascended to "a willing compliance with the workings of heaven."[67] In Act v, "his abnormally quick sympathy has acquired some of the quiet of the vision integrated and lived up to, some of the breadth of charity."[68]

Another group of critics demurs from Hamlet's redemption. Granville-Barker says that Hamlet "never regains a natural spiritual health, nor self-understanding."[69] Bradley, very sympathetic towards Hamlet, says that the "readiness" speech expresses "that kind of religious resig-

nation which, however beautiful in one aspect, really deserves the
name of fatalism, rather than faith in Providence."[70] Schucking calls
the speech "an admission that [Hamlet's] heart has grown old and
that life holds nothing more of value for him."[71] Parrott calls it "a
deadening fatalism,"[72] Stauffer, a "desperate stoicism."[73] H. B. Charlton says that "the recognition of the will's impotence is accepted as
. . . the calm attainment of a higher benignity, whereas it is nothing
more than a fatalist's surrender of his personal responsibility. That is
the nadir of Hamlet's fall."[74] And one might ask whether Hamlet's "If
it be now, 'tis not to come . . ." is not merely an elaboration of
Laertes' "Let come what comes" (IV.v.135).

We have, then, two Hamlets, one who ascends to become the agent
of providence, another who surrenders to the relentless gravity of
fate. And there *are* two Hamlets in Act v; it has been contrived so that
much of what he says or does can be interpreted in opposite ways.
His escape from the ship bearing him to execution in England can be
called a providential event proving (as it does to Hamlet) that
"There's a divinity that shapes our ends, / Rough-hew them how we
will" (v.ii.10–11), or a mere accident. Many of his words in the grave-
yard can be termed a calm acceptance of the inevitability of death, or
cynicism about the meaning of life. His outburst at Ophelia's grave
can be defined as genuine grief or as petulance that Laertes is playing
the part of chief mourner—"Nay an thou'lt mouth, / I'll rant as well
as thou" (v.i.306–307). Bradley calls Hamlet's apology to Laertes evidence of "all the nobility and sweetness of his nature":[75]

> . . . What I have done
> That might your nature, honour, and exception
> Roughly awake, I here proclaim was madness.
> Was't Hamlet wrong'd Laertes? Never Hamlet!
> If Hamlet from himself be ta'en away,
> And when he's not himself does wrong Laertes,
> Then Hamlet does it not, Hamlet denies it.
> Who does it, then? His madness. If't be so,
> Hamlet is of the faction that is wrong'd,
> His madness is poor Hamlet's enemy.   (v.ii.241–250)

"It is only the rarest of men," says Grebanier, "who are equal to the
honorableness of these words."[76] Hamlet's speech has a legalistic tone,
however. It is, in fact, a prototype of a modern lawyer's defense of
the psychopathic killer:

They did not reason; they could not reason; they committed the most foolish, most unprovoked, most purposeless, most causeless act that any two
boys ever committed . . . they killed him as they might kill a spider or
a fly. . . . Are they to blame for it? . . . It is one of those things that
happened . . . no human being could have done what these boys did,
excepting through the operation of a diseased brain.

This paraphrase of Hamlet's apology to Laertes is, of course, a portion
of Darrow's defense of Loeb and Leopold.[77] They killed him as they
might kill a spider or a fly. "Why, man, they did make love to this
employment," Hamlet says of his former school chums, "They are not
near my conscience" (v.ii.57–58). Of Polonius—"a certain convocation
of politic worms are e'en at him" (iv.iii.21). A spider or a fly. Which
is the true Hamlet—the sincerely repentant man or the clever defense
attorney defending the psychopath who happens to be himself?

Hamlet, it seems, has been written to prove the truth of Hamlet's
dictim that "there is nothing either good or bad, but thinking makes
it so" (ii.ii.256). Hamlet may interrupt *his* play and limit it only to
what he sees there; Shakespeare apparently does not. Shakespeare's
play has the dual potential of the mousetrap. *Hamlet* is designed to
catch our consciences in our providing the definitive comment which
Shakespeare avoids. As Harbage says, "Only a seer can deduce Shakespeare's *intention* unless that intention is defined as providing stimulus
in order to get a response."[78] The spectator, having been so deeply
stimulated, must attempt to define his response, although he knows
that he is bouncing a radar signal off the moon, getting back an echo
of his own transmission.

Clifford P. Lyons says that "the play obviously embodies conflicting
stresses; yet which emphasis does Shakespeare make primary in Hamlet's story? Not both."[79] Are the stresses so evenly balanced in Act v
that the spectator can emphasize either a redeemed or a fallen Hamlet and be at least half right? There *are* two Hamlets in Act v, but
one is primarily an appearance, a continuing reminder of the potential
we glimpsed in an earlier Hamlet who delighted in the coming of the
players and who devised a play himself. The other is the negative
reality emerging as the chaotic echoes of his disrupted drama circle
malignantly through himself and Denmark. That Shakespeare should
build such a dichotomy into his character is consistent with the play's
constant contrast between the angelic and bestial possibilities in man.
The dichotomy expresses profoundly Shakespeare's great theme—the

discrepancy between appearance and reality. Certainly many of Hamlet's speeches remind us of the Hamlet we have known. If we examine his actions, however, he is a murderer, responsible for the deaths of Polonius, Rosencrantz and Guildenstern (whose summary execution shocks even the impassive Horatio), and Claudius. He causes Ophelia's death indirectly and kills Laertes in self-defense. The only death of which he can be entirely absolved is Gertrude's, although she dies by drinking a toast to his dueling skill. Traces of a former Hamlet remain, but primarily to provide a dimension against which his fall may be measured. (Milton does something similar with Satan in Book 1 of *Paradise Lost.*)

It is imperative to note, however, that Shakespeare allows us to retain our sympathy for Hamlet. Sympathy, however, should not substitute for pardon, any more than sympathy for Othello condones his strangling of Desdemona. To claim that "what is not near Hamlet's conscience is not near our own because he is our moral interpreter,"[80] is to evade complexity, to dismiss the discrepancy between word and action which is one source of irony. Some critics, overcome by sympathy, quote Hamlet's words and apologize for him. Others coldly list his actions and condemn him. Each group ignores the interaction between word and deed on which any interpretation of drama must be based. While we continue to respond to Hamlet's better nature, we must also deplore its subversion.

The fall of Hamlet and a glimpse of a former Hamlet are captured in his description of the deaths of Rosencrantz and Guildenstern. To illustrate the divinity that shapes our ends, he invokes the discovery of the plot on his life and the execution of his Wittenberg friends, "Not shriving time allow'd" (v.ii.47). No divinity shapes *their* ends. Is this the "breadth of charity" Hamlet has supposedly attained? "Why even in that was heaven ordinant" cries Hamlet (v.ii.48), having consigned his victims' souls to hell. "What a piece of work is a man!" he had exclaimed (II.ii.315). Now he says, with a snap of the fingers, "And a man's life's no more than to say 'One'" (v.ii.74). Is this "a willing compliance with the workings of heaven"? Hamlet claims that Rosencrantz and Guildenstern are not near his conscience and suggests that it is "perfect conscience" (v.ii.67) to kill Claudius. Yet something troubles him: "Thou wouldst not think how ill all's here about my heart" (v.ii.222).[81] Why? He does not fear death. He is confident that he will achieve his revenge. What could trouble him?

". . . a kind of gain-giving," he says with some scorn, "as would perhaps trouble a woman" (v.ii.225), a last unexamined prompting of conscience, perhaps, for the blood he has and is soon to shed, a final reminder of a Hamlet who might have allowed his play to proceed? Laertes, weeping for Ophelia, suggests that such gain-giving is linked to Hamlet's better self:

> It is our trick. Nature her custom holds,
> Let shame say what it will; when these are gone,
> The woman will be out. (iv.vii.188–190)

As conscience is cowardly, tears are womanly; neither Hamlet nor Laertes will substitute tears for blood.

Several modern critics see Shakespeare, particularly the Shakespeare of *Hamlet*, as a non-Christian. "He did not write as a Christian," says D. G. James in his essay on *Hamlet*, "this seems certain."[82] Walter Kaufmann, extolling the virtues of an existential courage in the face of a meaningless cosmos, claims that Shakespeare's work "celebrates the riches of a world without God."[83] Laurence Michel says that "*Hamlet* depicts the destruction of homocentric humanism and its terrible aspect is to demonstrate how this value becomes corrupted before it goes down to defeat; it is rather appropriate than not, and an earnest of the uncompromising honesty of Shakespeare's deep tragic vision, that whatever of Christian humanism enters this abyss is perverted too, into diabolism. If *Hamlet* is any criterion the Tragic Vision and Christianity are incompatible."[84]

The play abounds in Christian usages and overtones. At Hamlet's most charitable moment, he employs an appropriate allusion to the Communion Service. At his *least* charitable moment he repeats the suggestion, but with a difference. Before he slumps towards death, he forces the contents of the poisoned chalice down the throat of the dying Claudius:

> Here, thou incestuous, murderous, damned Dane,
> Drink off this potion! Is thy union here? (v.ii.336–337)

In yet another perverted ritual, Hamlet becomes the devil's priest, conducting a macabre anti-communion. Seconds after this black mass, however, he magnanimously hopes that heaven will free Laertes of his sins. His hope for Laertes is a reminder of the alternative he rejected for Claudius during the Play Scene. The other alternative is represented by the corpses littering the throne-room floor. Immediately after Hamlet joins them, messengers from England add to the number with word "That Rosencrantz and Guildenstern are dead" (v.ii.382).

While Hamlet the man quite obviously rejects Christianity for the bloody destiny of Act v, does this mean that *Hamlet* the play does? Hamlet becomes a subject for tragedy precisely because he neglects the alternative of a potentially redemptive drama. As Jay Halio says, ". . . had Hamlet observed the calling of a Christian to return ill not with ill, but with good, he might not have plunged himself—and all of the principal characters—into the course of tragic catastrophe."[85] At the moment Hamlet makes the Christian approach irretrievable— on his interruption of the play—he suffers his fall and becomes a tragic figure. Michel is right, "the Tragic Vision and Christianity are incompatible," but to impute the rejection of the Christian alternative to Shakespeare is to forget that his character Hamlet makes the choice. The dichotomy between the alternatives and between the two Hamlets is summarized neatly by Horatio:

> Now cracks a noble heart. Good-night, sweet Prince,
> And flights of angels sing thee to thy rest!
> Why does the drum come hither?   (v.ii.370–372)

While the last line could be termed a turning back to the pressing affairs of this world, it is difficult not to see irony there. The first two lines, of course, are dear to the hearts of Hamlet's apologists. The next line, however, with its martial music, suggests the conflict which has worked in Hamlet since he met the ghost and perhaps before— the conflict between the creative son and the military father.

The spirit that I have seen may be the devil. It becomes the devil as soon as Hamlet accepts it as a true ghost and embraces the revenge thesis. Had he allowed his play to continue, the other potentiality of the ghost ("airs from heaven") might have been realized. Hamlet made the ghost the devil. There is nothing either good or bad, but thinking makes it so. As the signet ring of Hamlet's father sealed the deaths of Rosencrantz and Guildenstern, so a lingering reminder of the ghost is brought to the final scene. Long before, Bernardo had chided Horatio after the ghost's appearance: "How now, Horatio! You tremble and look pale" (i.i.53). Hamlet imputes the same reaction to the witnesses of the final bloodletting: "You that look pale and tremble at this chance . . ." (v.ii.345). Hamlet identified the ghost on the basis of his play, but in allowing the play to become a torture device, he automatically made the ghost the devil.

Hamlet may be a more Christian play than its "Christian" commentators, invariably apologists for Hamlet, recognize. If it is a Christian play, however, its full value does not reside in its central character. It shows, rather, what can happen to a supremely gifted man who ignores the way offered by "our Saviour." As Roy Battenhouse suggests, it "shows tragedy arising from various *un*Christian responses in Hamlet and others."[86] The play does not occur within the season Marcellus mentions, "Wherein our Saviour's birth is celebrated." Instead, a dying man forces poisoned wine down the throat of another dying man. What finer irony in a play which treats so pervasively the theme of appearance versus reality than to have its most sensitive character fail to recognize the alternatives struggling within him? "I have that within which passeth show" (I.ii.85), he had said. He had it within him to redeem the world and reign as its king by so working Claudius's soul that justice would have become the responsibility of an agency higher than that of Hamlet's will. And he had it within him to destroy the world and die amid its wreckage. For all his introspection, he never really asks himself the question with which the play opens: "Who's there?" He is the victim of tragic irony—the failure to recognize the central fact of his existence. He dies, as John F. Danby suggests, "a baffled . . . young man."[87] He may end depraved as well as baffled as Miss West and Madariaga suggest, but that does not mean that the play subscribes to the doctrine of man's depravity, or fails to suggest the alternative to moral destruction which Hamlet might have embraced.

Fortinbras's equation of the throne room to a battlefield (v.ii.411–412) would seem to support Eliot's contention that Hamlet "has made a pretty considerable mess of things."[88] Miss Gardner, however, objects to such censuring of Hamlet:

Mr. Eliot might, however, have noticed that it is not merely Hamlet who appears to feel at the close that if only the whole truth were known . . . the name which he leaves behind him would not be a "wounded name." Horatio's farewell to him and Fortinbras' comment make no suggestion that what we have witnessed is a story of personal failure and inadequacy; and Horatio's summary of what he will tell "the yet unknowing world" does not include any hint that these things have come about through the bungling of the dead Prince.[89]

But surely some of what Horatio says applies to Hamlet. ". . . acci-
dental judgements, casual slaughters" (v.ii.393) can be assigned to
the death of Polonius, and "deaths put on by cunning and forc'd
cause" (v.ii.394) to the deaths of Rosencrantz and Guildenstern.
". . . purposes mistook / Fall'n on the inventors' heads" (v.ii.395) can
pertain to Hamlet's disastrous play as well as to the deadly final
scene.

But those like Miss Gardner who feel instinctively that the final
scene represents a victory for Hamlet are partially right. While the
greatest Hamlet, the creative Hamlet, has been defeated, a lesser
Hamlet struggles through to a bloody victory. If Hamlet's actions
since the breakup of his play can be justified, they are justified in
terms of Fortinbras's command for Hamlet's funeral:

> . . . for his passage,
> The soldiers' music and the rites of war
> Speak loudly for him.   (v.ii.409–411)

While the funeral of a young soldier is invariably a ceremony of
wasted potential, it is also a celebration of heroism and sacrifice. Hamlet becomes a soldier. If that role is diminished compared to the
creative artist he had been, it becomes necessary once the man betrays the artist. Once he commits his tragic error, he does as well as
he can, as well as any human being could do in the struggle against
the evil working within him as well as in the world around him. The
creative son who once saw the cross in the hilt of the sword must
finally, like his soldier father, take the hilt in his hand.[90] Hamlet's own
life becomes necessary to the purgation of Denmark, but he gives
it willingly and can be said to have "parted well and paid his score."
Certainly he retains to the end the sympathy we have granted him
from the first. We continue to love him in spite of what he has done,
in spite of what he has become. "We love," as Robert Ornstein says,
"the suggestion of Hamlet's former self."[91]

We experience, at the end, pity and terror in proportion to our
celebration of Hamlet's greatness. We have witnessed the results of
a potentially good man's struggle with evil. What might have been
stays with us, even though Hamlet finds another ending. If Hamlet
purges the state, it is at the appalling cost of that potential Hamlet
we have glimpsed, the Hamlet which many insist on seeing—because
it is still there in brief flashes against the enclosing darkness—even at

the end. *Hamlet,* like many tragedies, explores the discrepancy between what a man might have been and what he becomes.

The ripeness is all. Prospero comes to recognize during his long exile that revenge is worse than meaningless—it reduces the revenger to the same corruption as that of the criminal. Unlike Hamlet, Prospero allows his production to find its meaning in the characters manipulated. His magic is primarily external; it can achieve no inward changes unless its participants have the capacity for change. It is this magic, this method of reaching the spirit, which Hamlet gets hold of and fails to recognize. Hamlet defines himself as modern man, very much as D. G. James defines him, oppressed and isolated, seeing the sacraments as a convention irrelevant to the soul of man. He is wrong about their power, as Claudius's belated efforts at prayer prove. Prospero recognizes that a reenactment of guilt *may* evoke a penitential response from guilty creatures and that it is the only method worth trying. He defines himself as medieval man, servant finally of forces larger than himself. He experiences at the end what he has known all along—that he is subject to those forces. Hamlet could not retain the conception of his play which he himself had expressed—that "guilty creatures" can be "struck so to the soul" that they must confess and plea for pardon. Hamlet destroys his play before it can explore this possibility. Prospero does not. "The rarer action is in virtue than in vengeance" because it can achieve a restoration to self and humanity not only for the guilty participant in a penitential drama, but for the dramatist as well.

Acknowledgments

I am grateful to the Bowdoin College Faculty Research Fund for assistance in preparing the manuscript of this monograph.

JANE AUSTEN'S NOVELS:
THE METAPHOR OF RANK

E. Rubinstein

JANE AUSTEN'S THEME AND JANE AUSTEN'S WORLD

N o wholly adequate one-sentence definition of "the novel" has yet been formulated, but for my purposes the following is at least as satisfactory as any other: "The novel, then, is a perpetual quest for reality, the field of its research being always the social world, the material of its analysis being always manners as the indication of the direction of man's soul." The writer is, of course, Lionel Trilling,[1] and since Jane Austen seems so nearly central to Trilling's whole conception of the art of fiction it is not surprising that his definition should be more directly apposite to Jane Austen's novels than to those of any other major English novelist. No writer of fiction has accepted "the social world" with less embarrassment or fewer qualifications than Jane Austen; none has relied more completely on the figurative force of ordinary social gestures and situations. None, in consequence, has been able to make richer use of the moral and psychological implications of social rank.

But metaphors* of rank, like any others, become fully operative

---

* Because the experience of "metaphor" is, for most readers, definitively associated with the experience of "imagery," it may seem improper to employ the word in relation to the less specifically sensuous aspects of prose fiction. When I speak of social rank as a metaphor, however, I take the word in its largest sense —that is, as the agency whereby any literary subject is clarified and redefined through analogy and extension. In this sense, metaphors derived from the observation of social change bear the same relation to the themes of fiction as metaphors derived from sensuous experience to the themes of lyric poetry.

Now, I recognize that, if one accepts my terms, any discrimination between "subject" and "metaphor" (or "tenor" and "vehicle") threatens to appear capricious—that, in fact, the activities of courtship in Jane Austen's fiction might better be dealt with as metaphors of growth and self-discovery than as the actual subject of that fiction. But by broadening the usual notion of metaphor, one is permitted to assert what most readers have always recognized—namely, that Jane Austen's novels, for all their meagerness of sensuous imagery, are as imaginatively rich as any verse in the language.

only when the matrix from which they are drawn is adequately defined: in order to apprehend the importance of rank in Jane Austen's work one must see that work in the context of the social history of Jane Austen's England, bearing in mind that the novelist lived in an age in which questions of rank were of obvious and immediate concern, an age in which the traditional class structure could still assert its historic meaning at the same time that a newer social order was quite irresistibly imposing itself. One must, in short, understand Jane Austen's novels as fictional microcosms of the England of her time.

Now, to think of any novel primarily in connection with the outside world it seems to picture is of course potentially dangerous; fiction, existing only in language, is different in kind from life, and I should say at the outset—though without wishing to become involved in larger questions of critical theory which I cannot hope to resolve in these pages—that I do not accept, or mean to perpetuate, the idea that novels are to be judged for their historical fidelity. Moreover, the novelist I am dealing with selected all the matter of her fiction with unexampled rigor and severity, and nothing could have been further from her intentions than a complete representation of the England she knew. Still, as Trilling suggests, the concern with social actualities, especially as expressed in "manners," has always (or at least until very recent times) been one of the definitive qualities of the novel as a genre, and before examining any of Jane Austen's works in detail, I must say something of the relation between Jane Austen's fictions and the world in which she produced them.

The nature of that relation is immediately suggested by the recurrent theme of her work. This theme, which points at once to Jane Austen's affinity with most of the major novelists of the nineteenth century, can be defined as the struggle between the claims of the rebellious ego and the claims of the normative world, between the individual protagonist's desire for active assertion and various external demands for passive submission. Each of Jane Austen's novels presents this theme in a very different light; just as the natures of the protagonists are radically unlike one another, so, too, are those ruling social and ethical values against which they revolt. Nonetheless, the theme—whether embodied as Catherine Morland versus good sense, or Mary Crawford versus piety and tradition, or Elizabeth Bennet versus the feudal ethic—is at the heart of each of the novels. And it is a theme which, as presented in Jane Austen's work, proclaims the major social and cultural trends of her time: the rise of the middle classes, marked by a new emphasis upon individual merit as opposed to the passive attributes of birth and rank; and the ascendancy of Romanticism, with its new emphasis upon the cultivation of the individual. There is, in fact, no line to be drawn in Jane Austen's mature work between personal and psychological relevance on the one hand and social or cultural relevance on the other, as both develop effortlessly and interdependently from the thematic crux of her work.

To so describe Jane Austen's theme is, as I have suggested, to announce her affinity with all those nineteenth-century novelists who describe the individual's perpetual battle with his world. But Jane Austen's method of extending her theme by reference to contemporary social actualities is not that of most of the French and English novelists who were her successors. She offers no explicit historical generalizations in an authoritative narratorial voice, nor does she (in the manner of George Eliot in *Middlemarch*, for example) place her *dramatis personae* in direct relation to historical events of unmistakable relevance to their personal affairs. What Jane Austen does do is at once simpler and more elusive: her larger "concerns," in Mark Schorer's phrase, "are so completely integrated in her individual characterizations and so little imposed upon them from without, that they tend, in fact, to go unnoticed." Schorer himself provides sufficient (if somewhat tentative) illustration: "Is not *Pride and Prejudice*," he asks, "in the very movement of its plot the representation of a great change that was overtaking society, the movement of a formerly depressed class into a position of power, and of a formerly powerful class into a position of compromise?"[2] In short, Jane Austen accepts English social history as one of her principal sources of metaphor, using birth and rank (as I explain more fully below) as the vehicles of thematic substance, and thus at the same time establishing what I have termed the microcosmic qualities of her small dramas.

However, Jane Austen's conception of the "social background" of her novels may be sufficiently different from that of the modern reader to require some preliminary discussion; perhaps the easiest way to approach the problem is to make clear what Jane Austen's view of society is not. If we compare her with any of the eminent French novelists of the nineteenth century, whose interest in the social background of their stories is so obtrusive, we may get the impression that Jane Austen's novels are in no way rooted in a specific historical moment. *Le Rouge et le Noir,* for example, is subtitled *Chronique de 1830,* and Stendhal's subtitle demands some attention; as Erich Auerbach has demonstrated, the representative characters and events of the novel would be very different had he set about to compose a *"Chronique de 1800"* or a *"Chronique de 1820."* Analyzing a scene from this novel, Auerbach concludes:

> The characters, attitudes, and relationships of the dramatis personae, then, are very closely connected with contemporary historical circumstances; contemporary political and social conditions are woven into the action in a manner more detailed and more real than had been exhibited in any earlier novel, and indeed in any works of literary art except those expressly purporting to be politico-satirical tracts. So logically and systematically to situate the tragically conceived life of a man of low social position (as here that of Julien Sorel) within the most concrete kind of contemporary history and to develop it herefrom—this is an entirely new and highly significant phenomenon. The other circles in which Julien Sorel moves—his father's family, the house of the mayor of Verrières, M. de Rênal, the seminary at Besançon—are sociologically defined in conformity with the historical moment with the same penetration as is the La Mole household; and not one of the minor characters—the old priest Chélan, for example, or the director of the *dépôt de mendicité,* Valenod—would be conceivable outside the particular historical situation of the Restoration period, in the manner in which they are set before us.[3]

Needless to say, Jane Austen does not think in terms of this kind of historical precision; indeed, it seems to me fair to assert that, on the whole, the more closely one attempts to read Jane Austen in light of specific observations of later social historians, the further one tends to move from what is essential in her work. It is true that the frequently mentioned quartering of troops at Meryton, a tacit reminder of the Napoleonic wars, roughly fixes the date of the action of *Pride and Prejudice;* it is equally true that certain details—the quality of the roads, for example—not only clearly indicate the difference between Jane Austen's world and that of Fanny Burney but, much more significantly, determine to a considerable extent the very possibilities of plot in Jane Austen's work. But such details remain part of what might be called the machinery of verisimilitude; they are seldom, if ever, selected for emphasis, and their implications are not consciously explored. For unlike Stendhal, Jane Austen did not in fact conceive each historical moment as an entity distinguishable from all preceding moments, nor did she understand and seek to explain human character by reference, implicit or direct, to historical causality. In Jane Austen's fiction, English society usually manifests itself to the reader as a fixed and settled thing.[4]

But if the society represented in a Jane Austen novel seems fixed, it must be fixed in a state of perpetual change. The social history of England in the eighteenth and early nineteenth centuries is largely a history of a great flux upward. As summarized by Elie Halévy—and the most general of summaries provides all the introduction one actually requires—the typical pattern is this: "The skilled labourer becomes in turn a skilled workman, an artisan, the head of a small business, and a business man possessed of a modest capital. . . ."[5] Then, increasing his capital and moving upward into and through the levels of the middle class, he educates his children in the ways of gracious gentility; if the capital grows sufficiently, he or his children will look to the country, purchasing land and entering the ranks of the established gentry, or perhaps becoming part of that gentry through marriage. Throughout Jane Austen's work, examples abound of city people who, through trade or other capitalistic enterprise, rise to mix with the country gentry: one need only mention Mrs. Jennings of *Sense and Sensibility,* and the Bingleys and the Gardiners of *Pride and Prejudice,* all very different in personality, in temperament, and in level of gentility achieved, but all sharing a common history. Moreover, upward movement is not exclusively the result of urban capitalism. It is also possible to rise in the counties, though the process tends to be slower and as a result more natural: Robert Martin in *Emma* can serve as a clear instance of the small farmer who, through diligence and good sense, is slowly but surely ascending. Then, too, there is the navy, through which Prices and Wentworths can, if they survive the perils of their profession, quickly establish themselves as gentlemen. But whatever the means, whether trade, farming, or the navy, with its vast resources of prize money, Jane Austen's characters are on the move, each generation coming closer and closer to an established place among the gentry.

And it is precisely this sense of social movement that provides Jane Austen with her most powerful social metaphors. The relation between this social situation and Jane Austen's recurrent theme is obvious: as dramatized in a social setting in which many different ranks and various levels of gentility are intermingled and contrasted to one another, the conflict between the established order and the individual often takes the form of a conflict between inherited rank and personal achievement, between merit as gauged by what one has the right to be and merit as gauged by what one makes of oneself, between tradition (to reapply Eliot's phrase) and the individual talent. Unlike the historian, however, Jane Austen employs a purely novelistic method, a method that concentrates all meaning in the affairs of private life.

But there is still more to Jane Austen's version of English social history: there is (above all in *Pride and Prejudice*) the confrontation of middle classes and nobility. And perhaps here I must interrupt my argument to offer some defense of my repeated use of the unfortunate term "middle classes" to characterize the milieu that Jane Austen describes. The term does serve to exclude both the peerage on the one hand and the urban and agricultural working classes on the other. In all other respects, it is at worst misleading and at best inadequate. If one recalls that it embraces long-established gentry as well as the latest parvenus—Sir Thomas Bertram as well as Mrs. Elton—one must condemn as wholly inappropriate the connotations of newly moneyed vulgarity which the term inevitably carries with it. Moreover, its very breadth undermines its usefulness to the social historian (let alone the literary critic): there is little to be said for the precision of a term which covers the ground from small farmer to baronet, or from self-made provincial lawyer to London gentleman-lawyer of notable birth and indisputable rank. One understands the complaint of a recent writer that "the conception of middle class [as employed by a prominent historian] attains all the rigor of a rubber band," and his consequent decision scrupulously to restrict his own use of the term to cover only the French *"estat moyen*—merchants, financiers, industrialists, the town rich, the *bourgeoisie"*[6]—a decision which, if universally followed, would render the term largely inapplicable to Jane Austen's scene.

Yet some such term as "middle classes"—and no better one happens to offer itself—is indispensable for the student of Jane Austen, serving as it does to point out both the diversity and the unity of her social scene, both the multiplicity of the parts which make that scene up and its actual coherence. For as so many historians remind us, the easy social intercourse that Jane Austen pictures was a fact; it stemmed not from the novelist's imagination but from the easy *bonhomie* and generous social freedom of English country life in the eighteenth century and after.[7] Moreover, by virtue of isolating the peerage, the term helps us to appreciate one of the fundamental prejudices informing all Jane Austen's work. Chapman notes that "English society as Jane Austen depicts it shows a sharp cleavage between the nobility and gentry."[8] Indeed, for many of Jane Austen's characters, the baronetcy marks not only the upper limit of the middle classes but the upper limit of moral trustworthiness; Elinor Dashwood and Elizabeth Bennet and the morally alert members of the Bertram family all counter aristocratic or quasi-aristocratic condescension with a recognizably middle-class mistrust of idleness and extravagance. We are often reminded that even the distinguished gentry of Jane Austen's novels are closer socially and spiritually to those just beneath them than to the nobility just above; the term "middle classes" proclaims this situation, and to some extent explains it, as a more precise word would fail to do.[9]

But let us return to the central point—which, briefly summarized, is this: the social scene to which Jane Austen limited herself, with its many degrees of rank and of gentility, provided the novelist with the material with which to dramatize one essential aspect of her contemporary society, namely the interplay of the old and the new, the tension between the established classes and those armed mainly with their own attainments. And this tension in turn provided one important means whereby to extend, often, indeed, to redefine, the implications of her recurrent theme.

THE EARLY WORK

The extensive use of metaphors of rank is not, by and large, characteristic of Jane Austen's early writings: it is above all the literary situation of the second half of the eighteenth century (rather than the circumstances of the English middle classes) that defines the larger scene of Jane Austen's work through the revision of *Sense and Sensibility*. In light of the parodic nature of the bulk of Jane Austen's juvenile writings, it was perhaps inevitable that, in *Northanger Abbey* and *Sense and Sensibility*, situations and personal characteristics deriving from contemporary literature should have offered themselves to the novelist's mind as the means by which to construct (and enjoy the metaphoric richnesses of) a fictional microcosm; and in light of the age in which she lived, it must also have been inevitable that, before attaining complete freedom in the use of her own gifts, she should have had to come to terms with the claims of subjectivity and unreason, asserted in her time with unprecedented vigor, and to investigate in her own way the privileges and limitations of the individual imagination.

I do not mean, of course, to lump together without discrimination all of Jane Austen's early work: the differences, in rhetoric and in narrative method, between the juvenilia and *Northanger Abbey,* and between *Northanger Abbey* and *Sense and Sensibility,* are no less palpable or illuminating than the cultural concerns that link them all together. No one would suggest that the scope of *Northanger Abbey* is, like that of "Love and Freindship," for example, limited to the exposition and exploitation of the absurdity, or at least the potential absurdity, of contemporary literary postures. But thanks to its general spirit of evasive sport, *Northanger Abbey* does have far more in common than *Sense and Sensibility* with the juvenile burlesques. The focal consciousness of the novel is, we are told at the outset, "about as ignorant and uninformed as the female mind at seventeen usually is" (18); the phrase is crucial, announcing the affectionate condescension that determines the characterization of Catherine Morland and assuring the reader that Jane Austen is prepared to exploit only the comic potential of her material. While the heroines of the later novels may, like Catherine, have much to learn, Jane Austen never suggests that they are ordinary or average or run-of-the-mill, yet this is precisely what she does affirm, again and again, of Catherine.

Sense and Sensibility, on the other hand, cannot justly be said to concern "the female mind at seventeen," even though Marianne Dashwood is indeed at that age for most of the action of the book. Her romantic tendencies, unlike Catherine Morland's, are not curbed by a modicum of worldly experience; they are sufficiently deep-rooted to bring her to the edge of the grave. And she is consistent—in her opposition to the use of calculated strategy in courtship, to hackneyed language, and to conventional forms of social civility; in her militant devotion to free expression, to whatever word or gesture best affirms the sovereign individuality of the human creature. Her tastes are the logical extension of these traits, and at the same time make known the superiority of her mind to Catherine Morland's; it is to music, to Cowper, to the picturesque in architecture and landscaping that she turns, and not to foolish Gothic titillation. There is, moreover, in Jane Austen's conception of Marianne, very little of the sense of universality implied by such a phrase as "the female mind at seventeen." Catherine Morland's addiction to Gothic fiction merely underscores her ignorance and lack of experience; what happens to Marianne, by contrast, is more nearly determined by the cultural trends of her time than by any other single isolable factor. She is unmistakably representative of what Northrop Frye calls "the age of sensibility," and a summary of the characteristics of that age could almost serve as a summary of the characteristics of Marianne: when, for example, Frye describes the definitive qualities of literary response in this period—when he speaks of emotions "without an object," emotions independent of, and anterior to, specific stimuli[10]—he helps us to understand Marianne's "moods," states of mind not exclusively engendered by causative circumstances (and therefore, as Elinor Dashwood sadly discovers, not to be cured by modification of such circumstances) but in a latent state pre-existent to, and merely stimulated by, exterior factors. Despair eventually engulfs Marianne just as joy and love engulfed her earlier; once she has made her suicidal submission to despair she remains within its power to the inevitable point of physical and psychological disintegration.

But the sophistication and seriousness manifest for the first time in this novel are not restricted to the treatment of cultural history: a similar, and, for my purposes, no less important advance is evident in the handling of those metaphors whose provenance is the movement of English society. Needless to say, social metaphors, born as they are of a novelist's unique ability to encourage the illusion of the continuity of fiction and life, depend as if by definition upon the conventions of formal realism, so that the very method of Jane Austen's parodic juvenilia precluded the possibility of their being used with any kind of freedom. Here is a representative passage from "Love and Freindship," the most *réussi* of the early works:

You may imagine how greatly we were surprised by the sudden departure of Lord St Clair. "Ignoble Grand-sire!" exclaimed Sophia. "Unworthy Grandfather!" said I, and instantly fainted in each other's arms. How long we remained in this situation I know not; but when we recovered we found ourselves alone, without either Gustavus, Philander, or the Banknotes. As we were deploring our unhappy fate, the Door of the Apartment opened and "Macdonald" was announced. He was Sophia's cousin. The haste with which he came to our releif so soon after the receipt of our Note, spoke so greatly in his favour that I hesitated not to pronounce him at first sight, a tender and simpathetic Freind. Alas! he little deserved the name—for though he told us that he was much concerned at our Misfortunes, yet by his own account it appeared that the perusal of them, had neither drawn

from him a single sigh, nor induced him to bestow one curse on our vin-
dictive Stars—. (92–93; page numbers throughout refer to the Chapman
edition; see n. 4 below)

In these sentences, Jane Austen in characteristic fashion sets standards
of "literary" behavior against a standard of actual behavior, and a
"literary" ethic against moral values endorsed by common sense and
familiarity. But the latter qualities in each case remain, for the most
part, merely implicit. And social metaphors obviously cannot assert
their effectiveness in works in which the actualities of a given external
social scene can only find oblique or referential expression.

Though the irony of *Northanger Abbey*, like that of "Love and
Freindship," is engendered in large part by the juxtaposition and
balance of irreconcilable norms, the "literary" rules and patterns are
employed mainly to provide an ironic perspective on characters and
situations essentially realistic in nature. Jane Austen's method is patent
enough:

When the hour of departure drew near, the maternal anxiety of Mrs. Morland will be naturally supposed to be most severe. A thousand alarming
presentiments of evil to her beloved Catherine from this terrific separation
must oppress her heart with sadness, and drown her in tears for the last
day or two of their being together; and advice of the most important and
applicable nature must of course flow from her wise lips in their parting
conference in her closet. Cautions against the violence of such noblemen
and baronets as delight in forcing young ladies away to some remote farm-
house, must, at such a moment, relieve the fulness of her heart. Who would
not think so? But Mrs. Morland knew so little of lords and baronets, that
she entertained no notion of their general mischievousness, and was wholly
unsuspicious of danger to her daughter from their machinations. Her cautions were confined to the following points. "I beg, Catherine, you will
always wrap yourself up very warm about the throat, when you come from
the Rooms at night; and I wish you would try to keep some account of
the money you spend;—I will give you this little book on purpose." (18–19)

Catherine's adventures at Bath and Northanger, though, of course, far
less prosaic than Mrs. Morland could have supposed, do indeed take
place in something quite different from a Radcliffean scene: what
Jane Austen introduces—and what Catherine must learn to inhabit
intelligently—is a world of actual manners (albeit a world in fact
hardly less frightening, hardly more predictable, than the world of
Gothic fiction). Hence the possibility of metaphors of rank is at least
introduced. But Jane Austen is in fact not yet ready to exploit the

opportunity she has created for herself, as we are reminded when, late in the novel, Mrs. Morland scolds Catherine for her dejection upon returning from Northanger:

"I hope, my Catherine, you are not getting out of humour with home because it is not so grand as Northanger. That would be turning your visit into an evil indeed. Wherever you are you should always be contented, but especially at home, because there you must spend the most of your time. I did not quite like, at breakfast, to hear you talk so much about the French bread at Northanger."
"I am sure I do not care about the bread. It is all the same to me what I eat." (240–241)

This speech illustrates perfectly both the advance of *Northanger Abbey* over such a piece as "Love and Freindship" and the limitations still present in the later work. The reference to "the French bread at Northanger," no less than the unmistakable, individualized voice of Mrs. Morland herself, points to a fictional world which asserts its verisimilitude by means of precise indications of actual manners. Yet we must recognize that Mrs. Morland's words suggest more than her own misunderstanding of Catherine's sorrows: distinctions of rank, implicit in Mrs. Morland's responses to Northanger, do not in fact figure very significantly in the moral scheme of the novel. We do not experience General Tilney's snobbishness or Mr. Thorpe's boorishness as anything other than very distasteful personal traits; by the same token, the unpleasantness of Bath and the preference of Henry Tilney and Catherine for a modest and genteel little home are not apprehended in social terms (as corollaries of a conflict between parvenu and established elements in a given social scene, for example).

In *Sense and Sensibility,* by contrast, the novelist does attempt to animate her fictive material by calling our attention to, and drawing her metaphors from, the difficult situation of the established gentry of her England. Consider, in this light, Jane Austen's new approach to the question of money, a subject no less prominent in *Sense and Sensibility* than in *Northanger Abbey.* From the first pages, which describe the death of Mr. Dashwood and the disposal of his property, money is a major motivating force in the novel. Now, wealth is not of primary importance to either of Mr. Dashwood's daughters. To be sure, when Elinor talks with her mercenary half-brother, John Dashwood, she betrays a clear awareness of how much people are worth (223 ff.). But neither she nor Marianne desires more than what Marianne calls a "competence" (91), and neither permits money to stand in the way of an accurate assessment of other people. Yet questions of money affect each of them profoundly, and in fact function for each as the obstacle in the way of marriage. It is Willoughby's extravagance which causes him to turn from Marianne to an heiress, and Mrs. Ferrars' passion for wealth which causes her to disapprove of Elinor as a match for her son Edward. Moreover, the girls' financial limitations are the result of the blinding avarice of the John Dashwoods, who, in the remarkable dialogue of the second chapter of the novel, contrive to cut the sisters off with much less than their father wished them to have. Thus, despite their own inclinations, the girls are inextricably involved in "the cash nexus."

Though avarice and extravagance, like any deficiencies of character, are not social but personal failings, they may of course be linked to social considerations, and in *Sense and Sensibility* Jane Austen makes explicit the relation. Mrs. Ferrars is concerned with rising socially as well as with increasing the family's wealth, as shown by her desire to effect a marriage between Edward and the daughter of Lord Morton:

Mrs. Ferrars at first reasonably endeavoured to dissuade him from marrying Miss Dashwood, by every argument in her power;—told him, that in Miss Morton he would have a woman of higher rank and larger fortune;—and enforced the assertion, by observing that Miss Morton was the daughter of a nobleman with thirty thousand pounds, while Miss Dashwood was only the daughter of a private gentleman, with no more than *three*. . . . (373)

Naturally enough, Mrs. Ferrars' children betray the results of their mother's aristocratic pretensions. Robert becomes a repellent dandy. We first see him in a shop, "giving orders for a toothpick case for himself" and proving himself not only absurdly finicky but rude and thoughtless (220–221). Later we are exposed to his general condescension and his almost Dickensian preoccupation with the superiority of his own education. Edward, on the other hand, does not gloat, but suffers. In one of the most interesting passages of the novel he connects his unhappiness with his quasi-aristocratic idleness:

"It has been, and is, and probably will always be a heavy misfortune to me, that I have had no necessary business to engage me, no profession to give me employment, or afford me any thing like independence. But unfortunately my own nicety, and the nicety of my friends, have made me what I am, an idle, helpless being. We never could agree in our choice of a profession. I always preferred the church, as I still do. But that was not smart enough for my family. They recommended the army. That was a great deal too smart for me. The law was allowed to be genteel enough; many young men, who had chambers in the Temple, made a very good appearance in the first circles, and drove about town in very knowing gigs. But I had no inclination for the law, even in this less abstruse study of it, which my family approved. As for the navy, it had fashion on its side, but I was too old when the subject was first started to enter it—and, at length, as there was no necessity for my having any profession at all, as I might be as dashing and expensive without a red coat on my back as with one, idleness was pronounced on the whole to be the most advantageous and honourable, and a young man of eighteen is not in general so earnestly bent on being busy as to resist the solicitations of his friends to do nothing. I was therefore entered at Oxford and have been properly idle ever since." (102–103)

Thus Edward's self-contempt and Robert's self-satisfaction may, no less than Elinor's frustrated love, be laid at the door of the Ferrars' pretensions.

Similarly, Willoughby's extravagance is but one symptom of his aristocratic leanings. We may cavil at the tone of Elinor's conclusion upon his behavior, but not at the truth it proclaims:

Her thoughts were silently fixed on the irreparable injury which too early an independence and its consequent habits of idleness, dissipation, and luxury, had made in the mind, the character, the happiness, of a man who, to every advantage of person and talents, united a disposition naturally open and honest, and a feeling, affectionate temper. The world had made him extravagant and vain—Extravagance and vanity had made him cold-hearted and selfish. Vanity, while seeking its own guilty triumph at the expense of another, had involved him in a real attachment, which extravagance, or at least its offspring, necessity, had required to be sacrificed. (331)

With his hunting-shooting ways, his graceful defiance of genteel social rules, indeed the very dash and animation which make him what he is, Willoughby is automatically suspect from the middle-class point of view; his treatment of Marianne is merely the logical outcome of his aristocratic charm.

The Dashwoods—at least the small family group consisting of Mrs. Dashwood and her daughters—stand in direct contrast to the "idleness, dissipation, and luxury" we have been considering. The novel opens with an affirmation of their gentility: "The family of Dashwood had been long settled in Sussex. Their estate was large, and their residence was at Norland Park, in the centre of their property, where, for many generations, they had lived in so respectable a manner, as to engage the general good opinion of their surrounding acquaintance." But since Calvinistic elements have always contributed significantly to the traditions of the British middle classes, the Dashwoods are not willing simply to be: they must do. Sir John is astonished at their busyness (40), and Elinor in turn is displeased by Mr. Palmer's idleness (305). Still more revealing is Marianne's vow upon recovering from her illness. She says of Willoughby: "His remembrance can be overcome by no change of circumstances or opinions. But it shall be regulated, it shall be checked by religion, by reason, by constant employment" (347). The religion of which she speaks is of little theological or mystical significance. Virtually inseparable from the "constant employment" that Marianne also cites, it is much more an agency of restraint than of edification; like Robinson Crusoe before her, Marianne will find in busy hands not only a release from the demands of the psyche but moral rectitude as well. To be sure, by the time the Crusoes had "settled in Sussex," drifted far from the ignobler aspects of capitalism, and become the Dashwoods, the duties of the women were to a great extent reduced to such impractical tasks as learning to paint water colors and to play music. But Marianne and the other heroines of Jane Austen are by no means freed from the sense that they are obliged, not merely expected, to work hard at such occupations as they have; the polite female "accomplishments" in Jane Austen's novels reflect morality as well as fashion.[11] Thus Marianne's vow is a gesture of renewed identification with the English middle classes, and at the same time a gesture of repudiation of Willoughby and his idle, aristocratic life.

It must be evident that the central social theme of *Sense and Sensibility* has to do with the contest between the genteel middle classes on the one hand and aristocracy or quasi-aristocracy on the other. The theme is reflected in ways other than those already mentioned, and most notably in the novelist's use of place—that is, of houses, setting, and other devices of background. The novel begins with Mrs. Dashwood and her daughters facing the necessity of moving from their Sussex neighborhood. The house they select, a so-called "cottage" on Sir John Middleton's Devonshire property, is exceedingly modest, and in their determination to be content with it they almost expressly deny the pretense and extravagance with which they are surrounded.

But once settled at Barton Cottage, Marianne and Elinor accept

Sir John's invitation to visit in London, and it is in the conflict between London and Devonshire that Jane Austen makes most vivid use of her social metaphors. Traditionally, of course, British gentry preferred the country. "England," in Halévy's words,

> was not a country in which the capital had proved the social death of the provinces. There was no absolute monarch in England, with his court and centralized administration. London was no more than a huge business centre where the representatives of the nation assembled yearly for a limited number of months, and that rather to dictate to the capital the wishes of the country than to issue orders to the provinces in the name of the central government. Nor was England a country where the town had proved the social death of the country. . . . The result was that, despite cold and fog, the modern Englishman regarded the country as the place to live if you would lead a life happy and worthy of a gentleman.[12]

Halévy goes on to relate the traditional resident ownership of land to many areas of English character, agriculture, and economics, but for the intentions of this study it is enough to say that the country gentlefolk entertained a feeling akin to mistrust of the ways of the metropolis. Hence we should not be surprised to find that in *Sense and Sensibility* the unpleasant *nouveau* types (such as Lady Middleton), who are insensitive to the implications of modest gentility and who wish to seize directly upon aristocratic ways, look to London, nor to find that the novelist considers this tendency as distasteful as London itself. The London of *Sense and Sensibility* is characterized by discomforts and indignities, by stifling parties, and by general rudeness, and neither Elinor nor Marianne can ever be happy there. Indeed, it can be said that from the moment the sisters go to London, their great underlying need—their "action," in what we understand as the Aristotelian sense of the word—is to get back to Barton Cottage, or, in larger terms, to return to the modesty and gentility of *la vie de campagne*.

A series of frustrating circumstances, climaxed by Marianne's illness, keeps them virtual captives in London, and the extent to which London has come to symbolize labyrinthine imprisonment (as well as the extent of Jane Austen's psychological prowess) may be gauged from a moment in Marianne's delirium. She cries out "with feverish wildness":

"Is mama coming?—"
"Not yet," replied Elinor, concealing her terror, and assisting Marianne

to lie down again, "but she will be here, I hope, before it is long. It is a great way, you know, from hence to Barton."

"But she must not go round by London," cried Marianne, in the same hurried manner. "I shall never see her, if she goes by London." (311)

In light of her experiences in trying to escape London, Marianne's confused terrors are not without palpable meaning. They derive, moreover, not only from Jane Austen's awareness of personality but also from her awareness of social history, for the London of this novel is the milieu of Lady Middleton and Robert Farrars, of the emulators of Willoughby and the challengers of everything for which Barton Cottage has come to stand.[13]

Especially when considered in light of Jane Austen's earlier work, the handling of the larger conflicts of *Sense and Sensibility* may appear rich and intricate. But when we recall the use to which such conflicts are put in the later work, the extensiveness of their applicability to all varieties of human behavior, their treatment here may cease to seem quite so impressive. Consider, for example, Mrs. Jennings and Sir John Middleton. While we immediately sense their vulgarity, this quality is not defined for us in terms of rank. When we discover at last (and from a curiously nasty authorial voice) that Mrs. Jennings' late husband was in trade in London (153), we are only confirmed in our assumption that that good woman has come up rather fast from the lower echelons of the middle class; what is really surprising is that Jane Austen presents the information almost incidentally and quite late in the novel, as if Mrs. Jennings (and her daughters, especially Lady Middleton) were to be understood quite without reference to the social context of the novel. Similarly, we are never even told what variety of "Sir" Sir John may be. Chapman's note identifies him as "no doubt Baronet" (428) but offers no grounds for the conjecture. At any rate, the metaphoric function of this presumed baronet, ostensibly situated at the highest and most secure level of upper middle-class gentility, is never adequately clarified. Such negligence is not to be found in the later works. To take but one obvious instance from *Pride and Prejudice*, it is hardly enough to know that Lady Catherine de Bourgh is a vulgar woman: she does not begin to exist meaningfully in the moral context of the novel until seen as a vulgar aristocrat. But in *Sense and Sensibility*, Jane Austen has not yet acknowledged the full metaphoric possibilities of rank and birth.

Not only are some of the threads left unwound, but the social metaphors in general are never tightly woven into the fabric of the novel. What have any of the issues I have been discussing to do with sense and sensibility? Beyond the rather Wertherian echoes of Edward Ferrars' hatred of himself, no answer appears. Some plausible connections might easily be set forth by any cultural historian: no less than the increasing social mobility of the eighteenth century, the cult of sensibility denied and threatened the traditional certainties of English life. But Jane Austen in *Sense and Sensibility* is unable to integrate her various awarenesses, and the novel never persuades us of its own thematic coherence; we must conclude that the relation between the social metaphors of the novel and the metaphors drawn from contemporary literature is at best doubtful.

Just as Jane Austen in her treatment of the Dashwood sisters has not yet reached the stage of artistic maturity which would permit her the full use of her wide ironic vision, so too she has not yet attained complete control of the social background of her narrative. *Sense and Sensibility* is full of intrinsically splendid moments, and what is more it shows Jane Austen for the first time seriously investigating the social implications of individual behavior. As a work of transition between the earlier and more mature modes of the novelist, it is of unique heuristic value. But when set beside the subsequent works it seems, from any standpoint, an uneasy, even a faulty production. The great Jane Austen novels are those yet to come.

It is not, in fact, *Sense and Sensibility* that most clearly prefigures Jane Austen's mature handling of social metaphors, but rather the fragment of 1804–1805[14] called *The Watsons*: one is fortunately not obliged to accept Mrs. Leavis' celebrated "critical theory" of *The Watsons* as an ur-*Emma*[15] to see in this tantalizing draft some of the characteristic methods of Jane Austen's later writings. For in *The Watsons* rank is very much an issue, and at the same time an important agency whereby to clarify and resituate the personal issues on which the plot is pivoted.

Emma Watson, the virtually penniless youngest daughter of a valetudinarian widower, is raised by an aunt and uncle of some means, and as a result enjoys considerable expectations. But the uncle dies, the aunt remarries, and Emma, bereft of her inheritance, returns to the cheerless home inhabited by her father, her three unmarried older sisters, and one unmarried older brother. Shortly after her return,

Emma attends a local "assembly" and is introduced to the society of the town of "D."; the story thereafter, briefly summarized, is concerned with Emma's developing responses not only to her own distressing family, but to the three marriageable men she encounters at the ball—young Lord Osborne; his friend Tom Musgrave, "a great flirt" (318) who has already toyed with the affections of all three of Emma's sisters; and Lord Osborne's former tutor and present vicar, Mr. Howard. (The last, according to Austen family lore, would have married Emma had Jane Austen completed the tale [363].)

As B. C. Southam has pointed out, the opening sentences—among the most finished and admirable of the fragment—at once effect a meaningful scene:

The first winter assembly in the Town of D. in Surry was to be held on Tuesday Octr ye 13th, & it was generally expected to be a very good one; a long list of Country Families was confidently run over as sure of attending, & sanguine hopes were entertained that the Osbornes themselves would be there.—The Edwardes' invitation to the Watsons followed of course. The Edwardes were people of fortune who lived in the Town & kept their coach; the Watsons inhabited a village about 3 miles distant, were poor & had no close carriage; & ever since there had been Balls in the place, the former were accustomed to invite the Latter to dress dine & sleep at their House, on every monthly return throughout the winter.—

Southam comments that:

The immediate function of the passage, to set the scene for Emma Watson's entry to this world, and to introduce the promise of action, is performed with economy and directness. It brings to our notice the ethos of the neighbourhood, alive to the assembly and responding to it with anticipation. The hope "that the Osbornes *themselves* would be there" renders the bated breath of D. in a single word.[16]

The most significant consideration, for my purposes at least, is the last. The reaction of D. to the presence of the Osbornes (communicated in an ironic voice of ostensible assent which looks forward to the narratorial voice of the opening paragraph of *Mansfield Park*) immediately introduces the question of rank—the question, in other words, of the respect actually due to Lady Osborne (a woman strikingly possessed of "all the Dignity of Rank" [329]) and to her two children as opposed to the respect due to three morally doubtful people—the question of intelligent judgment threatened by snobbishness and pride.

And it is largely in relation to such issues that Emma Watson must come to understand her place in D. and her marital possibilities. Herself bred to a much higher "situation" than she now enjoys (318), Emma, by dint of inherent beauty and charm, unintentionally forces Lord Osborne himself to an attraction which scarcely befits his exalted rank. But Lord Osborne's interest is marked, quite predictably, by considerable tactlessness and condescension, and Emma is not sufficiently respectful of rank to overlook his clumsiness in the name of his title. Indeed, she quite explicitly opposes rank to personal attractions when she says of Lord Osborne " 'that he would be handsome even, tho' he were *not* a Lord—& perhaps—better bred; More desirous of pleasing, & shewing himself pleased in a right place.—' " Tom Musgrave, balancing (in the italicized phrases) his characteristic sycophancy against his desire to please Emma by acceding to her own egalitarian standards, answers " 'Upon my word, you are severe upon *my friend!*—I assure you Ld Osborne is *a very good fellow*—' " (340). Unlike her sister Elizabeth, who, upon hearing that Emma danced with Mr. Howard, exclaims " 'I should have been frightened out of my wits, to have had anything to do with the Osborne's set' " (342), Emma is quite unwilling to adjust her feelings to standards determined by birth.

Needless to say, Emma's opinions of Lord Osborne point beyond the immediate confrontation of two fictional characters to the conflict in Jane Austen's time of older hierarchical social values and newer democratic ones. What sets *The Watsons* most clearly apart from the rest of Jane Austen's early work, however, is the centrality of these opinions to Emma's actions, the extent to which such opinions are integrated into a coherent and plausible personality, the extent to which they become incontrovertibly characteristic of Emma's unmistakable voice and gestures, and the extent to which they therefore develop the implications of all her other traits. In *The Watsons*, microcosmic connotations and personal features can be distinguished only by the most artificial means: Emma's tendency to minimize all claims but those of individual disposition and attainments is not experienced in isolation from the warm and kindly impulses by means of which Emma asserts herself in the world of D. It is in no sense fortuitous, for example, that these impulses are most dramatically rendered by contrast not with any of Emma's sisters but rather with Miss Osborne, who quite cruelly reneges on her promise to dance with Mr. Howard's ten-year-old nephew at the assembly while Emma herself "did not think, or reflect;—she felt & acted—. 'I shall be very happy to dance with you Sir, if you like it,' said she, holding out her hand with the most unaffected good humour—" (330–331). If in *Sense and Sensibility* the social issues seem imposed upon a fictional situation that does not easily accommodate them, in *The Watsons* Jane Austen effects a comfortable adjustment of personal qualities and microcosmic significance, drawing impressively for the definition of private behavior upon the metaphoric possibilities implicit in a social scene in which a rigid and redoubtable aristocracy can be confronted, indeed challenged, by someone who will overcome all the limitations of birth by excellences of person and character.

Unfortunately, *The Watsons* exists in such a fragmentary state that any further analysis of its use of the metaphor of rank would almost necessarily develop into fruitless speculation; and if we cannot know why Jane Austen abandoned it, or even be certain whether the reasons were personal or artistic in nature, we should find no difficulty in contenting ourselves with the obvious consideration that these reasons are of relatively small importance in light of what the novelist did manage to complete in the last few years of her life. It seems enough to observe that, of all Jane Austen's early or unfinished work, *The Watsons* in at least one way prepares us best for what was to come—not only because its heroine is a girl named Emma, living in a small town with a valetudinarian father, but much more significantly because in this piece Jane Austen has begun to find the most suitable means whereby to situate her fictions in a wider social context without any hint of violence to their modest and restricted scope.

THE TWO SYMPATHIES

However clearly it prefigures the last four books, *The Watsons* does, in one important respect, give a very misleading impression of Jane Austen's social valuations. For even though there is some indication that Lord Osborne is capable of being instructed and improved by the example of an Emma Watson, the piece as a whole strongly suggests that the writer's sympathies are wholly on the side of the spirited individual and wholly opposed to the very idea of privileged classes. The rest of Jane Austen's work makes clear that nothing could be farther from the truth. D. J. Greene suggests the complexity of the problem when he writes of Jane Austen that "as a child of her times, the contemporary of William Pitt and Walter Scott and Edmund

Burke, the disciple of Dr. Johnson and Cowper, she found it possible
to be enthusiastic both for the notion of *noblesse oblige* and for the
notion of *la carrière ouverte aux talents*. If she sometimes found the
two sympathies hard to reconcile, she was neither the first nor the last
'Tory democrat' to do so."[17] Greene's generalization (which incidentally amplifies my own restatement of Jane Austen's central theme) is
just and far-reaching, and furthermore indicates why even the most
acute study of any single Jane Austen novel is likely to be deceptive.
Jane Austen's sympathies with respect to thematic issues definable in
terms of rank and birth were indeed "hard to reconcile"; *Pride and
Prejudice* and *Mansfield Park*, the latter so obviously written in direct
response to the former, demonstrate the novelist's difficulties. As
Trilling has put it, *Pride and Prejudice*

> celebrates the traits of spiritedness, vivacity, celerity, and lightness, and
> associates them with happiness and virtue. Its social doctrine is a generous
> one, asserting the right of at least the good individual to define himself
> according to his own essence. It is animated by an impulse to forgive-
> ness. . . .
>   Almost the opposite can be said of *Mansfield Park*. Its impulse is not to
> forgive but to condemn. Its praise is not for social freedom but for social
> stasis. It takes full notice of spiritedness, vivacity, celerity, and lightness,
> but only to reject them as having nothing to do with virtue and happiness,
> as being, indeed, deterrents to the good life.[18]

The contrast between the two novels, underscored both by the striking
thematic similarities and by the radically different moral stance that
each seeks to provoke, suggests the author's engagement with personal
and social ethics. But only close attention to the use of the metaphor
of rank in each novel can suggest the success with which that engagement found expression.

The "Problem" Novels

PRIDE AND PREJUDICE: THE ARGUMENT REDEFINED

According to her usual practice, Jane Austen devotes the final
chapter of *Pride and Prejudice* to what may look like mere tidying up.
Elizabeth Bennet has become Mrs. Darcy of Pemberley, and the effect
of the marriage upon the other characters of the novel is dutifully
outlined. Mrs. Bennet enters a state of perpetual rapture; Mr. Bennet
misses his favorite daughter and visits her often, preferably when

"least expected" (385); Jane Bennet and Mr. Bingley, who have also been married, eventually purchase an estate near Pemberley; Kitty spends much time with her older married sisters and improves; Mary remains at home with her books; Lydia and Wickham live beyond their income, take advantage of the generosity of Elizabeth and Jane, and become quite bored with each other; Miss Bingley continues to fawn upon Miss Darcy; and Miss Darcy and Elizabeth become fast friends, despite the latter's shocking habit of teasing her husband.

Arriving at the concluding paragraphs, we find this place of honor reserved for characters who might not be thought important enough to merit such preferential treatment:

Lady Catherine was extremely indignant on the marriage of her nephew; and as she gave way to all the genuine frankness of her character, in her reply to the letter which announced its arrangement, she sent him language so very abusive, especially of Elizabeth, that for some time all intercourse was at an end. But at length, by Elizabeth's persuasion, he was prevailed on to overlook the offence, and seek a reconciliation; and, after a little farther resistance on the part of his aunt, her resentment gave way, either to her affection for him, or her curiosity to see how his wife conducted herself; and she condescended to wait on them at Pemberley, in spite of that pollution which its woods had received, not merely from the presence of such a mistress, but the visits of her uncle and aunt from the city.

With the Gardiners, they were always on the most intimate terms. Darcy, as well as Elizabeth, really loved them; and they were both ever sensible of the warmest gratitude towards the persons who, by bringing her into Derbyshire, had been the means of uniting them. (388)

Though the reasons may only be suggested by these paragraphs, Jane Austen's conclusion cuts to the heart of *Pride and Prejudice:* Darcy's imperious aunt and Elizabeth's London relatives represent the principal obstacles in the path of a Bennet-Darcy union, and deserve their prominence at the end of the novel.

Lady Catherine, of course, from the beginning wished Darcy to honor his unofficial engagement to her own daughter, Darcy's first cousin and thus, like him, descended from an earl. But even without regard to the existence of Miss de Bourgh, Elizabeth Bennet could never, in Lady Catherine's eyes, have made an acceptable wife for a man like Darcy. The reasons are in part economic, for Elizabeth has no fortune. But the question of birth is much more serious. In the great scene in which Lady Catherine confronts Elizabeth with her disapproval, she cries:

"If you were sensible of your own good, you would not wish to quit the sphere, in which you have been brought up."

"In marrying your nephew, I should not consider myself as quitting that sphere. He is a gentleman; I am a gentleman's daughter; so far we are equal."

"True. You *are* a gentleman's daughter. But who was your mother? Who are your uncles and aunts? Do not imagine me ignorant of their condition."

"Whatever my connections may be," said Elizabeth, "if your nephew does not object to them, they can be nothing to *you*." (356)

The dialogue tells us much about both participants. Elizabeth is not without respectable connections. She can assert her father's unquestioned gentility in face of any attack, and can easily bring Lady Catherine to admit her claims. But when Lady Catherine turns to her mother's family, Elizabeth has no defense—none, that is, that Lady Catherine might be expected to understand. Her mother's brother-in-law Philips is a country lawyer. Even worse, Elizabeth's uncle Gardiner is in London trade, living within walking distance of his warehouses —that is, not even far enough along the path to Lady Catherine's kind of respectability to have moved to the country and purged himself of the uglier connotations of capitalistic enterprise.

However, the full significance of the Gardiners becomes clear only when we recall that they are, on personal rather than social merits, much the most admirable characters in the novel, the only members of the large cast of *Pride and Prejudice* (including Elizabeth herself) who do not suffer from ironic or openly castigatory treatment from the novelist. Consider their introduction:

Mr. Gardiner was a sensible, gentlemanlike man, greatly superior to his sister [Mrs. Bennet] as well by nature as education. The Netherfield ladies [Bingley's sisters] would have had difficulty in believing that a man who lived by trade, and within view of his own warehouses, could have been so well bred and agreeable. Mrs. Gardiner, who was several years younger than Mrs. Bennet and Mrs. Philips, was an amiable, intelligent, elegant woman, and a great favorite with all her Longbourn nieces. Between the two eldest and herself especially, there subsisted a very particular regard. They had frequently been staying with her in town. (139)

Nowhere else in the book is Jane Austen so respectful as this. And she goes on to show the Gardiners to be not only pleasant and cultivated, but in addition quite honorably and endearingly aware of their own social inferiority. When Mrs. Gardiner invites Jane (whom Bingley appears to have abandoned) to visit in London, she adds:

"I hope that no consideration with regard to this young man will influence her. We live in so different a part of town, all our connections are so different, and, as you well know, we go out so little, that it is very improbable they should meet at all, unless he really comes to see her."

[Elizabeth answers:] "And *that* is quite impossible; for he is now in the custody of his friend, and Mr. Darcy would no more suffer him to call on Jane in such a part of London! My dear aunt, how could you think of it? Mr. Darcy may perhaps have *heard* of such a place as Gracechurch Street, but he would hardly think a month's ablution enough to cleanse him from its impurities, were he once to enter it; and depend upon it, Mr. Bingley never stirs without him." (141)

That they can participate in this kind of raillery gains the Gardiners the reader's respect and affection more effectively than any of the novelist's abstract commendations, and—at least temporarily—renders hateful and arbitrary the aristocratic objections of Lady Catherine and Darcy.

These, then, are the polar forces of the novel: Lady Catherine, distasteful and vulgar, insisting only upon passive qualities of rank and "connections"; and the Gardiners, not yet risen from a relatively low level of the bourgeoisie yet personally ingratiating and morally impeccable, representing the active qualities of individual achievement. The burden of the drama itself, however, does not lie with them, but with Elizabeth and Darcy. Their courtship involves much more than personal discoveries and adjustments, and their marriage is a synthesis of the Lady Catherine and Gardiner principles: Darcy comes to realize that he cannot have Elizabeth without the Gardiner element in her blood and Elizabeth learns that there is more than condescension to being the descendant of an earl.

Since, as we have seen, Jane Austen's sympathies appear to lie with the good Gardiners, it is not surprising that Darcy's adjustment appears the more obvious. At first he seems every inch the aristocrat, making no attempt to conceal his distaste for the undistinguished milieu into which his friendship with Bingley has drawn him.[19] It is this apparent pride which first arouses Elizabeth's anti-aristocratic prejudice, and which persists even through his first profession of love for her: "His sense of her inferiority—of its being a degradation, of the family obstacles which judgment had always opposed to inclination, were dwelt on with a warmth which seemed due to the consequence he was wounding, but was very unlikely to recommend his suit" (189). Elizabeth's resentment at the strong element of condescension in Darcy's proposal causes their extended breach, which, but for two events, would surely have been permanent.

In both of these events the Gardiners play an important role, as is necessitated by the nearly symbolic use to which Jane Austen puts them. The first, mentioned in the concluding paragraph of the novel, is the visit to Pemberley which Elizabeth and the Gardiners make as tourists. They assume, of course, that Darcy is not at home, but he arrives earlier than expected and all are obliged to meet. The Gardiners stand "a little aloof" (251) while he and Elizabeth make an embarrassed attempt at civilities. But when Darcy (to everyone's surprise) later returns, he asks Elizabeth

if she would do him the honour of introducing him to her friends. This was a stroke of civility for which she was quite unprepared; and she could hardly suppress a smile, at his being now seeking the acquaintance of some of these very people, against whom his pride had revolted, in his offer to herself. "What will be his surprise," thought she, "when he knows who they are! He takes them now for people of fashion."

The introduction, however, was immediately made; and as she named their relationship to herself, she stole a sly look at him, to see how he bore it; and was not without the expectation of his decamping as fast as he could from such disgraceful companions. That he was *surprised* by the connexion was evident; he sustained it however with fortitude, and so far from going away, turned back with them, and entered into conversation with Mr. Gardiner. Elizabeth could not but be pleased, could not but triumph. It was consoling, that he should know she had some relations for whom there was no need to blush. She listened most attentively to all that passed between them, and gloried in every expression, every sentence of her uncle, which marked his intelligence, his taste, or his good manners. (255)

Having discovered that the Gardiners are in fact more genteel than their rank might suggest, Darcy invites Elizabeth's uncle to fish on his property, and later brings his sister to call upon the family group. In a word, he judges the Gardiners on the basis of what they have become, not on the basis of what they were born to become.

Then comes the elopement of Wickham and Lydia. Since Wickham's evil inclinations were already well known to him, Darcy assumes partial responsibility for the calamity and provides the funds necessary to restore Lydia's honor. What is more, as Mrs. Gardiner informs Elizabeth in a letter (321–325), Darcy in the course of his negotiations passes much time with the Gardiners, and even dines at their Gracechurch Street house. His learning to like the Gardiners is the quintessential change apparently brought about by his love for their niece, and serves to efface most of Elizabeth's objections to his aristocratic blindness.

Elizabeth, meanwhile, has learned that Darcy is not as inflexible in his opinions as she once supposed. At her first sight of Pemberley, for example, she is overwhelmed by its beauty, and her emotions are tinged by the memory of her having refused Darcy's offer of marriage:

> "And of this place," thought she, "I might have been mistress! With these rooms I might now have been familiarly acquainted! Instead of viewing them as a stranger, I might have rejoiced in them as my own, and welcomed to them as visitors my uncle and aunt.—But no,"—recollecting herself,— "that could never be: my uncle and aunt would have been lost to me: I should not have been allowed to invite them."
>
> This was a lucky recollection—it saved her from something like regret. (246)

But we have already seen her reaction to Darcy's first encounter with that "uncle and aunt," her initial amusement and subsequent satisfaction. Darcy, as both Elizabeth and the reader discover, needs but to be shown that Elizabeth "had some relations for whom there was no need to blush" in order to capitulate to the claims of personal attainment.

But Elizabeth learns much more than this: she comes to see that Darcy's position (even without reference to the man himself) merits more respect than she has been accustomed to pay. At the beginning of the novel, while she cannot deny what her friend Charlotte Lucas calls Darcy's "*right* to be proud," she adds "I could easily forgive *his* pride if he had not mortified *mine*" (20). Her attitude is of course defensible: Darcy should not mingle with his inferiors unless able to treat them with the respect required by their rank, however much below his. What Elizabeth fails to see is the qualitative difference between the position and pride of a Fitzwilliam Darcy and an Elizabeth Bennet. She does not seem to sense quite how meaningful and how impressive Darcy's position really is, and continues in her ignorance until the visit to Pemberley. There, under the tutelage of Darcy's housekeeper, she not only discovers his kindness to his many dependents, but realizes the very number of those dependents and the consequent hugeness of Darcy's responsibility: "As a brother, a landlord, a master, she considered how many people's happiness were in his guardianship!—How much of pleasure or pain it was in his power to bestow!—How much of good or evil must be done by him!" (250–251) The role of the feudal lord (as opposed to the mere small-scale country gentleman, like her father) at last comes clear to Elizabeth. Moreover, as she finds that Darcy lives up to his responsibilities with honor and benevolence, she can no longer even refrain from honestly applying her own standards of personal achievement to him and, whatever his past deficiencies in civility, admiring the man no less than she respects the rank. In the end, Darcy's behavior toward Lydia and Wickham puts the finishing touches on this new portrait of the honor-bound seignior, and his advances are at last received with all the "gratitude" (251) due to a man of his rank—to the nephew of Lady Catherine de Bourgh.

Elizabeth's admiration and gratitude also cause her to begin to worry over Darcy's aristocratic sensibilities, and, in the last section of the novel, more than ever to suffer humiliation at the vulgarity of her mother and Aunt Philips. In a word, the novel has taken its principal characters full cycle: Darcy patiently endures the more trying members of Elizabeth's family, while Elizabeth herself bemoans their vulgarity, not only selfishly but in deference to Mr. Darcy of Pemberley. And as the final paragraphs of the novel tell us, Darcy comes to love the Gardiners while Elizabeth urges him to effect a reconciliation with the same Lady Catherine who so recently covered her with insult and disparagement. Order and balance have been realized.

Now, the synthesis in which *Pride and Prejudice* finds its resolution admits of many analogues and implications, some of which are explored in an important study only now beginning to claim the attention it merits: I refer to Samuel Kliger's *"Pride and Prejudice* in the Eighteenth-Century Mode," originally published in 1947.[20] Kliger's piece, which had not until recently found much acceptance on the part either of the old or new schools of Austenian criticism,[21] is in truth open to some valid objections—it tends, for example, to confuse suggestive parallels in philosophy and history with the actual facts at hand, as when it threatens Elizabeth Bennet with such terms as "prelapsarian" and "Leveller"—yet it is at the same time one of the most ambitious attempts yet made to read Jane Austen's work in the context of the intellectual background of her time.

Dominant in *Pride and Prejudice*, Kliger asserts, is the antithesis of "nature" and "art" which, stemming from the humanistic criticism of the Renaissance, was still central to much late eighteenth-century thought. These polar terms are illustrated at a relatively simple level by the contrast between Elizabeth's musical performances and those of her sister Mary. The former, though technically wanting, are "easy and unaffected"; the latter, on a higher plane of accomplishment, are afflicted by "a pedantic air and conceited manner" (25). Elizabeth's "natural" performance is evidently much more to Jane Austen's taste, but Kliger points out that this is not to be taken as a complete condemnation of "art"; in a sentence that Kliger quotes from R. S. Crane, "The rationalistic temper of the period required that excellence be found in a mean between two extremes." The need for adjustment and compromise takes on more direct relevance to *Pride and Prejudice* if we follow eighteenth-century criticism in extending the "nature-art" antithesis to the ethical level, and arrive at a parallel and closely related antithesis between "feeling" and "reason." Thus, of a piece with Elizabeth's musical performance is her three-mile walk through the mud to tend to her sister, taken sick during a visit to the Bingleys. Both testify to her inherent spontaneity and emotionality, and the latter especially "is purposely presented in the novel in such a way as to suggest possibilities of both praise and censure." As much as we enjoy and even admire Elizabeth, we are expected to understand that she will become all the more attractive as she tempers her innate warm impulsiveness with more scrupulous judgment.

Traits directly opposed to Elizabeth's are primarily embodied not in a secondary figure like Mary but in Darcy himself, the other pole in the "nature-art" and "feeling-reason" dichotomies. This is immediately evident if we recall his standing "in silent indignation" at the thought of passing an evening in so "savage" an amusement as dancing, "to the exclusion of all conversation"[22] (25); berating Bingley's effusive style of letter-writing on virtually ethical grounds; and (at least in Elizabeth's view) being willing "to allow nothing for the influence of friendship and affection" in his judgments of others (47–50). Just as Elizabeth needs to become less impulsive, more cautious, and more disciplined, so Darcy apparently needs to come more under the sway of "nature" and mercy and less under that of "art" and justice.

Even this brief account of Kliger's study points to the place of Jane Austen's theme in a broad intellectual context. And when Kliger offers his widest definition of the "art-nature" conflict, he reveals how natural it was for Jane Austen to comprehend the opposition of such a man as Darcy and such a woman as Elizabeth in microcosmic terms:

The issues are clear: (1) A tension is created between the conceptions of man-in-nature and man-in-society; the first deals with humans *qua* humans, the second deals with humans as the "art" of society directs their activities. (2) Pride in class is a proper and justifiable human trait; superiority, so far from being a usurped right, is actually a heavy burden of duties which one assumes; the essential meaning of *noblesse oblige* is this willingness to serve. (3) Since no class exists for itself but is bound by reciprocated rights and duties to classes above and below, social non-compliance is represented either in improper respect for classes above or in delinquency in duty to classes below. (4) The system embodies the universal criterion of the mean between the two extremes; the individual's worth *qua* individual is adjusted to his worth as a member of a social class, whatever his class may be; a dialectic separates the natural man from man as the art of society has created him; nature and art are the juxtaposed terms.[23]

In a word, the intellectual system in itself suggests the connections between social and personal values, as well as the way in which the fundamental oppositions will find resolution; as compromise is effected, Elizabeth not only tempers her innate vivacity but "learns that we must not scorn the accumulated wisdom of past experience which has shaped during centuries the institution of class"; Darcy, on the other hand, not only unbends but learns in effect that "conservatism need not be impervious to new ideas." Without wishing to ascribe to Jane Austen a philosophical sophistication she doubtless did not possess, one can easily accede to Kliger's conclusion:

And here, perhaps, we have the sufficient answer to those critics of Jane Austen who claim that she was politically and socially obtuse. A livelier appreciation among readers of Jane Austen's novels of the potency of the terms "art" and "nature" in the thinking of such typical eighteenth-century political writers as Burke, Rousseau, Priestley, and Paine, would make it clearer that the art-nature antithesis was an explicit intellectual formulation growing out of the rationalistic spirit of the age. Developed now in aesthetic discussion and now in political discussion, the terms at the bottom were the same since the century sought a universal criterion of a mean between extremes common to art and morals alike.[24]

If Jane Austen declines to provide an explicit commentary on the particular trends of contemporary social history, she deals in her own way with the major issues at stake, and without ever forcing the limits of her chosen fictional metaphors.

PRIDE AND PREJUDICE: THE SECONDARY FIGURES

Elizabeth Bennet, as we have seen, must discover for herself the real burden of the aristocracy, the meaning and function of *ordo* in traditional society. That she has reached maturity without this knowledge tacitly announces that she is part of a milieu which, functioning side by side with what is left of the traditional feudalism, nonetheless operates in ignorance of the significance of the feudal order. This ignorance is, of course, fully reciprocated by the aristocracy, which fails to see the positive virtues of the social mobility enjoyed by those whose rank is not rigidly fixed at birth. Though bourgeoisie and nobility are often joined in casual social intercourse at a common level of gentility, a comfortable, lasting union of the two is not easily attained, and in *Pride and Prejudice* Jane Austen for the first time makes extended novelistic use of the difficulties.

"The social setting of this, like that of Jane Austen's other novels," writes Schorer, "is one in which a feudalistic order that does not know it is dying and a bourgeois order that is not yet confident that it is quite alive, meet and conflict and sometimes merge."[25] The crucial word in Schorer's sentence is the last: though the conflict between social classes has been a subject of European literature for centuries, what links Jane Austen's treatment of it to her time is the depiction of a *merger* between the opposing forces. In their steady rise throughout the eighteenth century, the middle classes both challenged and joined those established above them. Eighteenth-century literature of course reflects this, nowhere more clearly than in the work of Richardson. It is true that Richardson often obscures the issues—by his ambiguous relation to the actual motives of his heroines, especially of Pamela; by his ostensible endorsement of the middle-class view of the "aristocrat" as idle, essentially evil, yet irresistibly seductive; and by his invention of such social improbabilities as that of a girl in service, however "respectable" and unservantlike her background, marrying her master. But he anticipates Jane Austen in his depiction of the union, or at least the possibility of the union, of distinctly different social levels; both novelists reflect similar social data. Needless to say, Jane Austen never enunciates the conflict in the abstract, as Balzac, for instance, might well have done. Rather, she demonstrates the moral and psychological issues implicit in that which her observation has taught her to regard as a natural social phenomenon, and she does this in two principal ways: by demonstrating the personal characteristics of the major *dramatis personae* in terms of social rank, and by seeing that the minor characters, in addition to their function in advancing the plot, operate meaningfully with respect to the central social theme.

Mr. Collins comes immediately to mind. Not only the heir to Longbourn, the suitor of Elizabeth, and finally the husband of Charlotte Lucas, Collins also functions as the embodiment of the kind of abject submission to feudal authority that Lady Catherine expects. His profession encourages, even necessitates this: a clergyman without notable family connections, he is utterly dependent upon Lady Catherine's generosity. And personality no less than profession decrees Collins' pleasure in humbling himself before his seignorial patroness. Fawning, sycophantic, completely negating his own will and his own individuality, Collins is a caricature of the attitudes Lady Catherine expects of Elizabeth, and the personification of everything Elizabeth despises in the traditional order.

Sir William Lucas is another figure who sometimes approaches caricature, and he too provides insight into the conflicting values which separate Elizabeth and Darcy.

Within a short walk of Longbourn lived a family with whom the Bennets were particularly intimate. Sir William Lucas had formerly been in trade in Meryton, where he had made a tolerable fortune and risen to the honour of knighthood by an address to the King, during his mayoralty. The distinction had perhaps been felt too strongly. It had given him a disgust to his business and to his residence in a small market town; and quitting them both, he had removed with his family to a house about a mile from Meryton, denominated from that period Lucas Lodge, where he could think with pleasure of his own importance, and unshackled by business, occupy himself solely in being civil to all the world. For though elated by his rank, it did not render him supercilious; on the contrary, he was all attention to everybody. By nature inoffensive, friendly and obliging, his presentation at St. James's had made him courteous. (18)

Having tasted of the Court of St. James, Sir William for all his benevolence begins to move toward absurdity. His one blessed moment of acceptance by the nobility turns him into "a courtier" (126), a *bourgeois gentilhomme*. Moreover, it blinds him to the huge gulf that separates his Longbourn friends (and himself) from the genuine aristocracy: in a beautifully suggestive scene early in the novel (26), he tries, to the great discomfort of those concerned, to force Elizabeth to dance with Darcy, an abortive metaphoric attempt at yoking together by violence Mr. Darcy of Pemberley and Miss Nobody of

Nowhere that may be taken as a paradigm of his insensitivity to social realities. To bring these two together is not a task to be accomplished by good will alone; it requires sacrifice and introspection on both sides. But Sir William, having confused honorary recognition with total social acceptance on the part of the feudal remnant in England, assuming that he is perfectly equipped to straddle the old order and the new, is wholly insensitive to the complexity of the novel's central drama.

The Bingleys—that is, Mr. Bingley and his two sisters—provide an interesting parallel to the Gardiners. Of the sisters, we are told:

They were in fact very fine ladies; not deficient in good humour when they were pleased, nor in the power of being agreeable where they chose it; but proud and conceited. They were rather handsome, had been educated in one of the first private seminaries in town, had a fortune of twenty thousand pounds, were in the habit of spending more than they ought, and of associating with people of rank; and were therefore in every respect entitled to think well of themselves, and meanly of others. They were of a respectable family in the north of England; a circumstance more deeply impressed on their memories than that their brother's fortune and their own had been acquired by trade. (15)

The besetting sin of the Bingley sisters is impatience. Their "proud and conceited" ways are, unlike Darcy's, inexcusable; the society of Longbourn is in no sense beneath them, and their desire to step immediately beyond the company of the genteel middle class to that of the nobility displays more vulgarity than any connection with trade.

A large fortune and the fanciest education, however, are not enough to cement their place in society. They need land, and resent their unhurried brother's satisfaction with merely renting Netherfield. Their pretensions are manorial, for without an estate linked to their name they cannot successfully appear, let alone become, fully worthy of a Darcy. Thus, only one step beyond the Gardiners on the social ladder, they have, as much as Collins himself, utterly sacrificed their justifiable pride to a slavish acquiescence to feudal values. From the equivalent of Gracechurch Street they wish to leap to the equivalent of Pemberley, and in so doing they cut themselves off from the representatives of both places: in their hatred of their origins they offend Elizabeth, and in their unwarranted familiarity they repel Darcy.

Perhaps the most subtle and striking comment upon the central conflict of *Pride and Prejudice* is provided by the unscrupulous Wickham. The son of Darcy's steward, he is born a dependent, a cog in the great feudal machinery. Yet, as he tells Elizabeth (realizing no doubt that such information is sure to win her favor), his father willingly chose his place: "'*My* father began life in the profession which your uncle, Mr. Philips, appears to do so much credit to—but he gave up everything to be of use to the late Mr. Darcy, and devoted all his time to the care of the Pemberley property'" (81). Thus Wickham's father has been both a man of independent profession and a feudal retainer; by heritage alone, Wickham himself joins the opposite principles associated with the Gardiners and Lady Catherine respectively. And in his own life, he continues to reflect both principles. He adopts a profession (the military) calling for individual excellence, but rises only by Darcy's eventual interference. Moreover, as he turns from an attempt to ruin Darcy's sister to an attempt to ruin Lydia Bennet, his actions parallel his curious and ambiguous social position in a beautifully ironic way. To quote Schorer once again:

Between Lydia and Miss Darcy, dramatically linking them stands Wickham, in whom charm and villainy go hand in hand. And he is an especially instructive figure: with his ambiguous initial attachment to one class, he has the aspirations of the other, and he feeds upon both: the immoral opportunist, he represents the acquisitive, the materialistic impulse at its worst, which is to say when it moves out beyond all social restraint whatever.[26]

Wickham's function in the plot is vital, but Jane Austen does not allow him to do his dishonorable work without also defining his role in terms of rank.

Much more could be said of the manner in which Jane Austen brings the minor characters into alignment with the issues of the Elizabeth-Darcy conflict; indeed, a section of at least the length of this one might be devoted to the ways in which the characters cluster around the "active" and "passive" qualities illustrated at the extreme by the Gardiners and Lady Catherine respectively.[27] It is enough here to assert that no novelist in English has erected a more subtle or more elaborate structure upon the perquisites and obligations of social rank, and that none has gone farther in the direction of demonstrating personal tendencies by reference to a larger social situation.

WHAT HAPPENS AT MANSFIELD PARK

As I have already suggested, the place of *Mansfield Park* in the Jane Austen canon is fixed to a considerable extent by its connections with *Pride and Prejudice;* and these connections, along with the differences between the two novels, are put into focus by the treatment of Mansfield itself. In *Pride and Prejudice,* the novelist contrives that a house alert Elizabeth to the restrictions of her own judgment: Pemberley, innocent of Darcy's sometimes distressing (and often misleading) manners, embodies all that is urgent in Darcy's claims upon Elizabeth. In similar manner, Mansfield transcends the limitations of its inhabitants and stands for certain values that could not clearly be represented through ephemeral personality. At the same time, *Mansfield Park* is a very different kind of book, one much less susceptible to discursive schematization: Mansfield, to a far greater degree than Pemberley, functions as something far beyond the mere sum of its parts. Indeed, the implications of Mansfield are very nearly mystical, and are expressed in voices that suggest figures in a cult. Sir Thomas Bertram, especially in the early parts of the novel, is made to seem not only a patriarch but very like the God of the Old Testament:[28] consider, as an instance of his characteristic tone and diction, the fiat "Let her home be in this house," by which he authorizes Fanny Price's residence at Mansfield (9). But terror is not the only quality of the Mansfield cult: if Sir Thomas is justice made flesh (or at least impresses himself, Edmund, and Fanny as such), Edmund embodies mercy; each, in his way, signifies one aspect of the morality which, both cruel and humane, keeps Fanny in her subservient place while at the same time allowing her to participate in the heavenly blessings of Mansfield Park.

And so it is less surprising than it otherwise might seem that Fanny, like the reader, should find herself unable to put into words the precise meaning of Mansfield Park. Why does she refuse Henry Crawford with such finality? To be sure, his flirtatious behavior to Maria Bertram in full view of her suitor, Mr. Rushworth, is appalling. But this is a symptom, not the disease itself. Fanny can only sense incoherently that, by his proposal, Henry "had insulted—she knew not what to say —how to class or how to regard it" (302). The sympathetic reader— he who has allowed the symbol of Mansfield Park to work its full and perhaps unwelcome effect—can only agree that Henry's attempt to connect himself with that house is indeed an "insult," an act of sacrilege. Moreover, Fanny's stammerings set forth another palpable difference between *Mansfield Park* and *Pride and Prejudice:* Elizabeth Bennet's awareness is so central to her novel that the symbolic implications of Pemberley can fairly be defined by the effect it produces upon her, but the drama of *Mansfield Park* is not played out in the arena of Fanny's developing awareness. Though Fanny of course sees much, she participates rather little in the major conflicts of the novel. Unlike the other Jane Austen heroines (with the single exception of Elinor Dashwood, who is only one of the two central figures of *Sense and Sensibility*), Fanny is not really the active protagonist of her novel. With respect to most of the conflicts of the book, she is much more an onlooker than a doer. Never seriously deluded by the superficial allure of the urbane but deadly crowd that profanes Mansfield Park, she has few painful revaluations to undergo; if some of her personal loyalties are threatened it is precisely because her most cherished values are so little subject to revision. Even the marvelously rendered visit to Portsmouth is more in the nature of reaffirmation than of discovery, for none of Fanny's own standards is profoundly or meaningfully altered by the visit: she only finds her family more vulgar than she had allowed herself to imagine or to remember. Once molded in childhood by Edmund and Sir Thomas, Fanny is, so to speak, a finished product, and she is only strengthened in her fixed convictions by the difficulties she faces—by having to watch the Bertram children, even Edmund, straying from the Mansfield code, and by having to refuse Henry Crawford without daring to describe to Sir Thomas the impropriety of Henry's past conduct with Maria.

For this reason, there are long passages in *Mansfield Park*—most of Chapter V, for example—in which Fanny does not appear (and in which her absence is in no way so striking as that of the heroine from Chapter V of *Emma*). Indeed, even when present, she rarely speaks or acts unless called upon; her innate sense of unworthiness has been too carefully nurtured by her foster family. Hence the typical scene in *Mansfield Park* consists of two major elements. First we have the dialogue and actions of the principal participants, and then, interrupting or following them, Fanny's reflections, which serve to remind us of those Mansfield ideals that the conversation has challenged. The following sentence, taken from the scene in which the young people decide to produce their play, illustrates Fanny's role in the novel:

> Fanny looked on and listened, not unamused to observe the selfishness which, more or less disguised, seemed to govern them all, and wondering how it would end. For her own gratification she could have wished that something might be acted, for she had never seen even half a play, but every thing of higher consequence was against it. (131)

Fanny at one point is called "a quiet auditor of the whole" (136), and the phrase applies throughout most of the book.

Hence it is almost inevitable in dealing with *Mansfield Park* to pass beyond character and to consider the conflicts of the novel in wider symbolic terms than those explicit in Fanny's assertions and gestures. Mansfield itself is, after all, the major force in the plot, no less subject to spiritual and physical dangers than the human protagonists of most other novels. Its sanctity, so richly demonstrated, is threatened from without by the intrusion of the Crawfords and from within by the failure of Tom Bertram and his sisters to meet its standards. Its physical reality—scarred by the theatricals—is as strongly felt as that of any of the *dramatis personae,* even though it is only scantily described. Unlike the other novels, *Mansfield Park* is set much more in a house than in a village or larger community. Even the human appurtenances of that house are really alive: the servants are present not merely as spectral functionaries but as living beings, real enough to interrupt conversations (270) or to be silently aware of the amatory situations of the young Bertrams (325). Moreover, it is now a critical commonplace that those forces which oppose Mansfield are themselves centered in and symbolized by architectural (or at least geographical) actualities. For Mansfield is not the only meaningful and vividly rendered house in the novel, and it is through other houses and places, and through talk of other houses and places, that we can, by effect of contrast, specify some of those values attached to Mansfield that any summary of plot must allow to remain elusive.

Important among the other houses is Rushworth's country seat, Sotherton Court, the goal of a pilgrimage made by the entire Mansfield party early in the novel. Rushworth's mother offers to show the house "to such of them as have not been there before":

The whole party rose accordingly, and under Mrs. Rushworth's guidance were shewn through a number of rooms, all lofty, and many large, and amply furnished in the taste of fifty years back, with shining floors, solid mahogany, rich damask, marble, gilding and carving, each handsome in its way. Of pictures there were abundance, and some few good, but the larger part were family portraits, no longer any thing to any body but Mrs. Rushworth, who had been at great pains to learn all that the housekeeper could teach, and was now almost equally well qualified to shew the house. On the present occasion, she addressed herself chiefly to Miss Crawford and Fanny, but there was no comparison in the willingness of their attention, for Miss Crawford, who had seen scores of great houses, and cared for none of them, had only the appearance of civilly listening, while Fanny, to whom every thing was almost as interesting as it was new, attended with unaffected earnestness to all that Mrs. Rushworth could relate of the family in former times, its rise and grandeur, regal visits and loyal efforts, delighted to connect any thing with history already known, or warm her imagination with scenes of the past. (84–85)

By suggesting Mrs. Rushworth's lack of personal or even familial connection with the great past of her house, this paragraph makes a mockery of the tradition in the Rushworth family and at the same time reminds us that tradition is one of the first tenets of the cult of Mansfield Park. Moreover, by showing us Mary Crawford's boredom with tradition (directly contrasted to Fanny's awed and rapturous reverence for things of the past), it makes us immediately perceive Mary's inability to adopt that tenet. We may be dazzled and refreshed by Miss Crawford's wit, so sharply different from the sobriety of Fanny and Edmund; we may be touched by her sensitivity to Fanny's situation; but we have only to see her in relation to tradition to recognize (as even Edmund comes to recognize) her fundamental corruption.

Mary is not alone in betraying her shortcomings through her attitude toward houses. Though perhaps less to be blamed because of his stupidity, Rushworth is no better than she. In the scene in which Maria, Henry, and Fanny discuss "improvements,"[29] for example, Rushworth "scarcely risked an original thought of his own beyond a wish that they had seen his friend Smith's place" (97). For Rushworth, houses are places to show, a means of impressing others with wealth and station, and are thus to be subjected to continual renewal and modification; possession of Mansfield Park, for him, could be no more than grounds for ostentation. Henry Crawford, too, though in a far more sophisticated way, shares Rushworth's love of the impressive façade. Having stumbled upon Thornton Lacey, the parsonage originally intended for Edmund upon his ordination, Henry lectures Edmund (during a rubber of "Speculation") on the improvements necessary to make the house habitable. He concludes:

"The air of a gentleman's residence, therefore, you cannot but give it, if you do any thing. But it is capable of much more. (Let me see, Mary; Lady Bertram bids a dozen for that queen; no, no, a dozen is more than it is worth. Lady Bertram does *not* bid a dozen. She will have nothing to say to it. Go on, go on.) By some such improvements as I have suggested, (I do not really require you to proceed upon my plan, though by the bye

I doubt any body's striking a better)—you may give it a higher character. You may raise it into a *place*. From being the mere gentleman's residence, it becomes, by judicious improvement, the residence of a man of education, taste, modern manners, good connections. All this may be stamped on it; and that house receive such an air as to make its owner be set down as the great land-holder of the parish, by every creature travelling the road; especially as there is no real squire's house to dispute the point; a circumstance between ourselves to enhance the value of such a situation in point of privilege and independence beyond all calculation." (243–244)

Here the badges of urbanity—"education, taste, modern manners, good connections"—are set above the qualities of gentlemanliness. To be modern, in this case, is quite literally to destroy the marks of age, in short to deny tradition. Even worse, the very purpose of this modernity is deception, the inaccurate representation of rank and land. This one speech, its elegant and playful treatment of serious subjects skilfully underscored by the interruption referring to the game of cards, might suffice to turn Fanny forever from Henry's advances.

Country houses such as Sotherton Court and Thornton Lacey are only part of the architectural scheme of *Mansfield Park*. In addition, Jane Austen provides us with something quite different, Fanny's father's house in Portsmouth. And however unlike the rich country houses of the novel, the Price home serves like them to underscore the importance of tradition at Mansfield. For tradition, involving subservience of the individual to ways of thinking and acting handed down through the generations, implies an imposed and permanent order, just as the selfish and wholly disrespectful wit of the Crawfords implies anarchy. And at Portsmouth Fanny encounters anarchy of another kind. Household duties are not assigned according to a fixed plan: the result is dirt and confusion. Order within the family is ignored: the result is children who squabble among themselves and show no deference to their parents. Order within ranks of society is denied: the result is servants who defy their masters and respond to commands with rudeness. Immersed in this chaos, Fanny

could think of nothing but Mansfield, its beloved inmates, its happy ways. Every thing where she now was was in full contrast to it. The elegance, propriety, regularity, harmony—and perhaps above all, the peace and tranquillity of Mansfield, were brought to her remembrance every hour of the day, by the prevalence of every thing opposite to them *here*. (391)

For Fanny, the disorder is most directly represented by, and most painfully perceived through, the intolerable noise:

The living in incessant noise was to a frame and temper, delicate and nervous like Fanny's, an evil which no superadded elegance or harmony could have entirely atoned for. It was the greatest misery of all. At Mansfield, no sounds of contention, no raised voice, no abrupt bursts, no tread of violence was ever heard; all proceeded in a regular course of cheerful orderliness; every body had their due importance; every body's feelings were consulted. (391–392)

The calm and silence of Mansfield Park are sensuous manifestations of its essential and precious order, to which the spiritual anarchy of the Crawfords and the physical anarchy of Portsmouth are both contrasted.

The final contrast to Mansfield Park is provided not by a house but by a larger symbol. In this novel, as in *Sense and Sensibility*, London comes alive as a wholly undesirable place, the appropriate setting for the Crawfords, for dissolute Tom Bertram, and for Maria, who no sooner marries Rushworth than she moves away to his Wimpole Street house. The admirable qualities of independence and personal achievement that Jane Austen links to London through the Gardiners in *Pride and Prejudice* are here largely overlooked; London is (as in *Sense and Sensibility*) not so much a place for rising enterprisers as for the idle rich.

Early in the novel, Jane Austen vividly illustrates the essential incompatibility of London and Mansfield Park. Scarcely settled at the Grants' parsonage, Mary Crawford challenges the pattern of life in the Mansfield Park country by requesting a horse and cart to transport her harp. Edmund discusses the situation with her:

"You would find it difficult, I dare say, just now, in the middle of a very late hay harvest, to hire a horse and cart?"

"I was astonished to find what a piece of work was made of it! To want a horse and cart in the country seemed impossible, so I told my maid to speak for one directly; and as I cannot look out of my dressingcloset without seeing one farm yard, nor walk in the shrubbery without passing another, I thought it would be only ask and have, and was rather grieved that I could not give the advantage to all. Guess my surprise, when I found that I had been asking the most unreasonable, most impossible thing in the world, had offended all the farmers, all the labourers, all the hay in the parish. As for Dr. Grant's bailiff, I believe I had better keep out of *his* way; and my brother-in-law himself, who is all kindness in general, looked rather black upon me, when he found what I had been at."

"You could not be expected to have thought on the subject before, but when you *do* think of it, you must see the importance of getting in the grass. The hire of a cart at any time, might not be so easy as you suppose; our farmers are not in the habit of letting them out; but in harvest, it must be quite out of their power to spare a horse."

"I shall understand all your ways in time; but coming down with the true London maxim, that every thing is to be got with money, I was a little embarrassed at first by the sturdy independence of your country customs." (58–59)

This conversation says a good deal and suggests a good deal more. It identifies Mary with London and London with money. The great leveller, money challenges birth as the major determinant of status, and thereby defies the traditional social order, the order associated in this novel with "country customs." From this point of view, London not only disturbs the everyday order of the country but offers no order of its own in recompense. Though she may be ironically aware of the impropriety of her "true London maxim," Mary is inextricably caught up in the tangle of her London background. And nowhere more clearly than in this passage, London is made to stand with Sotherton and the Price house as inimical to the harmonies and traditions of Mansfield Park.

MANSFIELD PARK AND THE BARONETCY

An acute sense of responsibility in light of an established order, submission of individual preference and response to an ancient but vital tradition: these can now be included among the Mansfield values. But there is still further to go in the search for the ultimate "meaning" of Mansfield Park. As the preceding paragraphs suggest, personal qualities cannot be separated from the position of Mansfield Park within the ranks of English society; Mansfield is, unmistakably, the house of a baronet.

The baronet, at least as Jane Austen presents him in this novel, plays a curious role in the drama of English society. With his quasi-feudal function in the rural economy, a baronet of ancient title like Sir Thomas Bertram is hardly distinguishable from a nobleman; he cannot but mingle with the aristocracy, whose equal he is in breeding, in education, perhaps even in fortune. At the same time (to quote Chapman's key sentence once again) "English society as Jane Austen depicts it shows a sharp cleavage between the nobility and the gentry." Sir Thomas, as we shall see, is scrupulously aware of this "cleavage," never forgetting that his place is not at the bottom of the peerage but at the upper limit of the gentry. Moreover, given both this anti-aristocratic prejudice and the social freedom among middle classes that Jane Austen describes, it is not surprising that Sir Thomas' closest connections are with somewhat lower orders, not only with lesser country gentry but with the urban bourgeoisie as well. Hence, as Jane Austen portrays it, Sir Thomas' status is unique and his responsibility twofold: it is his obligation as guardian of the Mansfield code to check both the bourgeois vulgarity of Mrs. Norris and the aristocratic amorality of his own overindulged children.

To be sure, this representation of the baronetcy depends less upon an impersonal application of the data of social history than upon the novelist's own very personal response to these data.[30] Nonetheless, it is characteristic of all Jane Austen's mature work in that it proclaims the possibility, indeed the necessity of expressing ethical values in terms of social rank.

The opening paragraph offers a revealing instance of the rhetoric by means of which Jane Austen seeks to persuade the reader to accept the new sense of English society that engenders her crucial set of metaphors. Profound in its irony, this paragraph must be studied closely.

About thirty years ago, Miss Maria Ward of Huntingdon, with only seven thousand pounds, had the good luck to captivate Sir Thomas Bertram, of Mansfield Park, in the county of Northampton, and to be thereby raised to the rank of a baronet's lady, with all the comforts and consequences of an handsome house and large income. All Huntingdon exclaimed on the greatness of the match, and her uncle, the lawyer, himself, allowed her to be at least three thousand pounds short of any equitable claim to it. She had two sisters to be benefited by her elevation; and such of their acquaintance as thought Miss Ward and Miss Frances quite as handsome as Miss Maria, did not scruple to predict their marrying with almost equal advantage. But there certainly are not so many men of large fortune in the world, as there are pretty women to deserve them. Miss Ward, at the end of half a dozen years, found herself obliged to be attached to the Rev. Mr. Norris, a friend of her brother-in-law, with scarcely any private fortune, and Miss Frances fared yet worse. Miss Ward's match, indeed, when it came to the point, was not contemptible, Sir Thomas being happily able to give his friend an income in the living of Mansfield, and Mr. and Mrs. Norris began their career of conjugal felicity with very little less than a thousand a year. But Miss Frances married, in the common phrase, to disoblige her family, and by fixing on a Lieutenant of Marines, without education, fortune, or connections, did it very thoroughly. She could hardly have made a more untoward choice. Sir Thomas Bertram had interest, which, from principle as

well as pride, from a general wish of doing right, and a desire of seeing all
that were connected with him in situations of respectability, he would have
been glad to exert for the advantage of Lady Bertram's sister; but her
husband's profession was such as no interest could reach; and before he
had time to devise any other method of assisting them, an absolute breach
between the sisters had taken place. It was the natural result of the conduct
of each party, and such as a very imprudent marriage almost always produces. To save herself from useless remonstrance, Mrs. Price never wrote
to her family on the subject until actually married. Lady Bertram, who was
a woman of very tranquil feelings, and a temper remarkably easy and
indolent, would have contented herself with merely giving up her sister, and
thinking no more of the matter: but Mrs. Norris had a spirit of activity,
which could not be satisfied till she had written a long and angry letter
to Fanny, to point out the folly of her conduct, and threaten her with all
its possible ill consequences. Mrs. Price in her turn was injured and angry;
and an answer which comprehended each sister in its bitterness, and
bestowed some very disrespectful reflections on the pride of Sir Thomas,
as Mrs. Norris could not possibly keep to herself, put an end to all intercourse between them for a considerable period.

At first glance, we seem to find ourselves in the realm of the wholly
objective, impartial account.[31] The narrator proposes, without apparent qualm or qualification, a calculating, essentially financial interpretation of marriage. Miss Maria Ward's conquest of Sir Thomas
Bertram is, in light of her small dowry, a major coup; "the rank of a
baronet's lady" which she attains is defined not by the new responsibilities of her elevated station but by "the comforts and consequences
of an handsome house and large income." The reaction of the Huntingdon community to Miss Maria's success, reported without commentary, assumes dowry and beauty as commodities to be bartered
for a life distinguished by the "comfort" and "large income" attendant
upon "rank." Indeed, the narrator participates so completely in the
Huntingdon point of view as to be able to construct a resonant universal statement upon the foundations of the Huntingdon conception
of the marriage mart: "But there certainly are not so many men of
large fortune in the world, as there are pretty women to deserve
them." The narrator goes on to judge the "contemptibility" of a marriage (in this case, Miss Ward's) by the income of the male partner,
making clear that contempt is reserved for a bad matrimonial bargain. And for the "imprudent" marriage of Miss Frances, the narrator
shows no sympathy whatever: joined to a man "without education,

fortune, or connections," Miss Frances cannot expect that mere ties of blood should suffice to keep her within her sisters' affections.

Obviously, the narrative voice of the paragraph is not wholly re-liable—or, to use somewhat less anachronistic terms, the function of its rhetoric is that of calling into doubt its ostensible assertions. But where is the line to be drawn to separate common sense and cruelty, hardheadedness and moral obduracy? It may be well here to recall those commentators who point out Jane Austen's essentially bourgeois, capitalistic bias and underscore her clear-eyed, unemotional aware-ness of the economic realities of the modern world,[32] as well as those who demonstrate the extent to which Jane Austen's mercantile back-ground influences the very texture of her prose, causing her to fall back upon words and metaphors drawn from the world of business and finance: from "possession," "affairs," and "establishment" to "good fortune," "taxed her patience," and "take into account."[33] However persuasive, these studies do not prove, nor in some cases even suggest, that Jane Austen's immersion in mercantile values ever caused her to accept these values unquestioningly as appropriate to all people in all situations. The first paragraph of *Mansfield Park*, in fact, delib-erately introduces through its narrator a viewpoint that the novel as a whole vehemently denies, a viewpoint which in fact is connected with the most disagreeable character in the novel.

For the narrator here is the spiritual cousin of Mrs. Norris herself. If we look again at the last part of the paragraph, we notice that the narrator ascribes Mrs. Norris' interference in her sister's life to "a spirit of activity" lacking in Lady Bertram. No reader of *Mansfield Park* will accept so pleasant an explanation of Mrs. Norris' noxious of-ficiousness. We notice, too, the narrator's tacit approval of Mrs. Norris' self-righteous inability to "keep to herself" her sister's "very disrespect-ful reflections on the pride of Sir Thomas": we are reminded of both Mrs. Norris' viciousness and her fawning snobbishness. Clearly the narrator represents Jane Austen at her most ironic, completely assum-ing the *persona* of her most unpleasant creation. And there is no reason to assume that Jane Austen has changed her method in mid-para-graph. The voice which approves Mrs. Norris' behavior is pitched no differently from the earlier voice which regarded marriage as a purely mercenary proposition and the rank of baronet's lady as nothing more than the fruit of a triumphant transaction: Mrs. Norris herself is precisely the sort of petite bourgeoise who might have dictated this whole paragraph. But for Jane Austen the baronetcy cannot be defined in financial terms any more justly than courtship in terms of either having "the good luck to captivate" or else finding oneself "obliged to be attached."

I have devoted this much space to the first paragraph because the intolerable judgments it ironically assumes are so characteristic of the great majority of the characters in the novel—because, in a word, it proclaims the hostility of the modern world to the Mansfield standards. Consider, for example, Mary Crawford's point of view:

> Tom Bertram must have been thought pleasant, indeed, at that rate: he was the sort of young man to be generally liked, his agreeableness was of the kind to be oftener found agreeable than some endowments of a higher stamp, for he had easy manners, excellent spirits, a large acquaintance, and a great deal to say; and the reversion of Mansfield Park, and a baronetcy, did no harm to all this. Miss Crawford soon felt, that he and his situation might do. She looked about her with due consideration, and found almost every thing in his favour, a park, a real park five miles round, a spacious modern-built house, so well placed and well screened as to deserve to be in any collection of engravings of gentlemen's seats in the kingdom, and wanting only to be completely new furnished—pleasant sisters, a quiet mother, and an agreeable man himself—with the advantage of being tied up from much gaming at present, by a promise to his father, and of being Sir Thomas hereafter. (47–48)

Like the narrator of the opening paragraph, Mary accepts the baronetcy as a means of social and economic advancement, ignoring the ethical imperatives Jane Austen now attaches to that rank.

Mary's insensitivity to the subtler values of rank clearly points to a sense of society in which the social scale exists only as a ladder to be climbed. But the danger to Mansfield Park is not only from the ambitious middle classes below. Tom Bertram, with neither profession nor scruples, is an embodiment of the conventional English vision of the idle, sybaritic aristocrat. His friends, moreover, include Mr. Yates, (later Julia Bertram's husband) who enters the book with this description: "The Honourable John Yates, this new friend, had not much to recommend him beyond habits of fashion and expense, and being the younger son of a lord with a tolerable independence; and Sir Thomas would probably have thought his introduction at Mansfield by no means desirable" (121). It is Yates who, fresh from "Ecclesford, the seat of the Right Hon. Lord Ravenshaw," brings to Mansfield

Park the idea of the theatricals, and whose reaction to the death of Ravenshaw's dowager grandmother consists only of regret that it interrupted similar theatricals at Ecclesford (121–122). Sir Thomas' instinctive dislike and mistrust of the nobility is Jane Austen's own, and together they damn the fashionable world in which Tom meets and learns to ape his noble friends, the world in which Yateses and Ravenshaws and Bertrams and Crawfords and (if they but have some money) Prices meet as equals, the socially chaotic world symbolized in this novel by London.

Thus the baronetcy emerges from this novel as the last bastion of English country tradition, surrounded and challenged by a grasping lower bourgeoisie and by an aristocracy which no longer participates (if ever it did) in the country traditions. Not only must the baronet maintain a way of life in which rank counts for something more than mere wealth, but he must maintain this way of life with little sympathetic support from any other social class. In light of these difficulties, it is not surprising that those committed to act as agents for the baronetcy are led astray. Edmund loses sight of his responsibilities when he begins to make excuses for Mary Crawford. Sir Thomas, despite his mistrust of the nobility, fails in the opposite direction from Edmund by providing his children with an easygoing, quasi-aristocratic upbringing and in effect exempting them from his own code of personal achievement—ruining them in the process. Only Fanny—the poor relation, the outsider—manages, despite the affecting generosities of Henry Crawford, to keep faith with the spirit of Mansfield Park. But this does not mean, as Margaret Kennedy for example would have it, that Jane Austen is showing the lower-born to be morally superior to the baronet. Miss Kennedy says of Fanny that "where Mansfield standards clash with her own she will have none of them";[34] it seems to me that, on the contrary, Fanny's standards *are* the Mansfield standards, so well learned through suffering and self-denial as never to be forgotten. When Sir Thomas urges Fanny to marry Henry Crawford, it is Sir Thomas who falls short of Mansfield Park and Fanny who lives up to it by refusing. The faith persists though priests may fail.[35]

THREE CRUXES: MISS CRAWFORD, THE THEATRICALS, AND THE CHURCH

Inseparable from Jane Austen's reassessment of tradition in *Mansfield Park* is her justification not of compromise but of orthodoxy, not

of common sense but of intuition and faith. *Pride and Prejudice,* with
its ineluctable movement toward synthesis and balance, has justly
been situated "in the eighteenth-century mode." In *Mansfield Park,* by
contrast, the movement of dialectic is stilled by the urgency of certain
moral absolutes, and the end of the novel is in its own beginning;
motivated by the same impulses which brought about the anti-
capitalist, anti-modernist aspects of Romanticism, and later the Oxford and Young England movements, *Mansfield Park* is in one of those
modes we think of as "nineteenth-century" or even "modern." The
relevance of Scott to the reactionary spirit in nineteenth-century
England hardly needs mention; what I now want to show is that, in
its deceptively modest way, *Mansfield Park* stands for a similar reaction.

The Romantic qualities of the novel are perhaps most immediately
suggested by this assessment of Mary Crawford: "She had none of
Fanny's delicacy of taste, of mind, of feeling; she saw nature, inani-
mate nature, with little observation; her attention was all for men
and women, her talents for the light and lively" (81). The sentence
could easily serve as a textbook specimen of the Romantic response
to the preceding century of literature: both in its substance and in
the evaluations implicit in its rhetoric it merits a place in that series
of Romantic documents of which Wordsworth's *Preface* is merely the
best known. My own emphasis, however, is not on trends of taste but
on Jane Austen's handling of rank, and Mary Crawford's inadequacies
are defined no less by her notions of society than by her insensitivity
to "nature."

Comparisons between Mary Crawford and Elizabeth Bennet are
practically inevitable. Like Elizabeth, Mary depends almost completely upon her vivacious intelligence, basing her judgments of men
and women upon acute observation of individual faults and virtues.
But one important difference between the two is perhaps best suggested by Erich Auerbach's description of the great *salon Rambouillet*
of the later seventeenth century. Auerbach says that

what held this *salon* together was not its culture—that would be too modern
and one-sided a view—but the much discussed and much defined notion of
honnêteté. This was not a class ideal, for essentially it was not contingent
on birth or on the manner of living of any particular caste. Such phrases as
un honnête homme aux Indes or *les honnêtes gens de l'antiquité* show that
the word referred to a purely personal ideal. In the course of the century,

it came to be applied to members of a larger and larger section of society. Indeed, the concept of *honnêteté* had nothing to do with class or economic position. Anyone could become an *honnête personne* who was willing and able to cultivate his inner and outer person in accordance with the spirit of the times. The product was a man cleansed of all particular qualities, no longer a member of a class, a profession, a religion, but precisely an *honnête homme*.

Up to this point in Auerbach's description, both Elizabeth Bennet and Mary Crawford seem to subscribe to the *salon* standards. What sets them apart is the ability to go beyond these standards. For Auerbach goes on to point out that the *salon* ethic also "implied a recognition and observance of distances; an *honnête homme* was expected to know himself, *se connaître,* and this meant knowing his position in society . . . ."[36] Implicit in this assertion is the sense of a moral significance in the social structure itself: Elizabeth can eventually arrive at a "recognition and observance of distances" precisely because she has come to realize that one's "position in society" is meaningful in other than purely personal terms. But Mary is trapped by her habits and unable to accommodate the traditional values. When she wrote *Mansfield Park,* Jane Austen was of a mind to see worldly acuteness not as a transitional stage of personal development but as a prison from which even the most gifted are unable to escape.

Those absolutes in light of which the insufficiencies of Mary Crawford must be understood thus depend as much upon a sense of society as upon standards of individual behavior; and unless we bear this in mind we cannot expect to understand the implications of the difficult and puzzling episode of the theatricals.

Many reasons can be adduced to justify the horror with which Fanny and Edmund react to the production of a play at Mansfield. Edmund himself enunciates two: upsetting the physical order and "decorum" of the great house, the production clearly represents the rejection of the authority of the absent Sir Thomas (127); it shows, moreover, a lack of concern both for Sir Thomas in his dangerous voyage from the West Indies and for the betrothed Maria, "whose situation is a very delicate one, considering every thing, extremely delicate" (125). Unexpressed by Edmund, and doubtless too subtle and too fundamental to be expressed, is what Trilling describes as "a traditional, almost primitive, feeling about dramatic impersonation . . . . It is the fear that the impersonation of a bad or inferior character will have a harmful effect upon the impersonator, that, indeed, the impersonation of any other self will diminish the integrity of the real self."[37]

None of these reasons touches upon the particular nature of the play selected for representation, Kotzebue's *Lovers' Vows*, in the English version of Mrs. Inchbald. (Chapman reprints it as an appendix to *Mansfield Park*, 474–538.) It is evident that Jane Austen expected the reader to be familiar enough with *Lovers' Vows* to comprehend her characters' reactions to it. The plot is this: Agatha, a sick and destitute woman, is evicted by a heartless innkeeper and forced to beg in the streets. A young soldier, Frederick, takes pity on her, and, in the course of his ministrations, discovers that he is her natural son. She tells him her sad story: Frederick's father, the great Baron Wildenhaim, was her seducer, but threw her over in order to marry a woman of his own station. Now the penniless Frederick and Agatha accept the hospitality of poor-but-honest cottagers, but their future looks grim. At the same time, Baron Wildenhaim, now a widower, is arranging for the marriage of his daughter, Amelia. Courted by the foppish Count Cassel, Amelia prefers her clergyman-tutor, Anhalt. The remainder of the plot holds neither interest nor surprises; by the end Amelia has her Anhalt and Baron Wildenhaim clears his conscience by a public marriage to the woman he ruined long ago.

One objection to *Lovers' Vows* has to do with the opportunities it provides for daring behavior on the part of the actors: as one commentator puts it, "the would-be actors are not seriously interested in the play as an artistic production, but as an opportunity for showing off and bringing themselves into various piquant and intimate relationships under the pretense of acting."[38] This is particularly true of Maria and Henry, who, playing Agatha and Frederick, are required to cling to each other in several scenes. Moreover, Amelia's forwardness with Anhalt offers Mary Crawford an excuse for toying with Edmund (who is at last persuaded to read Anhalt's lines) and makes light of their budding courtship. But even these instances do not fully explain Edmund's and Fanny's reaction to *Lovers' Vows*. The use of the Kotzebue-Inchbald drama in *Mansfield Park* is so rich and complex that one is reminded of another work of literature centering upon another wretched little play.

The play in *Hamlet*, says Francis Fergusson, "reveals the malady of the regime in all its ambiguity, mystery, and spreading ramifications."[39] Similarly, *Lovers' Vows* reveals the general and growing licentiousness of the group at Mansfield. The world of *Lovers' Vows* is a world in which accepted values are replaced by what Jane Austen sees as the fundamental anomie of those insensitive to the traditional restraints. The whole play is built around a seduction. In addition, seduction is a frequent topic of conversation, and, as Count Cassel suggests to the sanctimonious baron, can even be understood as the characteristic pursuit of a true gentleman. Amelia, for her part, sins in another but similar way: showing forth all the worst of Mary Crawford (who naturally plays her), she is outrageously forward in her courtship of Anhalt. Moreover, though Jane Austen (like Shakespeare) eschews any attempt at consistent identification of characters inside and outside the play-within-the-play, *Lovers' Vows* like Hamlet's "Murder of Gonzago" reflects specific situations and actions of the major characters of the work in which it appears, not only past and present actions but those yet to come. Agatha's early situation is embarrassingly like Fanny's: the daughter of "poor but reputable farmers," young Agatha was invited by the elder Lady Wildenhaim to live in the castle. The noblewoman promised to "provide for Agatha through life," and "took pleasure to instruct her in all kinds of female literature and accomplishments . . ." (487). Though it must be distasteful to Fanny and Edmund to have Fanny tacitly likened to a woman ruined by the son of her benefactors, it is even worse to see Maria's present situation reflected in Amelia's. Like Maria, Amelia is courted by a man of wealth and position, but a man everyone can identify as a fool. Yet unlike Maria, Amelia has sufficient sense to refuse the man about whom she can say "I love to laugh at him myself" (495). Thus the parallel is not only potentially humiliating to Rushworth: it also makes public the cruelty and immorality of Maria's consent to marry him. Similarly, Amelia's refusal looks forward to Fanny's own refusal to marry Henry Crawford solely for advantage, and the Baron's advice to Amelia on the subject foreshadows Sir Thomas' speeches to Fanny. Finally, Count Cassel, with his citified manners (496) and his cavalier attitude toward sexual matters, seems to reflect Henry Crawford and to prepare us for Henry's subsequent seduction of Maria.

But the danger of *Lovers' Vows* cannot adequately be defined by any particular set of correspondences: in a much larger sense, the whole play challenges the traditional social scheme. Eighteenth-century German domestic drama (like the eighteenth-century novel) tended to cater to a middle class defiant of the old order,[40] and the story of Agatha teaches the same lesson as the story of Pamela Andrews. Unlike Pamela, Agatha makes the great mistake of succumbing to the Baron's advances; a life of misery is hardly too much punishment for her stupidity in squandering her principal resources. Once her long and terrible penance is done, however, Agatha succeeds in closing up the apparently meaningless gap which separates farmer's daughter (turned beggar) from Baron Wildenhaim. And the tone of the play is no less subversive than its argument: Kotzebue and his translator consistently communicate a sense of smug contempt for the well-born. Not only morally defective (first in his licentiousness, then in his wholly unjustified self-righteousness), the Baron is made to seem more than a little fatuous. Even the leading comic character of the play, a butler who insists upon expressing himself in doggerel, challenges the manorial order by defying the Baron's commands and reducing him to a series of spluttering, unheeded directions (517–518).

Ultimately, however, the function of *Lovers' Vows* differs from that of Hamlet's playlet, for neither its specific situations nor its general atmosphere of immorality ever produces much effect on those characters who need most to be shown their own sins. So morally insensitive are most of the young people at Mansfield Park that they accept the play either blindly or (as is doubtless true of both Crawfords) with positive delight in its improprieties; they are, indeed, not the audience but the actors. Only Fanny and (for a time) Edmund sense the ruin of Mansfield in *Lovers' Vows*.

There is still greater scope to the meaning of social tradition at Mansfield Park than is suggested by the episode of the theatricals. Once again, Mary Crawford provides a useful point of departure. Mary's single-minded "attention . . . for men and women" cuts her off from another important theme in the novel and another important aspect of the Mansfield complex: I mean the whole question of religion. This is immediately apparent in her discussions with Edmund of his forthcoming ordination. Utterly insensitive to otherworldly considerations, Mary sees the clergy not as a calling but as a profession. While Edmund dwells upon the magnitude of the clerical office, Mary insists only upon the frumpiness and hypocrisy of the officeholders. Since they are arguing on different levels and from very different premises, Mary and Edmund are doomed never to reach an agreement. Moreover, seeing only the worldly attributes of religion and wholly unsusceptible to the claims of faith, Mary even adopts an anti-clerical view of religion as an oppressive social force, though of course she couches her objections in terms appropriate to the experience of an English gentlewoman—for example, in terms of servants finding themselves forced to attend chapel against their own inclinations.

Now, the religion of Mansfield Park—the religion that Mary Crawford in effect categorically denies—has often been associated with the rising Methodism of Jane Austen's time; like so many of the other errors of Jane Austen criticism, this one stems primarily from a passage in a letter. At the time of composition of *Mansfield Park,* she wrote to her niece Fanny Knight that "I am by no means convinced that we ought not all to be Evangelicals, & am at least persuaded that they who are so from Reason and Feeling must be happiest & safest."[41] What Jane Austen in fact intended her niece to understand by this is not my concern (the quotation appears not in a general statement on religion but in connection with a young man of supposedly Evangelical inclinations then courting Fanny); what is important is that the religion in *Mansfield Park* looks very different from Wesleyan. In its pervasive sobriety, in its insistence upon the responsibilities of the clergyman, *Mansfield Park* does challenge the conventional notion of the eighteenth-century hunting-shooting Church of England parson. But, as Margaret Kennedy points out, one of the major reasons why so many second sons of gentlemen entered the Anglican clergy in Jane Austen's time was precisely the desire to counteract, from within the Church, this unfortunate stereotype, and thus to bolster the Established Church against the dangers of Wesleyan non-conformity.[42] In all his speeches on religion, Edmund underscores the importance of maintaining and even reviving within the Established Church the old, neglected customs of Church observance.

In short, the religious values of Mansfield, firmly rooted in tradition and history, are not to be divorced from the social values. Fanny idealizes the clergyman not as a preacher among independent workingmen but as "a chaplain" attached to "a great house." A few lines earlier, she shows disappointment at her first sight of Sotherton chapel:

They entered. Fanny's imagination had prepared her for something grander than a mere, spacious oblong room, fitted up for the purpose of devotion—with nothing more striking or more solemn then the profusion of mahogany, and the crimson velvet cushions appearing over the ledge of the family gallery above. "I am disappointed," said she, in a low voice, to Edmund. "This is not my idea of a chapel. There is nothing awful here, nothing melancholy, nothing grand. Here are no aisles, no arches, no in-scriptions, no banners. No banners, cousin, to be 'blown by the night wind of Heaven.' No signs that a 'Scottish monarch sleeps below.'" (85–86)

No passage in *Mansfield Park* is more difficult to interpret: to what extent is Fanny herself—let alone the novelist—aware of the dubious-ness of a religious experience that gains from the proximity of royal corpses? Is the paragraph intended ironically or does it merely reflect the inadequacy of Fanny's (or Jane Austen's) rhetoric? The latter, in light of the values asserted by the novel as a whole, and more particu-larly in the context of the general metaphoric significance of the visit to Sotherton, seems a more likely answer; it appears that Jane Austen is really allowing Fanny to indulge her Gothicizing instincts, even to borrow a line from Walter Scott, to express herself on the subject of what a church should be. For Fanny's notion of religion, though a vulgarization of Edmund's, has the virtue of being no less reactionary.

MANSFIELD PARK: CONCEPTION AND FULFILLMENT

To admire *Mansfield Park* is not to deny the irreconcilable gap that separates the sobriety of its subject from the brilliance of Jane Aus-ten's style at its most characteristic. There is truth to the claim that that description of Mary Crawford upon which I have leaned so heavily in this discussion is, paradoxically, a valid (if partial) descrip-tion of Jane Austen herself; the beliefs and sympathies that forced Jane Austen to imagine a Mary Crawford so as to be able to condemn her also forced her to place impossible restrictions upon her own greatest gifts.

But the stylistic discomforts of *Mansfield Park* are only symptom-atic; the real difficulty lies in the very conception of the book—a conception which, I submit, depends to a considerable extent upon the reactionary vision of English society by means of which Jane Austen sought to define and evaluate the conflicts of the novel. The effective realization of such a vision was perhaps impeded by personal limitations, above all by Jane Austen's anti-aristocratic prejudices and concomitant faith in the country gentry. But even more serious were the obstacles implicit in the only form that Jane Austen could possibly adopt: one wonders if it is possible, in theory or in practice, to deny, with consistent logic and vigor, the familiar modern social and ethical premises in the uniquely modern genre of the novel. Moreover, having accepted, by necessity, the genre, Jane Austen also accepted its most common and most anarchic narrative convention: I mean hypergamy. Outrageous as it may seem, Fanny Price is in her way a faithful daughter to Pamela herself, another nobody who gets her Mr. B.

"This novel," as one acute critic has stated, "is not a failure: it is an unachieved masterpiece."[43] This does not simply mean that Jane Austen began with a masterful conception and then went on to bungle it here and there: the "unachieved" quality is no less evident in the general conception than in details of execution. The ultimate intellectual failure of *Mansfield Park* is, I suppose, characteristic of all those reactionary theories which seek to idealize the past yet are able to do so only in the context of the present. It is characteristic, too, of that Romantic mind which, by crying out for tradition and by choosing to deny the chaotic modern world, is merely accepting one of the innumerable choices offered by that world, assuming a posture no less personal or eccentric than that of the most radical anti-traditionalist. No novelist has ever confronted a more difficult task than Jane Austen in *Mansfield Park;* the measure of her skill is the extraordinary extent to which she managed to accomplish it.

RETROSPECT AND REVALUATION

The differences between *Emma* and *Persuasion* are as fundamental as they are immediately evident. The contrast is in part tonal, for if *Emma* is admirable throughout for its ironic brilliance, *Persuasion* seduces by its dim glow; indeed, much of the ironic rhetoric that does find its way into *Persuasion* strikes us as bitter, gratuitous, even uncontrolled. And this suggests another major difference between the books—the difference in quality of craftsmanship. While in *Emma* Jane Austen lifts her old subject matter to a new plane of interest, in *Persuasion* she seems dissatisfied with the familiar *données,* and her impatience is manifest in some unprecedentedly humdrum writing.[44] Compare, for example, Miss Bates of *Emma* with Mrs. Smith of *Persuasion.* The former is a magnificent creation in her own right, who, as if incidentally, provides us with information necessary for our understanding of the plot; the latter is a lifeless functionary who does little more than fill us in on some important data. Virginia Woolf's familiar summary is indisputable as far as it goes:

> There is a peculiar beauty and a peculiar dullness in *Persuasion*. The dull-ness is that which so often marks the transition stage between two different periods. The writer is a little bored. She has grown too familiar with the ways of her world; she no longer notes them freshly. There is an asperity in her comedy which suggests that she has almost ceased to be amused by the vanities of a Sir Walter or the snobbery of a Miss Elliot. The satire is harsh, and the comedy crude. She is no longer so freshly aware of the amusements of daily life. Her mind is not altogether on her object.[45]

Yet despite the great individual interest of each novel, despite the many differences between the two, *Emma* and *Persuasion* are, like *Pride and Prejudice* and *Mansfield Park*, best considered together, because each in its way embodies a resolution of the conflicts that animate Jane Austen's earlier work. Virginia Woolf is of course cor-rect to stress the transitional nature of *Persuasion*, but "dullness" and impatience need not be the only hallmarks of transition, and if one looks at *Emma* in light of Jane Austen's earlier productions one may feel that it too marks a significant new stage in the novelist's develop-ment: in its very perfection it indicates Jane Austen's recently won detachment from her traditional subject matter. Not only in *Sense and Sensibility*, but, as we have seen, in *Mansfield Park*, even in *Pride and Prejudice*, the writer's own sympathies for one side or the other in the struggle she dramatizes lead to deficiencies in composition, above all to failures in balance and emphasis. But in *Emma* there is no longer any sense of strain. Not since the Catherine Morland of many years before has Jane Austen created a heroine whose errors are so patently indefensible. From the beginning, the reader—like the novelist—is above and beyond the field of conflict. The psychological and moral struggle in *Emma* is Emma's alone; the rest of us are free to focus our attention upon the elegance of the methods by which the novelist goes about satisfying our expectations. Like the impa-tience of *Persuasion*, the detachment of *Emma* announces the final period of Jane Austen's career.

Earlier I have said something of Jane Austen's growth, from the ironic detachment of *Northanger Abbey* to the larger questions and deeper commitments of *Sense and Sensibility*; and then from the compromise of *Pride and Prejudice* to the uneasy glorification of tradition and rigidity in *Mansfield Park. Emma* and *Persuasion* together constitute another stage in Jane Austen's art; they are, for all their differences, at least as closely bound to each other as either of the preceding pairs. And their underlying kinship is perhaps most clearly demonstrated by attention to the novelist's changing vision of her England and to the many consequent changes in the metaphoric manifestations of social rank.

HIGHBURY AND ITS LIBERTIES

Most critics, in dealing with *Emma,* concentrate upon its heroine. The novelist seems to demand this approach of her readers, first by proclaiming the subject of the book in its title, and then by going on to show us much of the action through Emma's eyes. Moreover, Emma is a creation of unique interest among Jane Austen's heroines: "handsome, clever, and rich," she alone enters the scene in such full possession of "the best blessings of existence" that she is in effect obliged to create her own major difficulties. This she does—and most effectively—through the agency of her own imagination. It has often been observed that, unlike Elizabeth Bennet, Emma does not merely jump to conclusions on the basis of insufficient evidence: she is genuinely, profoundly perverse. Blinded by romantic imaginings, she chooses to believe that Harriet Smith—"the natural daughter of somebody" (22)—is better suited to a vicar like Mr. Elton, even to such a dashing gentleman as Frank Churchill, than to a mere "farmer" like Robert Martin; given over to foolish and ingenious suppositions concerning Jane Fairfax, she ignores the most obvious clues to Jane's real relation to Frank; above all, she refuses to understand her own feelings toward Mr. Knightley. Now, even this sketchy history of Emma's misjudgments should suggest that Jane Austen is motivated in *Emma* as nowhere else by a kind of pure delight in the difficulties of her craft, attempting to make us accept, not only as credible but as attractive, a heroine who denies her own considerable intelligence by setting out to mold other people's lives according to patterns drawn from her own mistaken observations.

Moreover, while most novelists in dealing with an Emma Woodhouse—with a protagonist addicted to audacious and unreasonable imaginings—might be expected to situate her in an unfamiliar and confusing milieu, Jane Austen complicates her own task by making

of Emma her only heroine who never leaves home;[46] Emma, we are
asked to believe, is capable of deceiving herself repeatedly about the
facts of life in the village that has always been her home. In light of
the job that Jane Austen has undertaken, and in light of the success
with which she has completed it, it is in no sense surprising that so
many commentators have devoted their attentions to the characterization of Emma Woodhouse.

There is, however, another way to confront *Emma,* and here I intend to shift the usual emphasis and concentrate upon the reverse
side of Jane Austen's achievement: I intend to look primarily not at
Emma but at Emma's principal antagonist. As several recent studies
(all to be quoted in this discussion) have demonstrated, that antagonist is not any single character in the novel, not even Emma's principal teacher and critic, Mr. Knightley. The antagonist is the real world
that surrounds Emma; it is the whole complex of truths and moral
values against which Emma sets herself; it is the village of Highbury
itself. And the novelist is aware that, if we are to understand Emma's
mistakes, we must see not only Emma herself and Emma's distorted
picture of Highbury but Highbury itself as a real place and as a vital
force. So it is that, aside from the characterization of Emma, the
characterization of Highbury is the most detailed and extensive in
the novel.

The physical reality of the town is, first of all, elaborately established. Highbury is given a more precise geographical location than
any of Jane Austen's other imaginary places.[47] We are told that it is
sixteen miles from London, nine miles from Richmond, and seven
from Box Hill. Chapman warns us that no real English town exists at
precisely such a location and that no attempt to identify Highbury
with a real place can be successful, but Jane Austen's carefully
planted geographical details are more than a tease for *aficionados:*
they intensify the reality of Highbury by making us feel that we could
place it instantly on a map of Surrey. Similarly, we are aware to an
uncommon extent of what Highbury looks like. Again, Chapman
warns us that we lack the evidence to chart Highbury "with certainty," but he acknowledges that the novelist herself is responsible
for any attempt to do so when he points out that "The topography of
Highbury is given in such detail that many attempts have been made
to construct a map" (521). In short, Jane Austen has situated and
described Highbury in enough detail that it can enjoy its own identity,

yet left it typical enough to allow the reader to imagine such details as the author herself omits.

But the real identity of the town ultimately depends more upon its people than upon its physical characteristics, and by the end of the novel we feel that we have been surrounded by a swarm of real townspeople. Not only Emma and Mr. Woodhouse, Mr. Knightley and the Westons, the Eltons and the Bateses—all of these, of course, are directly connected with all or most of the major events of the book —but also Mrs. Goddard and the girls at her school and the Coles and the Perrys and Mrs. Ford and a score more with whom even Chapman enjoys but a nodding acquaintance (519–524). They function in the novel as the vital accessories of village life, some no more than vague presences whom the novelist evokes primarily to remind us that Highbury is more than an inert backdrop for Emma's misadventures. When, for example, Frank Churchill, in his desperation to find acceptable social pretexts for being with Jane Fairfax, mobilizes the town's meager social forces, the names of the major figures in the novel mix with names which seldom if ever reappear: enumerating the party at his proposed ball, Frank tells Emma that

"You and Miss Smith, and Miss Fairfax, will be three, and the two Miss Coxes five. . . . And there will be the two Gilberts, young Cox, my father, and myself, besides Mr. Knightley. Yes, that will be quite enough for pleasure. You and Miss Smith, and Miss Fairfax, will be three, and the two Miss Coxes five; and for five couples there will be plenty of room." (248)

At such moments as these, we are in a sense urged to imagine the *dramatis personae* of this novel in situations that our economical novelist has chosen to suppress in favor of other situations which comment upon and clarify the central problems of her tale. We are reminded that our "populous village" is exactly that, full of "Gilberts" and "Miss Coxes" who are, if irrelevant to the major action, no less part of Highbury than the leading characters.

Frank Churchill's frantic party-making is a rare phenomenon in Highbury; what draws the town together in its quieter moments is everyone's rich knowledge of everyone else. This knowledge may take the form of a common mythology: "Mr. Frank Churchill," we are told long before he appears on the scene, "was one of the boasts of Highbury, and a lively curiosity to see him prevailed, though the compliment was so little returned that he had never been there in his life"

(17). Generally, however, knowledge is based more on acquaintance
than on speculation, and the latest facts and rumors about familiar
Highbury folk are sped throughout the village. When Harriet Smith
is attacked by gypsies and rescued by the now-present Frank
Churchill,

> Emma's first resolution was to keep her father from the knowledge of
> what had passed,—aware of the anxiety and alarm it would occasion: but
> she soon felt that concealment must be impossible. Within half an hour it
> was known all over Highbury. It was the very event to engage those who
> talk most, the young and the low; and all the youth and servants in the
> place were soon in the happiness of frightful news. (335–336)

And with an event of the most colossal importance—the engagement
of Highbury's leading citizens, Mr. Knightley and Miss Woodhouse—
the news travels with the speed of sound itself:

> The news was universally a surprize wherever it spread; and Mr. Weston
> had his five minutes share of it; but five minutes were enough to familiarize
> the idea to his quickness of mind.—He saw the advantages of the match,
> and rejoiced in them with all the constancy of his wife; but the wonder of
> it was very soon nothing; and by the end of an hour he was not far from
> believing that he had always foreseen it.
> "It is to be a secret, I conclude," said he. "These matters are always a
> secret, till it is found out that every body knows them. Only let me be
> told when I may speak out.—I wonder whether Jane has any suspicion."
> He went to Highbury the next morning, and satisfied himself on that
> point. He told her the news. Was not she like a daughter, his eldest daugh-
> ter?—he must tell her; and Miss Bates being present, it passed, of course,
> to Mrs. Cole, Mrs. Perry, and Mrs. Elton, immediately afterwards. It was
> no more than the principals were prepared for; they had calculated from
> the time of its being known at Randall's, how soon it would be over High-
> bury; and they were thinking of themselves, as the evening wonder in many
> a family circle, with great sagacity. (468)

Needless to say, critical commentary follows hard upon the text itself:

> In general, it was a very well approved match. Some might think him,
> and others think her, the most in luck. One set might recommend their all
> removing to Donwell, and leaving Hartfield for the John Knightleys; and
> another might predict disagreements among their servants; but yet, upon
> the whole, there was no serious objection raised, except in one habitation,
> the vicarage.—There, the surprise was not softened by any satisfaction. Mr.
> Elton cared little about it, compared with his wife . . . .—But Mrs. Elton
> was very much discomposed indeed. (468–469)

Such is Highbury, and in another state of mind Jane Austen might have made us look upon *Emma* as an antecedent not of *Cranford* but of *Madame Bovary* and *Main Street*. Yet it is imperative to see that, for all the gossip, Highbury is not to be taken for a malevolent place. Through the agency of laughter, Jane Austen makes certain that even the constant chatter does not turn ominous. Here, as so often in Jane Austen's novels, the most loquacious characters are fundamentally comic, and those gossips we should otherwise despise are provided with what might be termed comic immunity. Even Mrs. Elton, whose endless flow of talk depends upon snobbishness and real malice, is so absurd in her pretensions, so ineffectual in her desperate attempts to seem impressive, that she amuses more than she angers. Utterly without Mrs. Elton's defects, and blameless in their own garrulous simple-mindedness, are Mr. Woodhouse and Miss Bates. Indeed, by calling Miss Bates a mere gossip one fails completely to suggest the extraordinary range of her knowledge at the same time that one denies her irresistible comic benevolence. Her mind (in general wholly indistinguishable from her voice) is the great treasury of Highbury lore, a comic, incoherent, but complete index to Highbury history. Though focused only upon a single village, her semi-choate consciousness is a modest premonition of the mind that will absorb the history of a race in *Finnegans Wake*. Here is that mind at work:

"Ah, here's Miss Woodhouse.—Dear Miss Woodhouse, how do you do?—Very well I thank you, quite well. This is meeting quite in fairy-land!—Such a transformation!—Must not compliment, I know—(eyeing Emma most complacently)—that would be rude—but upon my word, Miss Woodhouse, you do look—how do you like Jane's hair?—You are a judge.—She did it all herself. Quite wonderful how she does her hair!—No hairdresser from London I think could.—Ah! Dr. Hughes I declare—and Mrs. Hughes. Must go and speak to Dr. and Mrs. Hughes for a moment.—How do you do? How do you do?—Very well, I thank you. This is delightful, is not it? Where's dear Mr. Richard?—Oh! there he is. Don't disturb him. Much better employed talking to the young ladies. How do you do, Mr. Richard? —I saw you the other day as you rode through the town—Mrs. Otway, I protest!—and good Mr. Otway, and Miss Otway, and Miss Caroline.—Such a host of friends!—and Mr. George and Mr. Arthur!—How do you do? How do you all do?—Quite well, I am much obliged to you. Never better.— Don't I hear another carriage?—Who can this be?—very likely the worthy Coles.—Upon my word, this is charming to be standing about among such friends!" (323)

For Miss Bates, living in the village and living off the village, "Dr. Hughes" and "dear Mr. Richard" and a whole flock of "Otways" assume full-bodied reality, yet her universal good will always prevents us from fearing that her strange knowledge will ever be put to destructive ends.

That the bristling, inescapable actuality of Highbury does not induce loathing in the reader is part of Jane Austen's larger design in her characterization of the town; as I hope to show later, Highbury is to be understood not merely as embodying an absence of evil but as embodying an ideal of good. But before approaching the question of what Highbury means I must continue to explore the question of what Highbury is. For the re-creation of the village and its inhabitants is only a small (if necessary) part of Highbury's function in the novel, of about the same expressive value as the physical description of any single character. In order to understand the fundamental role of Highbury in *Emma*, we must go on to consider the social makeup of the town.

Highbury represents Jane Austen's most concentrated use of what I have called her microcosmic approach to English society: within the confines of this one town Jane Austen has assembled a catalogue of the English middle classes. There are no noblemen in *Emma*; though the man who comes closest is named "Knightley," his nobility is, strictly speaking, personal rather than social. Nor are there souls below the middle rank, save as the natural accoutrements of village life: servants, of course, and the indigent farm laborers whom Emma visits as part of her duties, none of them individually characterized or individually significant. But within the middle classes nearly every imaginable possibility is dramatized, from long-established gentry (Knightleys and Woodhouses) to the yeomanry (Robert Martin), from gentleman lawyer (John Knightley) to the counterpart of Mrs. Bennet's lawyer brother Phillips (William Coxe), from the vulgar *nouveaux riches* of Bristol trade (Mrs. Elton) to the shabby genteel (the Bateses) and the penniless young gentlewomen-governesses (Mrs. Weston and Jane Fairfax)—in sum, from a young woman of impressive rank and fortune to "the natural daughter of somebody" who is being given a respectable education.[48] The list could, of course, be extended; it is enough to say that each of the Highbury presences has his place in it.

Earlier in this study I apologized for my use of the term "middle classes," admitting that it served primarily to exclude and only very roughly and deceptively to define. Yet the term, I argued, was needed to describe the unity of the social milieu of Jane Austen's novels, one *sine qua non* of our novelist's mature work. I raise these points once again because none of Jane Austen's novels illustrates both the shortcomings and the usefulness of the term "middle classes" as neatly as does *Emma*. The imprecision of the term I have tacitly demonstrated in the preceding paragraph, by showing how much ground it covers; the necessity of the term is manifest in the social freedom which the Highbury denizens enjoy, a freedom that results in a Miss Woodhouse, a Mrs. Elton, and a Miss Bates repeatedly attending the same parties, and in Mr. Knightley stating that Robert Martin "knows that I have a thorough regard for him and all his family, and, I believe, considers me as one of his best friends" (59). Not that Highbury is a seat of social anarchy: one is expected to recognize one's place at the same time that one recognizes one's liberties, and the next part of my discussion will show the bitter results of errors in the appreciation of rank. Moreover, social fluidity does not extend to marriages, as Mr. Elton's foolhardy and unthinkable proposal to Emma makes clear. Nonetheless, one of the most important Highbury traits is the *bonhomie* that binds all its middle ranks together.

By the end, of course, the spirit of Highbury carries all before it, and the "small band of true friends" spoken of in the last paragraph of the novel as the witnesses of Emma's marriage undoubtedly represents a good cross-section of the Highbury middle classes. This triumph is all the more impressive in that Highbury's most influential foe is its own great and revered Miss Woodhouse. For most of the book, the easy social intercourse of Highbury fills Emma with disgust, as we see for example when Jane Austen tells us that a visit to the Bateses' humble rooms calls forth in Emma "all the horror of being in danger of falling in with the second rate and third rate of Highbury, who were calling on them for ever . . ." (155). This is much more than a case of simple condescension. It is partly to be explained by Emma's notorious verdict upon Robert Martin:

"A young farmer . . . is the very last sort of person to raise my curiosity. The yeomanry are precisely the order of people with whom I feel I can have nothing to do. A degree or two lower, and a creditable appearance might interest me; I might hope to be useful to their families in some way or other. But a farmer can need none of my help, and is therefore in one sense as much above my notice as in every other he is below it." (29)

There is nothing for Emma to do for—that is, to make of—the "second rate and third rate of Highbury." They lack potential because—and this is the quintessence of Emma's reaction to them—they lack style. When confronted with a distinctly "third-rate" Harriet Smith, Emma feels no condescension, for she can imagine in Harriet's ancestry a hint of glamour and in Harriet's charming innocence the materials for a heroine. But until she comes to see friendship and a meaningful sense of community where she has been wont to see homeliness and frumpiness, Emma stands in open defiance of Highbury.

Highbury, then, is more than a neutral background for Emma's story. It is the vital corrective to all her imaginings. Emma Woodhouse is, as one critic has aptly observed, a "magnificent exception" to the prevalent nineteenth-century literary rule that "no one can learn much of anything at home."[49] And this is no reflection upon the breadth of Emma's learning: it is instead the result of Jane Austen's having made that "home" the embodiment of all that Emma has to learn.

HIGHBURY AND JANE AUSTEN'S ENGLAND

If Highbury can teach us a great deal about Emma Woodhouse, this is precisely because Highbury also teaches us a great deal about its creator's vision of the real England of her time: the juxtaposition of Highbury and that which lies outside it provides one of Jane Austen's principal means of defining and illustrating Emma's personal failures.

The plot of *Emma*, even more than that of *Pride and Prejudice*, depends upon the misinterpretation of rank. In Highbury, moreover, such misinterpretations are particularly dangerous. I have already discussed the freedom of social intercourse among the representatives of the many ranks found in Highbury; this very freedom is endangered by the failure of those within Highbury's society to recognize the distinction between social freedom and social anarchy. We have already observed the offensive forwardness of Elton's proposal of marriage to Emma. But it is in fact Emma herself who proves the worst offender in respect to matters of rank. Perhaps this is necessitated by Highbury itself, since, as G. Armour Craig points out, the village in its smallness and its openness "is a place where there can be nothing but rank for the imaginist—or the climber—to be mistaken about."[50] At any rate, there would be no story if the protagonist did not grossly misrepresent Harriet Smith's social qualifications, or if she did not deny the yeomanry its rightful and honorable place in Highbury society. But Emma's misunderstanding of rank is still more extensive. For rank, as Emma repeatedly forgets, entails responsibility. Though we may dote on Miss Bates while we recoil from Mr. Elton, we should be aware that Emma's behavior to both is of a kind. When Emma tells Mr. Elton that she is no more aware than Harriet (whose mind, on questions of rank, she has confused and corrupted) of the "very great inequality which you are so sensible of" between his own rank and Harriet's (132), she is of course wrong in failing to appreciate Elton's respectable situation as vicar of Highbury, and she is also asserting her natural superiority as cruelly and unnecessarily as in the great scene in which she makes fun of Miss Bates.

The most revealing aspect of Emma's errors about rank is implied by Craig's juxtaposition of "imaginists" and "climbers." If we list the climbers—those who, by failing to appreciate rank, are comparable to our "imaginist" heroine—we notice that they are all outsiders. The list includes Mr. Elton, the vicar who dares aspire to the hand of Miss Woodhouse; Mrs. Elton, the vulgar parvenu who suppresses the "Mr." when speaking of and to Mr. Knightley and who takes herself to be the equal of anybody in town; and Harriet Smith, the imaginist's befuddled protegee, who so far surpasses her own tutor that she believes herself ready not only for Mr. Churchill but for Mr. Knightley himself. Opposed to them all is Highbury's own Robert Martin, moving slowly but impeccably up the ladder by devoted attention to the duties of his situation and by quiet demonstration of his own worthiness. Opposed to them also are the Coles, relative newcomers both to Highbury and to respectability who invite the formidable Miss Woodhouse to dinner with all the appropriate deference and humility. Though Highbury occasionally opens its doors to immigrants and transients, they remain identifiable as outsiders until they have learned the accurate and selfless discriminations of rank that Highbury teaches, and which alone make possible its social freedom.

Highbury, then, stands in contrast to—and in danger from—something beyond itself, and misjudgment of rank is only one of the evils imported into Highbury from the outside world. Trilling observes that "It is from the outside that the peculiarly modern traits of insincerity and vulgarity come, in the person of Frank Churchill and Mrs. Elton."[51] The list might well be longer: Harriet, for instance, is a constant reminder of a sexual license that, as far as we know or even

dare suppose, is wholly foreign to her adoptive village. Even leaving
aside poor Harriet and concentrating upon Trilling's two "outside"
characteristics, one can easily extend his point: Jane Fairfax, for all
her goodness and patience (let us not forget that she is almost—not
quite—a Highbury regular), is an accomplice to all the "insincerity"
of Frank's secret engagement; Mr. Elton, somewhat less spectacular
in his vulgarity than his wife, is neither less presumptuous nor less
ambitious. Now, just as Emma allies herself with the outside world
through her errors about rank, so too does she participate in the outside plot against Highbury values by evincing both "insincerity" and
"vulgarity." The first quality is manifest in her whole predilection for
manipulating other people's lives; in this she is exactly like the dread
Mrs. Elton herself.[52] The second is evident not only in the scenes
already mentioned in which she humiliates Mr. Elton and Miss Bates,
but also in the incredibly cheap melodramas she concocts in order to
explain the mysteries that confront her: we see it in her conviction
that Harriet's questionable ancestry must involve glamorous and distinguished personages, a hopelessly absurd assumption that fixes
Emma's whole view of the match Harriet must make;[53] we see it later
in the outrageous theatricality of her assumptions about the inex-
plicable arrival of a piano for Jane Fairfax. Indulging her meretricious
imagination, heedless of the self-respect of those about her, Emma
seems indeed to be advancing the cause of the vulgar outside world.

Thus we have in *Emma* an elaborately wrought parallel between
the heroine's worst behavior and the behavior smuggled into Highbury by its immigrants. By the end of the novel, when Emma has renounced her anti-Highburian ways, this parallel disappears. What
remains, however, is a very real historical conflict that Jane Austen
cannot resolve so easily, the conflict pointed to by the disparities
between Highbury and the world beyond. Craig begins to describe
it when he says that

It is blindness not to see that the historical setting of *Emma* is a small community that is responding to some strange pressures from a strange outside
world. It is hard, indeed, not to use the inevitable "age of transition" in
reflecting on the kind of world this novel presents. Outside Highbury is
a mysteriously powerful institution called "trade" from which rich men like
Mr. Cole retire to a life of anxious respectability. Bath is a remote, fashionable haven for parvenus who reassure each other that tradition can be
manufactured by talk—or if not by talk, then by such items of conspicuous
consumption as the barouche-landau. . . . In Weymouth and Bristol con-

ventional social relations are queerly scrambled, and illicit flirtations have their proper habitation. London, where Emma's married sister lives . . . , is only sixteen miles but a much larger social distance away.⁵⁴

Beyond Highbury, in short, lies the anomie of Jane Austen's England, the realm of too much money and too little personal and social responsibility.

None of the characters in the novel clarifies the contrast between the two worlds of *Emma* as succinctly as Mr. Weston. He, more than anyone else, has one foot in each camp, and we should not fail to observe the extent to which his career (like Wickham's in *Pride and Prejudice*) is paradigmatic, demonstrating both the lures and the perils of the world outside Highbury. Weston is not predestined to the status of the Knightleys and Woodhouses: he is but "a native of Highbury, and born of a respectable family, which for the last two or three generations had been rising into gentility and property." The rate of rising in Highbury proves too slow, however, and Weston in his impatience turns to the outside means: "He had received a good education, but on succeeding early in life to a small independence, had become indisposed for any of the more homely pursuits in which his brothers were engaged; and had satisfied an active cheerful mind and social temper by entering into the militia of his county, then embodied" (15). In Jane Austen's novels, the military frequently provides the means of fast "rising," and in other moods, those of *Persuasion* or of *Pride and Prejudice,* Jane Austen might have shown approval of Weston's initiative. But in accordance with the prevailing values of *Emma,* Weston's combination of personal charm and ambitious restlessness brings him much grief before it brings him any joy.

For Weston not only rises, but also marries, outside Highbury:

Captain Weston was a general favourite; and when the chances of his military life had introduced him to Miss Churchill, of a great Yorkshire family, and Miss Churchill fell in love with him, nobody was surprised except her brother and his wife, who had never seen him, and who were full of pride and importance, which the connection would offend.

Miss Churchill, however, being of age, and with the full command of her fortune—though her fortune bore no proportion of the family-estate—was not to be dissuaded from the marriage, and it took place to the infinite mortification of Mr. and Mrs. Churchill, who threw her off with due decorum. (15)

Jane Austen does not waste words in announcing the failure of the union: "It was an unsuitable connection, and did not produce much happiness." Perhaps, we are led to believe, some marriages of this non-Highbury sort may work, but only when both parties demonstrate extraordinary courage and extraordinary intelligence:

Mrs. Weston ought to have found more in it, for she had a husband whose warm heart and sweet temper made him think every thing due to her in return for the great goodness of being in love with him; but though she had one sort of spirit, she had not the best. She had resolution enough to pursue her own will in spite of her brother, but not enough to refrain from unreasonable regrets at that brother's unreasonable anger, nor from missing the luxuries of her former home. They lived beyond their income, but still it was nothing in comparison of Enscombe; she did not cease to love her husband, but she wanted at once to be the wife of Captain Weston, and Miss Churchill of Enscombe. (15–16)

With richly ironic intonation, Jane Austen describes the marriage as an unfortunate business transaction, underscoring the social and monetary attractions and the more than social and monetary punishments of the world at large:

Captain Weston, who had been considered, especially by the Churchills, as making such an amazing match, was proved to have much the worst of the bargain; for when his wife died after a three years' marriage, he was rather a poorer man than at first, and with a child to maintain. (16)

The child is an "expense" from which "he was soon relieved"; the Churchills adopt young Frank and provide him with due "care" and due "wealth," while Weston, disembarrassed of the principal by-product of his impatient merger, "had only his own comfort to seek and his own situation to improve as he could."

For money, Weston now turns to London. But for happiness, he turns back to Highbury.

A complete change of life became desirable. He quitted the militia and engaged in trade, having brothers already established in a good way in London, which afforded him a favourable opening. It was a concern which brought just employment enough. He had still a small house in Highbury, where most of his leisure days were spent; and between useful occupation and the pleasures of society, the next eighteen or twenty years of his life passed cheerfully away. He had, by that time, realized an easy competence —enough to secure the purchase of a little estate adjoining Highbury, which he had always longed for—enough to marry a woman as portionless even as Miss Taylor, and to live according to the wishes of his own friendly and social disposition. (16)

Randalls, Weston's estate, is not quite in Highbury, and his chosen bride not quite a native; but both are close enough to the real thing, and Weston enters upon "a new period of existence with every probability of greater happiness than in any yet passed through." Though the novelist offers explicit reflections upon only the most directly personal benefits of his new marriage—the second Mrs. Weston proves "how delightful a well-judging and truly amiable woman could be," and provides "the pleasantest proof of its being a great deal better to chose than to be chosen, to excite gratitude than to feel it" (16–17)—there is clearly another moral to Mr. Weston's story: it has to do with the excessive worldliness and excessive ambition that characterize life outside Highbury, and with the perils of leaving a place where nature takes its wholly trustworthy course.

HIGHBURY IN PERSPECTIVE

Since it is, above all else, the tone of *Emma* that makes the novel what it is, and since no critic can duplicate this unique tone, any description of *Emma* must to some degree prove an exercise in falsification; I am aware that, in restating the social situation of *Emma*, I have made the novel sound too much like *Mansfield Park*. While in both novels Jane Austen makes use of a contrast between what she sees as traditional English ways and the wholly antithetical ways of the modern world, the tone of *Emma* betrays a completely different attitude toward her material.

Comparing Emma to some earlier Jane Austen characters who have failed to appreciate the rank of others, we realize that none of these earlier figures errs foolishly: their errors stem at worst from lack of experience with the rank they encounter. An appreciation of the nobility for Elizabeth Bennet, of the lower orders of the middle classes for Darcy, of the baronetcy for Mary Crawford—these are important and difficult lessons, even impossible in the last instance. In *Emma*, the sources of error are inexcusable, the outcome (for the reader at least) painless. Emma's misinterpretations of rank are outside our range of weakness: we might be as hasty as Elizabeth, we may even discover ourselves to be as cynical and corrupt as Mary Crawford, but we are never asked to believe ourselves as perversely self-deceiving as Emma. Like the novelist herself, for whom any serious moral difficulties definable in terms of rank seem wholly a matter of the past, the reader derives detached enjoyment from Emma's errors; the problems which, in the past, evoked Jane Austen's serious commitment (and hence the reader's) appear to have found resolution.

Jane Austen's attitude is even more evident in her treatment of Highbury, as Trilling suggests when he associates Highbury with the "idyll." Highbury, he says, is a place in which "we have been led to believe that man may actually live 'in harmony and peace with himself and the external world,'" a milieu of such limitless benevolence that even "fools" like Miss Bates and Mr. Woodhouse are saintly.[55] The contrast between Highbury and the world beyond is, in Trilling's view, no less the product of actual historical change than of the novelist's imagination: "in *Emma*," he says, "Jane Austen contrives an idyllic world, or the closest approximation of an idyllic world that the genre of the novel will permit, and brings into contrast with it the actualities of the social world, of the modern self."[56] Now, if we accept Trilling's key term and go beyond its specifically Schillerian usage to pursue its fullest meaning, we see that in all its implications the word "idyll" points to Jane Austen's new way of apprehending and expressing her theme in *Emma*. It connotes, first of all, a place of escape. The vantage point of anyone—Jane Austen or the reader—who sees Highbury as idyllic must be that of the harsh modern world against which the idyllic simplicities are set, for those whose lives are defined by the pastoral setting cannot be aware that that setting is idyllic; a person who has never experienced the world beyond Highbury may love his home but he cannot see it as a refuge. The word connotes, too, something temporary: like the heroes of Renaissance pastoral—Spenser's Calidore is an obvious instance—no one who sees Highbury as idyllic can avoid recognizing that he must eventually bow to the demands of life and return to the actualities he has temporarily renounced. And the word connotes finally a literary device: the idyllic scene in literature is not presented as an actual place, but rather is, at least in part, the writer's agency of dramatizing, through contrast, discontentment with that which does really exist. If Highbury is an idyllic place, then Jane Austen is not seriously suggesting that it represents a state of mind that she or her readers can be expected to attain, or ideals that she or we can pursue with any hope of success in the very unidyllic modern world. Unlike Mansfield Park, it is not experienced as a real alternative, and is not presented as such to those who were not born to enjoy it. It is a reminder and a scold, but it is not something really to be had.

Indeed, even as described within the novel, Highbury is in its last stages as an "idyllic" setting. The town is no longer what it was, as Craig points out:

Highbury may be small and serene, but like The Crown, its principal inn, it is just a little seedy. The quality of its neighborhood is declining; there are no longer enough county families even to provide a homogenous guest list for a ball. Emma's father, the first citizen, is a comic valetudinarian who rarely leaves his house and who cannot stand change. Highbury, in short, is no longer an eighteenth century county town nor is it yet a fashionable suburb like Richmond.[57]

Once this "large and populous village almost amounting to a town" (7) belonged to Knightley's estate; officially it still does, but it no longer has the character of a manorial village. Wealthy businessmen retire to it, those "without any alliances but in trade" cut a figure on its streets, and the "natural daughter of somebody" marries into it. As far as we can tell, there has never been anyone like them before, and they can only make a difference. All these are, moreover, recent arrivals: one cannot avoid the suspicion that the tentacles of the modern world are already around Highbury's throat. At the end of *Mansfield Park*, those who do not fit are removed: Maria is banished, Mrs. Norris follows after her, and, in the most desperate and unconvincing moment in the book, Tom Bertram is symbolically destroyed by a fever and then reborn in virtue. But at the end of *Emma*, Mr. and Mrs. Elton remain, and the novelist even insists that their horrid voices ring in our ear to the very last paragraph: Emma's wedding, we are told, "was very much like other weddings, where the parties have no taste for finery or parade; and Mrs. Elton, from the particulars detailed by her husband, thought it all extremely shabby, and very inferior to her own.—'Very little white satin, very few lace veils; a most pitiful business!—Selina would stare when she heard of it'" (484). We do not know what Highbury will become, but we are led to suspect that its days as a symbol of the old life are numbered.[58]

Moreover, the very small-town insularity of Highbury, and the severity of the punishment dealt out to those who are not wise enough to leave its confines unguided, are still further signs of Jane Austen's ultimate disengagement. For she often seems to be playing with her themes, moved by a spirit of comic exaggeration. For example, she presents marriage outside Highbury as a form of unthinkable miscegenation; even a newcomer like Elton must not go outside to marry, and his punishment for wandering is, of course, Miss Augusta Hawkins of Bristol and Bath. Even more *outré* is the celebrated affair of Harriet Smith and the gypsies. While everyone sees the narrative function of the scene—it throws Harriet into Frank Churchill's arms and thereby encourages Emma's worst scheme—no one appears to have understood it as a hyperbolic statement of one of the novel's major themes. Harriet, accompanied only by another, equally inexperienced "parlour boarder" at Mrs. Goddard's, no sooner leaves the safety of her adopted home than finds herself exposed to the dangers of the outside world: "about half a mile beyond Highbury" Harriet and Miss Bickerton meet violence and the most unmistakable form of avarice in a party of gypsy beggars (333). Seen beside the major situations of the novel, this episode serves as another symbolic demonstration of the relation between Highbury and the outside world; seen as an instance of Jane Austen's attitude toward her material, it illustrates the detachment that allows her to indulge in ironic overstatement.

Finally, there is the national element in the novel. It is commonly recognized that, of all Jane Austen's novels, *Emma* is the most explicit in its awareness of Englishness, on the part both of the narrator and of the characters themselves. When the Knightley brothers are re-united, " 'How d'ye do, George?' and 'John, how are you?' succeeded in the true English style, burying under a calmness that seemed all but indifference, the real attachment which would have led either of them, if requisite, to do every thing for the good of the other" (99–100). The Constable-like description of Martin's Abbey-Mill Farm is often cited:

The considerable slope, at nearly the foot of which the Abbey stood, gradually acquired a steeper form beyond its grounds; and at half a mile distant was a bank of considerable abruptness and grandeur, well clothed with wood;—and at the bottom of this bank, favourably placed and sheltered, rose the Abbey-Mill Farm, with meadows in front, and the river making a close and handsome curve around it.

It was a sweet view—sweet to the eye and the mind. English verdure, English culture, English comfort, seen under a sun bright, without being oppressive. (360)

When making clear to Emma his misgivings about Frank Churchill and his "watering-place" ways, Mr. Knightley says:

"No, Emma, your amiable young man can be amiable only in French, not in English. He may be very 'aimable,' have very good manners, and be very agreeable; but he can have no English delicacy towards the feelings of other people; nothing really amiable about him." (149)

And Frank himself proves to us the validity of Knightley's observations when, much later in the novel, he and Emma "were looking over views in Swisserland":

> "As soon as my aunt gets well, I shall go abroad," said he. "I shall never be easy till I have seen some of these places. You will have my sketches, some time or other, to look at—or my tour to read—or my poem. I shall do something to expose myself."
>
> "That may be—but not by sketches in Swisserland. You will never go to Swisserland. Your uncle and aunt will never allow you to leave England."
>
> "They may be induced to go too. A warm climate may be prescribed for her. I have more than half an expectation of our all going abroad. I assure you I have. I feel a strong persuasion, this morning, that I shall soon be abroad. I ought to travel. I am serious, Miss Woodhouse, whatever your penetrating eyes may fancy—I am sick of England—and would leave it tomorrow, if I could." (365)

The reader comes to sense the contrast between Mr. Knightley and Frank Churchill in such explicitly national terms that, when Emma finally echoes the Knightleyan principles of manly virtue in her condemnation of Frank and his deceit, she is not only decrying one man's behavior but the anti-English ethos embodied by that man:

> "Impropriety! Oh! Mrs. Weston—it is too calm a censure. Much, much beyond impropriety!—It has sunk him, I cannot say how it has sunk him in my opinion. So unlike what a man should be!—None of that upright integrity, that strict adherence to truth and principle, that disdain of trick and littleness, which a man should display in every transaction of his life." (397)

Now, many interpretations have been placed upon the English qualities of *Emma*, but for my purposes it is enough to concentrate upon the wide authorial point of view that these qualities proclaim. Jane Austen has come to see her material almost comparatively, in that both the limited scene of her little drama and the larger factors imposed upon and dramatized by that scene are more precisely defined than ever before, and are set against other modes of behavior and other ethical standards. To be sure, the non-English qualities are not described or analyzed in any but the most vaguely negative manner; we see them only as expressions of something bad and foreign that has somehow infiltrated the very heart of England, Highbury itself. Nonetheless, Jane Austen's tendency to see Highbury and Mr.

Knightley as English is significant in that it restricts the characters and situations of the novel to limits that do not seem to contain the novelist herself. Hence this tendency is inseparable from Jane Austen's choice of a heroine in whose problems she has no part. Both announce a distance and an objectivity which, in the past, were only seldom characteristic of the author. And both help us to understand why her next novel was to be of the kind of *Persuasion*.

The focus of *Persuasion*, even more than that of *Emma*, is upon one central consciousness.[59] But the difference between the two books can be gauged by the differing natures of the central consciousness in each. Anne Elliot is not so young as Emma Woodhouse—given Jane Austen's chosen subject, seven years means a great deal—nor is she in any sense so foolish. A perceptive woman in her late twenties, Anne is plagued not by present misjudgments but by a single great error committed long ago. At the age of nineteen, she was persuaded by her friend and adviser, Lady Russell, to renounce her suitor, Commander Frederick Wentworth, because of his uncertain prospects. The fullness of her mistake is revealed to Anne when, early in the novel, Wentworth comes into her life once again. As attractive as ever, Wentworth is now in addition a Captain and a man of considerable means. Though Anne can no longer have any reason to refuse him, Wentworth, still resentful of the weakness she displayed in yielding to Lady Russell's advice, appears no longer to desire the match. *Persuasion* is the story of the gradual reconciliation of Anne and Wentworth; Jane Austen's concern in this novel is not the comic awakening of a benighted young mind but a sad woman's growing recognition that deliverance is still possible.

But the two novels are no less different in ambiance, physical and emotional, than in their central figures. And this diversity is of greater immediate concern since I wish to approach *Persuasion* as I approached *Emma*, primarily through analysis of its heroine's background. For the reader who turns to this novel from its predecessor suddenly quits a fading Arcadia and re-enters a scene as real and recognizable as it is unprepossessing.

Trilling, in his essay on *Emma*, warns of confusing "Jane Austen's England" with "the England of the years in which our author lived," repeating his contention that Jane Austen's England, "especially as it is represented in *Emma,* is an idyll," and adding that "All too often it is confused with the actual England, and the error of the identification ought always to be remarked."[60] It seems to me that the operative phrase here is "especially as it is represented in *Emma*"; in fact the extent to which any Jane Austen novel does or does not underscore the uglier actualities of life in the modern world is determined by its own particular emphases. And there is very little of the idyll in *Persuasion:* while in *Emma* the modern world is an ominous but distant force, only beginning to make itself felt in Highbury through its agents-in-residence there, in *Persuasion* the modern world is unmistakably the background of the major action. This is nowhere clearer than in the novel's unrelenting emphasis upon money—not only money as one factor in the marriage bargain but money as the guarantee of a tolerably genteel existence. Though in *Emma* we meet several characters beset by financial problems, they do not stand at the center of the tale; the fortunes of the major characters bear the expected concomitance to their respective stations. In *Persuasion,* however, financial problems are ubiquitous, and they affect not only the secondary figures but the leading figures as well. Wentworth's original poverty is the source of Anne Elliot's woes, and Anne herself is the only Jane Austen heroine who refuses a suitor on primarily financial grounds. The first major episode of the novel has to do with the painful decision of Sir Walter Elliot to rent the family seat of Kellynch Hall when his foolish spending at last renders him unable to maintain it. And the novel is permeated with reminders of even more serious financial problems. Poverty and dissipation bring Anne's former schoolmate, Mrs. Smith, to "a more cheerless situation" than has ever before been seen at first hand in a Jane Austen novel; when we first encounter Mrs. Smith at Bath, we are told that

She had been very fond of her husband,—she had buried him. She had been used to affluence,—it was gone. She had no child to connect her with life and happiness once again, no relations to assist in the arrangement of perplexed affairs, no health to make all the rest supportable. Her accommodations were limited to a noisy parlour, and a dark bed-room behind, with no possibility of moving from one to the other without assistance, which there was only one servant in the house to afford, and she never quitted the house but to be conveyed to a warm bath. (154)

The "thoughtless, gay set, without strict rules of conduct" (201) to which Mrs. Smith and her husband belonged is reminiscent of the

Crawfords *et al.* of *Mansfield Park,* but is even more reprehensible by reason of joining financial dishonesty to moral laxity. Moreover, through Mrs. Smith (her horizons broadened by the regular *comptes-rendus* of an all-knowing nurse named Mrs. Rooke), Anne and the reader are given further glimpses of poverty and sordor. Important among these are the descriptions of Anne's cousin (and present suitor) Walter Elliot, first in his impecunious student days and later in his calculated rise to wealth through a socially disgraceful marriage to the granddaughter of a butcher (199–202). In a word, poverty and the fear of poverty are to be met with throughout *Persuasion.*

The modern qualities of *Persuasion,* emphasized by these economic uncertainties, are further underscored by the homelessness of its heroine. A relatively fixed society leads to fixed residence, while social fluidity inevitably leads to movement from house to house; thus Anne Elliot is the most *déracinée* of all Jane Austen's heroines. Social movement in Jane Austen's fiction of course involves changes for the better on the part of those moving up, but it can also lead to the displacement of those unable to survive financially in the new order; thus the opening of *Persuasion* is dominated by Sir Walter's relinquishment of Kellynch to an admiral. To emphasize still further Anne's homelessness, Jane Austen cuts her off not only from a house but from all meaningful family ties, for while Sir Walter and Elizabeth (Anne's older sister) are always together in their passions for rank and for physical beauty, Anne is linked to her father and sister neither by similarities of taste and disposition nor by any hint of personal fondness. In contrast to the devoted Dashwoods, who, like the Elliots, find themselves displaced at the beginning of their tale, Sir Walter and his children need the physical solidarity of a house to which they are all personally attached in order to maintain anything more than purely formal family unity. Without Kellynch, Anne must wander, and even when Sir Walter and Elizabeth (accompanied by their sycophantic admirer, Mrs. Clay) remove to temporary lodgings at Bath, Anne does not immediately accompany them. Instead she joins her married sister, Mary Musgrove, at Uppercross, dividing her time between her sister's Cottage and the elder Musgroves' Great House. And she plans, even after joining Sir Walter at Bath, to spend much of her time with Lady Russell. The unmarried daughter of an uprooted baronet, Anne has no function, hence no fixed home, in the modern world; the daughter of a foolish and unsympathetic man, she cannot even settle into the temporary comforts of exile.

Anne Elliot's cheerless peregrinations are colored by the unique mood of *Persuasion,* the mood more often than not described as "autumnal." The tonal qualities of this novel have to do with much more than simply the time of year in which the greater part of the action is set[61] and the vividly rendered autumnal scenery. Anne Elliot is, at twenty-seven, if not in the autumn of life at least in the autumn of nubility; what is more, she is subject not only to a sense of lost youth but also to the painful memory of a chance for contentment which disappeared with the spring of her life. Her physical appearance naturally reflects this: we learn in the first chapter that "her bloom had vanished early" and that "she was faded and thin" (6). And the sense of the fading of the year is further intensified by the many deaths we hear of throughout the novel.

Those who choose to make too much of the limitations of Jane Austen's fictional material tend to insist upon the absence of death from the small world of her novels. It is of course true that none of Jane Austen's major characters is overtaken by death in full view of the reader (though Marianne Dashwood very nearly is); this could not be otherwise in light of Jane Austen's choice of subject. Since, for reasons already discussed, the novelist selected courtship as her subject and thereby stressed both its importance and its excitement, she could only have been acting in her own worst interests by allowing death to make a mockery of that importance and that excitement. In *Persuasion,* however, she uses death, and above all the deaths and near-deaths of young people, to underscore Anne Elliot's loss of youth and love.[62] The necrology of *Persuasion* is a long one. Anne's own mother died, according to Sir Walter's revered Baronetage, in 1800;[63] if we suppose her to have been about twenty years old at the time of her marriage in 1784 (Sir Walter was twenty-four), she was only thirty-six at the time of her death. Presumably William Elliot's first wife was even younger, since William himself is only "about thirty" during the action of the novel (105). Mrs. Clay's husband also appears to have died young (23). We first encounter Fanny Harville, the fiancee of Wentworth's friend Captain Benwick, in the following description: "They [Benwick and Fanny] had been a year or two waiting for fortune and promotion. Fortune came, his prize-money as lieutenant being great,—promotion, too, came at *last;* but Fanny Harville did not live to know it. She had died the preceding summer, while he was at sea" (96). And even beyond these particular instances, death is, like poverty, ever ominous and ever near. Most of the more admirable men in the novel—Admiral Croft, Wentworth, Benwick, Harville—are in the Navy, and the last paragraph reminds us that they and their wives must live in "the dread of a future war" and "must pay the tax of quick alarm for belonging to [the naval] profession . . ." (252).

The subject of death is, however, not always handled seriously or sympathetically. No one who has read the novel will forget "poor Richard" Musgrove, who died as a midshipman "before he reached his twentieth year" (50), or his mother's "large fat sighings over the destiny of a son, whom alive nobody had cared for" (68), or the following paragraphs:

> The real circumstances of this pathetic piece of family history were, that the Musgroves had had the ill fortune of a very troublesome, hopeless son; and the good fortune to lose him before he reached his twentieth year; that he had been sent to sea, because he was stupid and unmanageable on shore; that he had been very little cared for at any time by his family, though quite as much as he deserved; seldom heard of, and scarcely at all regretted, when the intelligence of his death abroad had worked its way to Uppercross, two years before.
>
> He had, in fact, though his sisters were now doing all they could for him, by calling him "poor Richard," been nothing better than a thick-headed, unfeeling, unprofitable Dick Musgrove, who had never done any thing to entitle himself to more than the abbreviation of his name, living or dead.
>
> He had been several years at sea, and had, in the course of those removals to which all midshipmen are liable, and especially such midshipmen as every captain wishes to be rid of, been six months on board Captain Frederick Wentworth's frigate, the Laconia; and from the Laconia he had, under the influence of his captain, written the only two letters which his father and mother had ever received from him during the whole of his absence; that is to say, the only two disinterested letters; all the rest had been mere applications for money. (50–51)

No less hard-hearted is Jane Austen's treatment of the near-fatal mishap of Louisa Musgrove when, during her short-lived flirtation with Wentworth, she insists once too often upon jumping from a stile. At the height of the excitement, the authorial voice participates in everyone's concern for Louisa: "There was no wound, no blood, no visible bruise; but her eyes were closed, she breathed not, her face was like death.—The horror of that moment to all who stood around!" (109) But three pages later we find that "Louisa's limbs had escaped. There was no injury but to the head." The thematic justifications for such savage sarcasm will be discussed below; for the moment it is enough to suggest that these notorious passages are the result of Jane Austen's ability to take fatal accidents to the young so completely in her stride that she even permits herself some grisly humor at the expense of unworthy sufferers.[64]

To summarize briefly: in subject and in mood, *Persuasion* seems to defy comparison with *Emma*. It is concerned with a gentlewoman who has been doomed to wander sadly through a world in which she has no place; it reflects at every turn the imminence of poverty and reminds us repeatedly of the imminence of death. Yet, as I hope to show, its theme is in fact the theme of all Jane Austen's work, and the attitudes it assumes toward that theme are in fact not unlike the attitudes of *Emma*. For again the contest between doing for oneself and submitting to outward forces is brought up only to be denied. In *Emma,* as we have seen, there is no real struggle whatever; in *Persuasion,* the struggle—expressed from the beginning through its social and economic analogues—no longer has any meaning. In the idealized world of *Emma*, only perversity and the most unmistakable vulgarity stand in the way of the natural order of things; in the real world of *Persuasion,* there is no natural order to command the respect and obedience of any intelligent person, for the old allegiances are at best moribund, at worst ridiculous, and always destructive, while individual achievement is always held up for unqualified approval. The two novels merely reflect two different solutions, one a wistful but ironic escape to the past, the other a serious and impatient assent to the difficult present.

PERSUASION: RANK AND PROFESSION

The opening and closing paragraphs of *Persuasion* succinctly set forth the personal and social polarities of the novel. They also illustrate the extent to which the inevitable opposition implied by these polarities has already been resolved in the novelist's mind.

Jane Austen never attempts to conceal her contempt for Sir Walter Elliot. But from her opening thrust she makes clear that she is giving us more than an ironic portrait of a vain and fatuous man: Sir Walter's absurdity is inseparable from, and most easily understood through, Sir Walter's rank.

> Sir Walter Elliot, of Kellynch-hall, in Somersetshire, was a man who, for his own amusement, never took up any book but the Baronetage; there he found occupation for an idle hour, and consolation in a distressed one; there his faculties were roused into admiration and respect, by contemplating the limited remnant of the earliest patents; there any unwelcome sensations, arising from domestic affairs, changed naturally into pity and contempt, as he turned over the almost endless creations of the last century—and there, if every other leaf were powerless, he could read his own history with an interest which never failed—this was the page at which the favourite volume always opened:

"ELLIOT OF KELLYNCH-HALL. . . ."   (3)

We have here in succinct form the repudiation of the attitudes and sentiments that Jane Austen held up for approbation—that Jane Austen perhaps forced herself to hold up for approbation—in *Mansfield Park*. The rank of baronet gave dignity and stature to Sir Thomas Bertram and secured for him a meaningful high place among the other characters of the novel. But now the same rank has become connected with pointless pride and ludicrous *amour-propre*. Nor does *Persuasion* anywhere show us an admirable baronet (or an admirable peer, that rarest of creatures in the works of Jane Austen) to offset our original impression of Sir Walter. The baronetcy comes to life in *Persuasion* as a fool's blind devotion to a book with his name in it.

Jane Austen strips the baronetcy not only of its eminence but also of its romance. Following the opening quotations from the pages devoted to Sir Walter in the Baronetage comes

> the history and rise of the ancient and respectable family, in the usual terms: how it had been first settled in Cheshire; how mentioned in Dugdale —serving the office of High Sheriff, representing a borough in three successive parliaments, exertions of loyalty, and dignity of baronet, in the first year of Charles II., with all the Marys and Elizabeths they had married; forming altogether two handsome duodecimo pages, and concluding with the arms and motto: "Principal seat, Kellynch hall, in the county of Somerset," and Sir Walter's hand-writing again in this finale:
> "Heir presumptive, William Walter Elliot, Esq., great grandson of the second Sir Walter." (3–4)

There is enough of English history here to set areel the mind of Fanny Price. As we learned in the first paragraph, Sir Walter's baronetcy is an old one, not one of the pitiable and contemptible "creations of the last century." "Ancient and respectable," the Elliot family harks back to the old England that Fanny adored; owing its title to services rendered in the cause of Charles II, it brings to mind the Tory orthodoxy of *Mansfield Park*. But in *Persuasion* this distinguished Tory tradition culminates in a man whom nobody can take seriously. And the irony arising from the incongruous juxtaposition of the Elliots' grand past and the absurd present bearer of the family honors is double-edged: if the past makes the present seem inadequate, the present makes the past seem futile. Indeed, in offhandedly reducing the history of the Elliots to a question of "the usual terms," Jane Austen is displaying the insouciant disrespect of Mary Crawford herself.

There is more at stake in this prologue to *Persuasion* than Sir Walter's fatuity, more even than the single rank of baronet that once Jane Austen asked her readers to take so seriously. The very possibility of respect for birth is challenged when this respect is brought down to the level of the comically effeminate worship of personal comeliness:

> Vanity was the beginning and the end of Sir Walter Elliot's character; vanity of person and of situation. He had been remarkably handsome in his youth; and, at fifty-four, was still a very fine man. Few women could think more of their personal appearance than he did; nor could the valet of any new made lord be more delighted with the place he held in society. He considered the blessing of beauty as inferior only to the blessing of a baronetcy; and the Sir Walter Elliot, who united these gifts, was the constant object of his warmest respect and devotion. (4)

Pride in rank becomes "vanity . . . of situation"; the cluster of meanings traditionally associated with the structure of feudal society is reduced to the vulgar delight of "the valet of any new made lord." And the mocking attitude toward the old *ordo* that Jane Austen establishes in this paragraph is resolutely maintained throughout the novel.

Jane Austen is perhaps most intolerant of the feudal order in her treatment of the performance of Sir Walter and Elizabeth vis-à-vis their cousins, "the Dowager Viscountess Dalrymple, and her daughter, the Honourable Miss Carteret." When he gets word of the arrival of the two ladies at Bath, Sir Walter leaps at the opportunity of setting right some past misunderstandings:

Sir Walter had once been in company with the late Viscount, but had never seen any of the rest of the family, and the difficulties of the case arose from there having been a suspension of all intercourse by letters of ceremony, ever since the death of that said late Viscount, when, in consequence of a dangerous illness of Sir Walter's at the same time, there had been an unlucky omission at Kellynch. No letter of condolence had been sent to Ireland. The neglect had been visited upon the head of the sinner, for when poor Lady Elliot died herself, no letter of condolence was received at Kellynch, and, consequently, there was but too much reason to apprehend that the Dalrymples considered the relationship as closed. (148–149)

This commentary upon the inhuman formality of the *haut monde* is only the first stage of Jane Austen's attack. It is not until Sir Walter succeeds in re-establishing relations with Lady Dalrymple—that is, until he writes "a very fine letter of ample explanation, regret, and entreaty, to his right honourable cousin" and is rewarded by "three lines of scrawl from the Dowager Countess" (149)—that he and his oldest daughter achieve the full measure of obsequious absurdity. Restrained irony becomes an inadequate vehicle for the novelist's disgust at their behavior; the bluntness of her attack is evident in the description of Elizabeth's entrance into a "concert room," when, "arm in arm with Miss Carteret, and looking on the broad back of the dowager Viscountess Dalrymple before her, [Elizabeth] had nothing to wish for which did not seem within her reach . . ." (185).

But Jane Austen communicates her new sense of rank still more clearly in the last chapter, when, passing beyond individual deficiencies of character, she assaults the very idea of a rigidly stratified social order. Mrs. Clay, perhaps sensing the futility of her attempts to ensnare Sir Walter through sheer sycophancy, runs off to London to become the mistress of William Elliot. We are then told:

It cannot be doubted that Sir Walter and Elizabeth were shocked and mortified by the loss of their companion, and the discovery of their deception in her. They had their great cousins, to be sure, to resort to for comfort; but they must long feel that to flatter and follow others, without being flattered and followed in turn, is but a state of half enjoyment. (251)

This then is the novelist's vision of the traditional social order in *Persuasion*. Rank is indeed honored, and distances observed. But to accept one's superiors is "to flatter and follow" with neither dignity nor self-respect; what should be a sense of responsibility toward social inferiors is no more than the smug pleasure of "being flattered and followed in turn." This passage is much more than a critique of some natural abuses in the traditional system; it is, in the context of *Persuasion,* an attack upon the system itself, upon the refusal to recognize individual merit and the willingness to tolerate stupidity in the name of rank.

For Jane Austen is now wholly and impatiently committed to a society in which recognition and reward stem from "merit and activity" in some profession. Demonstrating the fatuity of the landed class, Mrs. Clay insists to Sir Walter that virtually all professions leave unpleasant scars upon the face, and concludes:

"In fact, as I have long been convinced, though every profession is necessary and honourable in its turn, it is only the lot of those who are not obliged to follow any, who can live in a regular way, in the country, choosing their own hours, following their own pursuits, and living on their own property, without the torment of trying for more; it is only *their* lot, I say, to hold the blessings of health and a good appearance to the utmost: I know of no other set of men but what lose something of their personableness when they cease to be quite young." (20–21)

The novelist intends that Mrs. Clay's fawning speech cast suspicion upon the whole idea of a professionless gentry, and provides no central figure (such as Darcy or Sir Thomas Bertram or Mr. Knightley) to demonstrate the opposing viewpoint, no benevolent and solicitous landlord to offset the idea that the landed class is devoted chiefly to static contemplation of its own non-existent perfections.

The Navy is, of all professions, the one that most values intelligence and spirit over birth and "connexions"; it is the profession *par excellence* of the new and harshly competitive world. Just as it is through baronet and nobleman that Jane Austen dramatizes the injustice and absurdity of the old order, so it is through sailors (and above all through Wentworth) that she represents the accomplishments and the virtues of the new. Sir Walter affirms that the Navy

". . . is in two points offensive to me; I have two strong grounds of objection to it. First, as being the means of bringing persons of obscure birth into undue distinction, and raising men to honours which their fathers and grandfathers never dreamt of; and secondly, as it cuts up a man's youth and vigour most horribly; a sailor grows old sooner than any other man; I have observed it all my life. A man is in greater danger in the navy of being insulted by the rise of one whose father, his father might have disdained to speak to, and of becoming prematurely an object of disgust to himself, than in any other line." (19)

Jane Austen here is using one of her favorite ironic devices, that of denigrating the importance of birth by allowing Sir Walter to equate it with the condition of one's skin. In a larger sense, she is ascribing to her spokesman for everything foolish a negative view of the naval profession in particular and of social mobility in general.

However unfortunate in tone, Jane Austen's ruthless treatment of Dick Musgrove is thus perfectly adjusted to the severe ethical standards and concomitant professional symbolism of *Persuasion*. While the ways of Sir Walter, Elizabeth, and the Dalrymples are diametrically opposed to the ways of Captain Wentworth, Dick Musgrove tried to follow Wentworth's road to success. The Navy tested him (by the same standards applied to the triumphant Wentworth) and found him unworthy. Incompetent, selfish, and stupid, Dick deserved to be done away with and forgotten; the reader, like Anne, sees the stupidity of Mrs. Musgrove's belief that, "if it had pleased Heaven to spare my poor son," he would have become "just such another" as Wentworth (64). One is prompted to reflect that, while the new morality of individual "merit and activity" may be more democratic than the old, it is not necessarily more benign.

The movement away from traditional feudalism is, of course, economic as well as social. Though explicit remarks upon economic theory would be inconceivable in Jane Austen's work, in *Persuasion* she does seem to endorse an ethic as capitalistic as it is democratic. This is a point that several important critics of Jane Austen have refused to accept. Wayne C. Booth, for example, commenting on Schorer's elucidation of the pervasiveness of financial metaphors in *Persuasion*, says that "No one would deny that the novel is packed with such metaphors . . . . But the crucial question surely is: What precisely are these metaphors of the countinghouse doing in the novel? *Whose* values are they supposed to reveal?" Booth proceeds to answer his own questions, but his conclusions are highly questionable. The novel, he insists,

is really very clear about it all. The introduction, coming directly from the wholly reliable narrator, establishes unequivocally and without "analogy" the conflict between the world of the Elliots, depending for its values on selfishness, stupidity, and pride—and the world of Anne, a world where "elegance of mind and sweetness of character" are the supreme values. The commercial values stressed by Schorer are only a selection from what is actually a rich group of evils. And Anne's own expressed views again and again provide direct guidance to the reader.[65]

Booth errs first in his definition of the conflict in *Persuasion*, or at least in his definition of the economic conflict, which presumably should be the basis of his speculation about the role of money in the novel; the opposing forces are not, as he would have it, embodied in Anne and the other Elliots respectively, and are not identifiable by the presence or absence of such qualities as "elegance of mind and sweetness of character." Rather, the economic conflict is the logical extension of the social conflict, and has to do with money as a condition of birth versus money as a reward for individual achievement; the conflict is therefore between the Elliots and Wentworth. Needless to say, Jane Austen is wholly on Wentworth's side; merely to inherit money is no proof of intelligence or skill, but to earn and accumulate money through one's wit and daring is cause for admiration. In short, when Booth connects the "commercial values" of *Persuasion* with the Elliots and then baldly classifies them as "evils," he reveals much more about the ethics of twentieth-century American academicians than about the ethics of *Persuasion*. For if Booth and his readers (needless to say, I include myself) are loath to accept financial success as any kind of reliable gauge of virtue, the author of this novel was not.

Hence, the opening paragraph of the last chapter, in which Jane Austen describes the effect of Anne's reconciliation with Wentworth:

Sir Walter made no objection, and Elizabeth did nothing worse than look cold and unconcerned. Captain Wentworth, with five-and-twenty thousand pounds, and as high in his profession as merit and activity could place him, was no longer nobody. He was now esteemed quite worthy to address the daughter of a foolish, spendthrift baronet, who had not had principle or sense enough to maintain himself in the situation in which Providence had placed him, and who could give his daughter at present but a small part of the share of ten thousand pounds which must be hers hereafter. (248)

In the context of *Persuasion* as a whole, these sentences can, I believe, fairly be read as Jane Austen's ultimate gesture of deference to capitalist standards. The author of *Mansfield Park* (a novel to which Booth's general remarks apply much more accurately than they do to *Persuasion*) has come full cycle, to the point of identifying "principle" and "sense" with capitalistic prowess. (Notice that the Elliots see money only as a gauge of outward respectability, and not of character.) We may be distressed by the unqualified baldness of Jane Austen's judgment here, but it is of no use to deny its existence. According to the values of *Persuasion*, one is obliged to do, and if one vital measure of doing is monetary, Jane Austen seems perfectly content to apply it.

Booth's remarks also reveal what seems to me another serious misconception: I mean his statement of the relationship between the protagonist of *Persuasion* and her creator. If we wish to appreciate Jane Austen's treatment of the theme of the book, we must disabuse ourselves of the notion that Anne Elliot and Jane Austen are equally reliable guides to its values. Anne does, of course, approach Jane Austen's standards in most ways. Like the novelist, she is very much aware of the rightness of Wentworth and the wrongness of her father and elder sister; in other words, she is, like the novelist, above the major conflict, not choosing between Wentworth and the Elliots but merely hoping that the former will rescue her from a life with the latter. And Anne's preference for Wentworth is, like Jane Austen's, based upon something more than emotional response. Anne subscribes to the code of individual merit of which Wentworth is the leading exemplar, and she attaches relatively little importance to "rank and connexion" (148). Her feelings on the subject come into focus after she is married:

> Anne, satisfied at a very early period of Lady Russell's meaning to love Captain Wentworth as she ought, had no other alloy to the happiness of her prospects than what arose from the consciousness of having no relations to bestow on him which a man of sense could value. There she felt her own inferiority keenly. The disproportion in their fortune was nothing; it did not give her a moment's regret; but to have no family to receive and estimate him properly; nothing of respectability, of harmony, of good-will to offer in return for all the worth and all the prompt welcome which met her in his brothers and sisters, was a source of as lively pain as her mind could well be sensible of, under circumstances of otherwise strong felicity. (251)

Money as the Elliots might see it—as a factor in the marriage bargain —is of no interest to Anne, but more significantly, not even Sir Walter's baronetcy and her own kinship to a Viscountess are worth anything to her in comparison to the warmth of Wentworth's family, for she shares, on the whole, Jane Austen's disdain for details of high birth.

But Anne is not Jane Austen. First, she is closer to the events of the novel, so that her vision is less wide than her creator's, and her pronouncements, for the most part, less general. But even more pertinently, Anne must, by the very nature of her situation, display far greater tolerance than her creator toward the less worthy characters of the novel. Indeed, Jane Austen herself when dealing with these characters fails frequently to evince precisely those qualities of "sweetness of mind and elegance of temper" that she exhibits and praises in Anne. One example should serve to show the gulf between the heroine and the novelist: Anne manifests "shock and mortification" when she sees the letter containing young William Elliot's abusive repudiation of Sir Walter and the name of Elliot (203–204), yet William's contempt for Sir Walter and his station is hardly greater than that which Jane Austen herself feels and clearly expects the reader to share. Beyond question, Anne demonstrates exemplary conduct for a person in her situation, but Jane Austen and the reader, being free of Anne's personal and familial obligations, are morally free to hold and to express far more severe opinions.

Similarly, Jane Austen is obliged by dramatic necessity to paint a sympathetic portrait of the woman whom Anne trusted over her own instincts. Thus, despite her support of the moribund caste system, Lady Russell is shown to be a reasonable and warmhearted woman. At the same time, Jane Austen never suggests that Lady Russell is, for all her good intentions, anything but dead wrong in her antiquated beliefs. During the discussions, early in the novel, of the various possible solutions to Sir Walter's financial problems, Lady Russell is described as being

of strict integrity herself, with a delicate sense of honour; but she was as desirous of saving Sir Walter's feelings, as solicitous for the credit of the family, as aristocratic in her ideas of what was due to them, as any body of sense and honesty could be. She was a benevolent, charitable, good woman, and capable of strong attachments; most correct in her conduct, strict in her notions of decorum, and with manners that were held a standard of good-breeding. She had a cultivated mind, and was, generally speaking, rational and consistent—but she had prejudices on the side of ancestry; she had a value for rank and consequence, which blinded her a little to the faults of those who possessed them. (11)

The rhetoric is hardly subtle: even in this good woman, as Jane Austen makes clear, warm feelings toward "ancestry" are simply "prejudices," while a "value for rank and consequence" leads to partial blindness. By the end, Lady Russell "must learn to feel that she had been mistaken with regard to Wentworth . . . . There was nothing less for Lady Russell to do, than to admit that she had been pretty completely wrong, and to take up a new set of opinions and of hopes" (249).

Lady Russell's new "opinions" and "hopes" concern much more than Anne's marital situation: they apply, by implication, to a whole new way of seeing and judging.

In still another characterization, Jane Austen is obliged to offer certain qualifications of the values upheld by the experience of the novel. William Elliot makes too much capital of social fluidity; his marriage to the granddaughter of a butcher alerts us to the difference between enterprise and profiteering (and at the same time reminds us that Jane Austen's notions of social equality are after all a century and a half away from our own). But William is selfish and amoral, and his flouting of social rigidity, like his habit of speaking "most slightingly and contemptuously of the very blood he belonged to, and the honours which were hereafter to be his own" (9), is nothing more than proof of his fundamental dishonesty: once he has his butcher's fortune, he reconciles himself to Sir Walter and assumes opinions about his uncle's dignity which, if a bit less reverent than the Baronet's own, are likened to those of Lady Russell, and are, in his own words, "'only too strict to suit the unfeudal tone of the present day'" (139). In short, William is, like Wickham in *Pride and Prejudice*, ready to exploit either camp, and Jane Austen has not allowed the needs of characterization seriously to challenge the prevailing ethical sense of the novel.

It is possible that, with further revision, Jane Austen would have modified the tone of her authorial intrusions so as to adjust the balance between the values implied by some of her characterizations and the values explicit in certain authorial exhortations. But—short of making the most fundamental changes, changes that seem unlikely in light of the general direction of her earlier work—she could not have altered her basic theme, nor her encompassing view of it. If Jane Austen is, as Leavis and some other critics have called her, the first modern novelist, *Persuasion* is the most modern of her books. Nowhere else is the peculiarly modern sense of the intelligent, rootless individual in conflict with meaningless and moribund traditions set forth so vividly, nor with such complete sympathy for those who must learn that they have only themselves to trust.

FROM *PERSUASION* TO *SANDITON*

Though in the course of this study I have, for the most part, limited myself to those works which Jane Austen wished to see published and which can, as a result, be taken for a reliable index of her changing responses to, and representations of, the English macrocosm, it seems appropriate here to deal at least briefly with the draft traditionally known as *Sanditon*. Despite its fragmentary state, *Sanditon* invites and justifies comment by providing the major clue to the direction that Jane Austen's work might well have taken: it looks forward to still another stage of Jane Austen's development—to new modes of characterization, to new subjects, even to new themes—and thereby sheds further light upon the coolness and detachment of *Emma* and the impatience and warm commitment of *Persuasion*.

The reader of *Sanditon* is first struck by the openly physical nature of much of its comedy. While it might be argued that the seeds of this earthiness are discernible in the vividness of the physical descriptions in *Persuasion*, there exists between the two works a qualitative difference. *Sanditon* begins with a carriage overturning on a rough road; the scene is, rather surprisingly, essentially comic, and the reader suspects that, with further revision, it would have become even more so. And it sets immediately the comic mood of the book. Witness Jane Austen's treatment of hypochondria: long one of her favorite targets, it is no longer linked to—and excused by—the delicate, genteel charm of a Mr. Woodhouse, as we see in the letter written by Miss Diana Parker to her brother:

> "And neither of my dear Companions will leave me, or I wd promote their going down to you for a fortnight. But in truth, I doubt whether Susan's nerves wd be equal to the effort. She has been suffering much from the Headache and Six Leaches a day for 10 days together releived her so little that we thought it right to change our measures—and being convinced on examination that much of the Evil lay in her Gum, I persuaded her to attack the disorder there. She has accordingly had 3 Teeth drawn, & is decidedly better, but her Nerves are a good deal deranged. She can only speak in a whisper—and fainted away twice this morning on poor Arthur's trying to suppress a Cough. He, I am happy to say, is tolerably well—tho' more languid than I like—& I fear for his Liver." (387)

While such a passage would have done violence to the mood of any of the earlier books, in *Sanditon* it seems entirely appropriate, and one suspects that the novel if completed would have offered many more such effusive diagnoses on the part of Miss Parker.

Similarly, many of the central characters seem to have emerged from a comic world never before explored by Jane Austen. Lady Denham and Sir Edward are particularly arresting. The former— miserly, ill-educated, grandiosely repulsive—is often called Dickensian, though Chaucerian seems to me a more accurate description of a character who professes:

"I am not the Woman to help any body blindfold.—I always take care to know what I am about & who I have to deal with, before I stir a finger.—I do not think I was ever overreached in my Life; & That is a good deal for a Woman to say that has been married twice.—Poor dear Sir Harry (between ourselves) thought at first to have got more.—But (with a bit of a sigh) He is gone, & we must not find fault with the Dead. Nobody could live happier together than us—& he was a very honourable Man, quite the Gentleman of ancient Family.—And when he died, I gave Sir Edwd his Gold Watch.—" (399–400)

If Lady Denham has certain affinities with the Wife of Bath, Sir Edward, the defective child of literature, looks forward to the characters of *Nightmare Abbey*. Not only is his language the echo of the most sententious literary criticism—" 'You will never hear me advocating those puerile Emanations which detail nothing but discordant Principles incapable of Amalgamation, or those vapid tissues of ordinary Occurrences from which no useful Deductions can be drawn' " (403)—but the very conduct of his life constitutes a distillation of literature into personal madness. His "great object in life," we are told, "was to be seductive," yet his motives are wholly asexual:

He felt that he was formed to be a dangerous Man—quite in the line of the Lovelaces.—The very name of Sir Edward he thought, carried some degree of fascination with it.—To be generally gallant & assiduous about the fair, to make fine speeches to every pretty Girl, was but the inferior part of the Character he had to play.—Miss Heywood, or any other young Woman with any pretensions to Beauty, he was entitled (according to his own views of Society) to approach with high Compliment & Rhapsody on the slightest acquaintance; but it was Clara alone on whom he had serious designs; it was Clara whom he meant to seduce.—Her seduction was quite determined on. Her Situation in every way called for it. (405)

Catherine Morland is the temporary dupe of romantic fiction, but Sir Edward is a hopeless lunatic, an aberration of nature in its relentless imitation of art.

Even more startling than the intrinsic tenor of these characterizations is the prominence they command: Lady Denham and Sir Edward stand near the center of Jane Austen's canvas, while the middle-aged entrepreneur of Sanditon, Mr. Parker, is no less than its focal point. In short, Jane Austen's very subject seems to have changed. As in all the novelist's earlier work, marriageable girls—in this case Charlotte Heywood and Clara Brereton—occupy a good deal of the

writer's attention, but they do not occupy all or even most of it; courtship, except as practiced by Sir Edward, himself an extraordinary
departure from the suitors in Jane Austen's earlier work, seems to be
no more than one of the several subjects of the book, and not necessarily the major one. At least as important is the subject of business,
not as epitomized in social and marital relations but as represented
directly: Mr. Parker's plan for exploiting Sanditon—an unusually direct
reference on the author's part to the specifically contemporary growth
of seaside resorts (in itself a reflection of the growth of a new leisured
class)—is more nearly at the heart of the action than Clara's or even
Charlotte's matrimonial prospects. Once again, the roots of *Sanditon*
are to be found in *Persuasion,* but once again the difference is qualitative, here reflected in the very subjects at hand.

But it is in thematic possibilities that *Sanditon* most clearly inaugu-
rates a new period in Jane Austen's work. The change becomes clear
if we set *Sanditon* beside the only comparable Jane Austen fragment,
The Watsons. The latter, even in its rough state, already betrays Jane
Austen's familiar theme of the individual versus fixed tradition: Emma
Watson's undistinguished station is directly opposed to her attractive
traits of compassion and sensitivity, and anyone familiar with Jane
Austen's novels senses that this opposition would have assumed central
thematic importance had the piece been developed. But there seems
no possibility of this theme arising out of the given material of *Sanditon.* Jane Austen's interest appears to be centered in the gallery of
unpleasant, even grotesque types who populate *Sandition;* her theme
might have become one of those that Dickens worked on throughout
his life, namely the conflict between simple benevolence and bizarre,
twisted destructiveness as played out against the backdrop of a chaotic
commercial scene. Other possibilities also suggest themselves, but the
important point is this: the theme of all Jane Austen's earlier work
does not appear to be among them.

Admittedly, no discussion of *Sanditon* can ever rise above the level
of speculation. But if *Sanditon* the fragment cannot certainly tell us
what *Sanditon* the completed novel would finally have been like,[66] it
can tell us what Jane Austen was thinking about after finishing *Persuasion;* if the fragment does not prefigure the future with absolute
clarity, it does comment upon the past. Her preoccupations, as recorded in her last extended piece of writing, are not what they once
were. All her work after *Mansfield Park* shows that her old interests

were waning, and as *Emma* and *Persuasion* record the demise of the old, *Sanditon* records the germination of the new; if in *Sanditon* many of the elements of Jane Austen's earlier work have undergone a marked alteration, the causes of that alteration are demonstrable in her last two completed masterworks.

Conclusion: The Pattern of the Canon

Few readers today would dispute the proposition that Jane Austen is—perhaps to an even greater extent than the other novelists in the Leavis "tradition"—a writer whose essential impulse is to judge, and a writer who demands that her reader be always ready to judge with her. To be sure, every novel ever written creates, explicitly or implicitly, its own standards of human behavior, and every successful novel seduces its reader into temporary acquiescence to those standards. But for Jane Austen and her reader, the simplest act of perception becomes an act of moral scrutiny; nothing illustrates this more dramatically than the extreme scarcity of those characters—Miss Bates and Mr. Woodhouse are virtually the only important ones—who seem to deny rather than encourage the reader's capacity for moral discrimination.

At the same time, it is well to remember what so many critics of an earlier age were wont to forget: that Jane Austen was a novelist with moral preoccupations, not a moralist; and that if in her work characterization and situation are inseparable from judgment, so too is judgment inseparable from character and situation, with the result that few general "principles" can be abstracted from her work. Even within the small range of six completed novels, all published within a span of seven years, one discovers much inconsistency, some of it quite surprising; each erects its own moral framework. Now, it has often been said that for Jane Austen certain traditional values were still fixed and settled, the values that C. S. Lewis imputes to Jane Austen because of her repeated use of those "great abstract nouns of the classical English moralists"—"courage" and "good sense," for example, or "fortitude" and "reason." In Jane Austen's work, Lewis contends (with evident pleasure), "we still breathe the air of the *Rambler* and the *Idler*."[67] Yet all my preceding chapters lead inevitably to the rather different conclusion that, in Jane Austen's novels, these nouns are largely defined by context, that each of the novels is in fact a personal attempt to rediscover or re-approximate their meaning. If the eighteenth-century moralists gave Jane Austen their vocabulary, they do not appear to have given her the certainty that Lewis implies they themselves enjoyed.

And because, in Jane Austen's mature work, the assessment of individuals inevitably extends to—is indeed co-essential with—the assessment of larger questions, in large as in small the novelist not only obeys the same necessity to judge but also displays the same surprising variations in judgment. As we follow Jane Austen's progress from novel to novel, from each complex of character and situation to the next, we are obliged always to align our vision of Jane Austen's England with the novelist's own, sometimes (as in *Emma*) hardly conscious of the effort, sometimes (as in *Mansfield Park*) only too aware of the novelist's present demands upon us. The frequency of these required adjustments is of course simply another symptom of the fact that Jane Austen was a novelist; her treatment of larger themes, unlike that of a social critic or historian, cannot be dissociated from her response to the characters and events by means of which the themes are dramatized. But it is also connected with Jane Austen's continuing interest in the world around her; in her search for a satisfactory synthesis between the warring claims of individual and environment, she was forced into repeated revaluation of that world. And this revaluation I take to be as much the cause as the effect of the specific personal dramas she creates: those varying attitudes which have been the subject of all the preceding chapters betoken neither evasion nor superficiality, but instead the novelist's thoughtful engagement in the task of reviewing the meaning of culture and of society at a time when traditional views had already been seriously challenged.

But while it is one thing to point to Jane Austen's inconsistency and its broad historical background, it is still another to arrive at some conclusions about the particular course of Jane Austen's individual development. First, then, we must begin to question the accepted notion of the Jane Austen canon. According to this view, Jane Austen's completed novels fall into two groups, those originally conceived in the 1790's (the first three) and those conceived and written during the novelist's last years at Chawton (the last three). But at least one of the novels seems to defy this chronological formulation: *Pride and Prejudice* as we know it must have been fundamentally rewritten before its publication, and is therefore doubtless closer in actual date of final execution to *Mansfield Park* than to the *First Impressions* of 1798.

Moreover, as I have argued in my discussion of *Mansfield Park,* Jane Austen's third and fourth novels are linked to each other by something more than the high quality of their art. Together they constitute Jane Austen's most intense examination of the structure and meaning of the English social hierarchy, an examination that the novelist had not yet embarked upon in *Northanger Abbey* and had only tentatively undertaken in *Sense and Sensibility.* If *Pride and Prejudice* and *Mansfield Park* mark a single stage in Jane Austen's career, so too do her first and third pairs of novels. The connections between *Northanger Abbey* and *Sense and Sensibility* are self-evident. And, as I have contended in the last portion of this study, *Emma* and *Persuasion* are also companion pieces, each offering a kind of resolution of the conflicts which animated *Pride and Prejudice* and *Mansfield Park* but which seem, by the time of *Sanditon,* to have disappeared from the center of Jane Austen's consciousness.

If then we see Jane Austen's novels as falling into three groups of two rather than two groups of three, we must also notice that the first work of each group is essentially comic, while the second is notably less lively and may even have tragic overtones; one might conveniently postulate that the second novel of each group is pitched in the relative minor key of the first. In *Northanger Abbey,* the novelist took as her point of departure the novel of Gothic sensibility, but it would appear that her first novelistic (rather than parodistic) inquiry into the literary scene had raised in her own mind more questions than it had answered, for in reworking *Sense and Sensibility* she attempted a much more serious exploration of the cult of sensibility in English life; and as her probing widened, so too did her insight into, and sympathy for, the individual's protest against the status quo. Turning next to the examination of English society in the revision of *Pride and Prejudice,* Jane Austen seems to have recaptured the confident comic spirit of *Northanger Abbey.* But this examination clearly opened many new and perhaps unexpected paths: responding more fully to the qualified claims for orthodoxy and rank made in *Pride and Prejudice,* Jane Austen in *Mansfield Park* found it necessary to explore what has been called the "Tory" side of her nature, to redefine some of her "great abstract nouns," and to offer her most sustained apology for tradition. *Mansfield Park* demonstrates how strong and how deep-seated Jane Austen's "Tory" sympathies really were; it was only after she had probed these sympathies to the full that she could look freshly at the conflict between the assertive individual and his restrictive environment. Thus, in *Emma,* she could review her theme from a newly attained distance, while in the nearly crepuscular pages of *Persuasion* she turned away almost completely from the romance of the past to an unprecedentedly realistic rendering of modern life and a nearly total capitulation to the creed of individual achievement. In the context of Jane Austen's earlier work, the sharp anti-traditionalism of *Persuasion,* like its autumnal scenery, points to the end of a cycle: even if one bears in mind the danger of imposing upon the course and direction of Jane Austen's work too much of our contemporary idea of historical development, one cannot resist the suspicion that *Persuasion* represents the novelist's final vision—not merely the last she lived to communicate—of the English social scene of her day.

Thus we have a tripartite division of Jane Austen's works, with the darker novel of each of the three units understood as a comment upon its lighter antecedent and each of the units understood as a stage to be passed before the next could be begun. Admittedly, this scheme is not the only possible one; there exist many valid considerations that it ignores. But any pattern discernible in the canon of a major writer's work must yield its share of insight: the design I suggest, having emerged from my concern in these pages with Jane Austen's changing vision of the English macrocosm, teaches us that this vision—which engendered the novelist's unmatched freedom to make expressive use of questions of rank and birth—was in no sense the haphazard outgrowth of the comic or dramatic material of her novels, but rather another sign of her unique sensitivity to the causes and implications of what people do.

Acknowledgments

My thanks go to Professors Carl Woodring and Carolyn Heilbrun of Columbia, who read the first version of this study with unusual attention and appropriate severity; to my friends and former colleagues, Daniel F. Howard and Thomas F. Van Laan of Rutgers, who made many sensible and useful suggestions about the present version; and to Ronald Christ of Manhattan College, who endured *both* versions. The Rutgers University Research Council provided a grant for the final typing of the manuscript.

REFERENCE MATTER

NOTES

Ross: Wingless Victory

1 C. R. Morey, *Christian Art* (New York, 1935), p. 62.

2 See Chrysostom, "Homily XI on the Epistle to the Romans," in *A Select Library of the Nicene and Post-Nicene Fathers of the Christian Church*, ed. Philip Schaff (Grand Rapids, 1956), XI, 409; also *Glossa ordinaria* on this place and Eph. iv.22, in *Biblia cum glossis* (Lyons, 1545), VI, fols. 15ʳ, 94ᵛ.

3 See *Glossa ordinaria* (in *Biblia*, VI, fol. 94ʳ) at Eph. iv.22: "Veterem hominem. Nonnulli putant, quod vetus corpus sit, & nouus alma. Sed corpus exterior homo est, alma interior: & in interiori agitur hæc vetustas & nouitas."

4 Interlinear gloss on *homo vetus* at Col. iii.9, in *Biblia*, VI, fol. 107ᵛ: "homo vetus, vita vetus in peccatis secundum Adam."

5 Cf. I John ii.29. Scriptural quotations in English are from the Authorized Version unless otherwise stated.

6 The inevitable use of youthful age to indicate or represent spiritual "newness" readily follows that of old age to signify "oldness" of the spirit; it begins early and was held to have scriptural warrant. See the Index in *Biblia*, VI, sig. mijʳ, s.v. *Iuuenes*: "scriptura non semper iuxta ætatem appellat, sed iuxta in stabilitatem animi." For a patristic text, see, e.g., Chrysostom, "Homily VIII on Colossians," in *A Select Library*, XIII, 295:

"And he calleth him 'old,' on purpose to show his deformity, and hideousness, and imbecility; and 'new,' as if to say, Do not expect that it will be with this one even as with the other, but the reverse: for ever as he farther advances, he hasteneth not on to old age, but to a youthfulness greater than the preceding. For when he hath perceived a fuller knowledge, he is both counted worthy of greater things, and is in more perfect maturity, in higher vigor; and this, not from youthfulness alone, but from that 'likeness' also, 'after' which he is. Lo! the best life is styled a creation, after the image of Christ: for this is the meaning of, 'after the image of Him that created him,' for Christ too came not finally to old age, but was so beautiful as it is not even possible to tell."

Cf. *Allegoriæ in sacram scripturam*, s.v. Rabanus Maurus, in *PL*, CXII, col. 975, s.v. *Juventus*; also Alanus de Insulis, *Distinctiones*, *PL*, CCX, col. 825, s.v. *Juvenis, Juventus*. For further discussion and illustration of the *vetus:senex* equation, see D. W. Robertson, Jr., *A Preface to Chaucer* (Princeton, 1962), p. 379 and Figs. 94, 104.

7 See *Glossa ordinaria* on Eph. iv.24, in *Biblia*, VI, fol. 94ᵛ.

8 See Carl Justi, *Michelangelo: Neue Beiträge zur Erklärung seiner Werke* (Berlin, 1909), p. 285.

9 See John Pope-Hennessy, *Italian High Renaissance and Baroque Sculpture* (London, 1963), I, 49; for reproductions of Giambologna's group, see ibid., I, Fig. 51, or Charles de Tolnay, *Michelangelo. IV: The Tomb of Julius II* (Princeton, 1954), Fig. 269.

10 Giorgio Vasari, *Le vite de'più eccellenti pittori scultori ed architettori,* ed. Gaetano Milanesi, Vol. VII (Florence, 1881), p. 166: ". . . ed a Fiorenza ne abozzò cinque, e finì una Vittoria con un prigion sotto . . . ."

11 In the absence of corroborative interpretation of the central attributes of the figures, this fact by itself is insufficient to support the suggestion "that the group should be interpreted as a political allegory (Justi)."— Pope-Hennessy, *Italian . . . Sculpture,* II, 24.

12 "Io mi truovo aver perduta tutta la mia giovineza, legato a questa sepultura . . ."—Letter "A Monsignore . . . ," Rome (October 1542), in *Le lettere di Michelangelo Buonarroti,* ed. Gaetano Milanesi (Florence, 1875), p. 490.

13 See Ascanio Condivi, *Vita di Michelagnolo Bvonarroti* (Rome, 1553), fol. 16ᵛ; Vasari, *Vite,* ed. Milanesi, pp. 163–165; and, for interpretative discussion, Erwin Panofsky, "The First Two Projects of Michelangelo's Tomb of Julius II," *Art Bulletin,* XIX (1937), 561–579, and his corrections of this reconstruction in his *Tomb Sculpture,* ed. H. W. Janson (New York, n.d.), pp. 88–89.

14 See Tolnay, *Michelangelo. IV,* pp. 23–24.

15 See Erwin Panofsky, *Studies in Iconology* (New York, 1939), p. 192.

16 Pico della Mirandola, *Oratio de hominis dignitate,* trans. Elizabeth Livermore Forbes (Lexington, Ky., 1948), p. 10.

17 See Panofsky, *Studies,* pp. 138–139, and references.

18 Letter from Florence, December 1523, to Ser Giovan Francesco Fattucci in Rome, No. 157 in *The Letters of Michelangelo,* trans. and ed. E. H. Ramsden (Stanford, 1963), I, 149. The sculptor later repeated this point in the October 1542 letter already referred to (n. 12, above), but because of their self-justificatory intent (as Pope-Hennessy, II, 17, remarks) "neither can be accepted at its face value." In point of fact the total number of statues would have been reduced by placing the tomb's back against a wall. For the details of this second contract, see *Le lettere,* ed. Milanesi, pp. 635 ff.

19 Condivi, *Vita,* fol. 16ʳ: ". . . altre statue legate, come prigioni, le quali rappresentauano l'arti liberali, similmente Pittura, Scultura, & Architettura, ogniuna colle sue note, si che facilmente potesse esser conosciuta, per quel che era, de notando per queste, in sieme con Papa Giulio, esser prigioni della morte, tutte le virtù, come quelle che non fusser mai per trouare da chi cotanto fussero fauorite et nutrite, quanto da lui."

20 Vasari, *Le Vite de piu eccellenti architetti, pittori, et scultori* (Florence, 1550), p. 960; (Florence, 1568), p. 727: ". . . questi prigioni erano tutte le prouincie soggiogate da questo Pontefice, & fatte obediente al la Chiesa Apostolica; et altre statue diuerse pur legate errano tutte le virtu, et arte ingegnose . . . ."

21 Tolnay, *Michelangelo. IV,* p. 24.
22 Edgar Wind, *Pagan Mysteries in the Renaissance* (London, 1958), p. 152.
23 See Horst W. Janson, *Apes and Ape Lore in the Middle Ages and the Renaissance* (London, 1952), pp. 295 ff.
24 See Tolnay, *Michelangelo. IV,* pp. 98–99, 38.
25 See, besides this sketch after the wax figures in the lost model, and the Berlin copy after the drawing for the 1513 contract, another studio drawing of the lower story of the 1505–1513 tomb in the Uffizi (in Tolnay, *Michelangelo. IV,* Fig. 97).
26 Tolnay, *Michelangelo. IV,* p. 34; see also the discussion in Luitpold Dussler, *Die Zeichnungen des Michelangelo* (Berlin, 1959), p. 122.
27 See Panofsky, *Studies,* pp. 194–197, and his illustrations of moralized fettered prisoners, Plate LXXV.
28 See *Le lettere,* ed. Milanesi, pp. 644 ff. For reasons for supposing that the 1516 reduction was at the instance of the heirs and not the artist, see Ramsden's discussion in *The Letters,* I, 252–255.
29 See Johannes Wilde, *Michelangelo's "Victory,"* The Thirty-sixth Charlton Lecture (Oxford, 1954), pp. 5–6.
30 This interpretation is by no means certain. In the contract (in *Le lettere,* ed. Milanesi, p. 646), the pertinent passage reads: ". . . ne quali in ogni uno [i.e., of the "tabernacoli"] . . . viene una figura simile a le supradite." The four slaves referred to "supradite" are there described only as "quatre figure tonde di marmo tre bracia et mezo l'una . . . ." But I do not see the evidence for Wilde's saying (in *Michelangelo's "Victory,"* p. 9) that the earlier Victory groups "were to be replaced by single figures which nevertheless have clearly the same meaning."
31 See *The Letters,* ed. Ramsden, I, 162 (Nos. 173 and 174).
32 Ibid., I, 166 (No. 178).
33 See the *Nuovo contratto* in *Le lettere,* ed. Milanesi, pp. 702 ff.
34 The contract was signed 29 April 1532; for the letter, of 15 March 1532, see *Les Correspondants de Michel-Ange,* ed. Gaetano Milanesi (Paris, 1890), I, 82: "Credo, Compare mio, queste parolle ve faranno fastidio, ma se le pigliate per el verso, non vi daranno noia alcuna, perchè a vui sta mandare quello pare piace a vui, se non fusse altro che doi pezzi de pietra abozata, loro non sanno quello c'è particularmente, pur che con qualche demostratione appara che ce sia qual cosa per detta opera."
35 Wilde, *Michelangelo's "Victory,"* p. 21.
36 These evidently were the figures assigned for execution by Raffaello da Montelupo in the contract of 27 February 1542 (*Le lettere,* ed. Milanesi, p. 709). Michelangelo, in his petition to Pope Paul III, 20 July 1542, recounts this disposition of three of the statues to Montelupo for "finishing," names them, and claims that "the said three statues . . . were well advanced" (*The Letters,* ed. Ramsden, II, 21). Wilde, in his reconstruction of the secret project (*Michelangelo's "Victory,"* Fig. 2), places the "Moses" on the second story directly above the "Victory." This disposition, especially for a figure originally designed for a corner, appears unlikely in such a full revision of the sculptural enterprise. But the point about the relative size of first and second story figures remains

unaffected. The "Moses" is 8 feet 3½ inches; the "Victory," 8 feet, 7 inches.

37 Panofsky, *Studies,* p. 196.

38 Tolnay, *Michelangelo. IV,* p. 59.

39 Hence the *Hermae,* or *Termini* (Condivi's and Vasari's name), the symbols of death (Carl Justi's interpretation) which mark the upper boundary of the first register in the completed tomb (Fig. 4), are half figures of old men (see Tolnay, *Michelangelo. IV,* Figs. 84–87). In the Berlin drawing (Fig. 5), the herms are females; they are old men in a drawing by Aristotile da Sangallo of the architecture of the tomb according to the projects of 1516 and 1532 (Uffizi, No. 525, 741A; in Tolnay, *IV,* Fig. 98).

40 Pico della Mirandola, *Commento,* ii.xv, in Girolamo Benivieni, *Opere* . . . (Venice, 1522), fol. 29ʳ:
   "Prima lo essere uerde, non e altro che permanere & durare la cosa nel suo essere integra & sanza labefattione alcuna, ne per altro si chiama la giouanezza uerde, se non perche alhora lhuomo ha lo essere suo integro & perfetto, ilquale del suo uigore & sua integrita con gli anni sempre poi piu & piu perdendo uiene ad annularsi il tutto, & conciosia che ogni cosa composta tanto duri nel suo essere, quanto dura quella proportione debita che unisce le parti sua ad unione di quella, ne sia Venere altro che questa proportione, meritamente essa Viridita non e altro che una proprieta consequente à essa Venere. Et pero doue e la prima & uera Venere, cioe nel mondo ideale, ui si truoua anchora la uera uiridita, per essere ogni natura intelligibile, intra mutabile dalla integrita dello essere suo, & in tutto insenescibile, laqual proprietà in tanto deriua alle cose sensibili in quanto essa Venera possono participare, perche mentre in loro dura quella proportione, in tanto durano & si mantengono uerde . . . ."

41 Condivi, *Vita,* fol. 12ʳ⁻ᵛ.

42 Pico, *Oratio de hominis dignitate,* p. 4: "'. . . Poteris in inferiora quae sunt bruta degenerare; poteris in superiora quae sunt divina ex tui animi sententia regenerari.'"

43 Wilde, *Michelangelo's "Victory,"* p. 20.

44 Marsilio Ficino, *Opera omnia* (Basel, 1576; reproduction, Turin, 1959), I, 481. The entire passage reads:
   "Itaque fratres, si Christus caput nostrum est in cœlo, nos membra, quatenus in terra sumus, tamquam membra seiuncta, motum, sensum, uitam amittimus, nisi quatenus fide, spe, charitate ad ipsum, quasi tribus neruis alligati, manemus. Quæramus igitur superius ascendendo arctius alligari Christo, qui sursum est, ne penitus pereamus. Sapiamus & gustemus, quæ sursum sunt. Terrenas escas passim paratas à Diabolo fugiamus: harum enim sapore uelut hamo nos illaqueat, & sapore detinet diuturno, ne euolemus ad Christum. Igitur quæ sursum sunt sapite. Animalis quidem & diabolicus homo, qui in nobis erat, iam per passionem et resurrectionem mortuus est. Interea spiritali homine uiuimus, donec uitæ gloriæ manifestetur in nobis, quæ nunc nobis est abscondita, & reseruatur in Christo apud Patrem."

45 See Panofsky, *Studies,* p. 211, Fig. 157, and citation.

46 For discussion, see Otto Demus, *Die Mosaiken von San Marco in Venedig, 1100–1300* (Baden, 1935).

47 See Ficino, *Opera*, I, 25.

48 The mature nude Christ in the Minerva and the tremendously massive and powerful Divine Judge of the Sistine wall do not invite meaningful comparison, though it is interesting that a sketch apparently based on the former work (Archivio Buonarroti, No. 101; ca. 1525–1530) has been viewed as preparing the way to the design of the Victory group (Charles de Tolnay, *Michelangelo. III: The Medici Chapel* (Princeton, 1948), pp. 92–93 and Fig. 138). More fruitful associations can be established, I think, with several of the Risen Christ figures in the drawings of the Resurrection treated by Wilde as a series dating from 1532–1533, "more especially from Michelangelo's ten months stay in Rome when he was given permission by the pope to resume his work on the Julius Monument."—Johannes Wilde, *Italian Drawings in the Department of Prints and Drawings in the British Museum: Michelangelo and His Studio* (London, 1953), pp. 89–90. Indeed, Wilde (p. 88) thinks the pen and ink drawing of Victory (Casa Buonarroti, No. 51F^r; my Fig. 18) "may have been copied from a lost variant of the figure of Christ" in one of the British Museum Resurrection drawings (No. 53). I incline, however, to an earlier date for the original of this copy.

49 See, e.g., Panofsky, *Studies*, pp. 155 ff.

50 See H. W. Janson, "The Image of Man in Renaissance Art: From Donatello to Michelangelo," in *The Renaissance Image of Man and the World*, ed. Bernard O'Kelly (Columbus, Ohio, 1966), p. 94, and his detailed discussion in *The Sculpture of Donatello* (Princeton, 1957), II, 77–86.

51 Colin Eisler, "The Athlete of Virtue: The Iconography of Asceticism," in *De Artibus Opuscula XL: Essays in Honor of Erwin Panofsky*, ed. Millard Meiss (New York, 1961), pp. 92–95.

52 Panofsky, *Studies*, p. 218n. Cf. Tolnay, *Michelangelo. IV*, p. 112; also (though he dissociated the group from the Julius Tomb) the earlier interpretation of this kind by A. E. Brinckmann, *Barockskulptur* (Potsdam, n.d.), pp. 57–60.

53 Panofsky, *Studies*, p. 218n. It should be recalled that Vasari says that ca. 1533, when Michelangelo was supposed to be busy with the cartoons for "The Last Judgment," he "segretamente lavorava sopra le statue che andavano a detta sepoltura."—*Vite*, ed. Milanesi, VII, 205.

54 See the sensitive discussion in Nesca A. Robb, *Neoplatonism of the Italian Renaissance* (London, 1935), pp. 239–261.

55 "Neque amor sine religione, neque religio sine amore laudatur."—Letter to Filippo Controni, in *Opera*, I, 632 (cited by Panofsky, *Studies*, p. 141): ". . . agnoscas & amorem meum religiosum esse, & religionem amatoriam."

56 Wind, *Pagan Mysteries*, pp. 133–134.

57 Pico, *Commento*, II.xxi, in Benivieni, *Opere*, fol. 34^{r-v}:
". . . Venere non è altro che lordine di quelle idee, dalquale depende lordine mondano chiamato Fato, seguità che Venere domini à esse Fato, ilquale Fato in tre parti è diuiso, & disegnato per è nomi delle tre parce, Cloto, Lachesis, & Atropos, perche quello che è unito nella prouidentia & misurato da una indiuisibile misura della eternita fatto gia nel fato temporale, si diuide in tre parti, cioè presente, preterito, & futuro . . . ."

Di qui si puo intendere che al fato non sono sottoposte se non le cose temporale, & queste sono quelle che son corporee, & pero essendo lalma rationale incorporea non è sottoposta al fato, anzi domina à quello, ma bene è sottoposta alla prouidentia & serue à quella, ilquale seruire è una uera libertà, perche se la uolunta nostra obedisse alla legge della prouidentia . . . ."

58 Ficino, *Commentary on Plato's "Symposium,"* trans. Sears Reynold Jayne, University of Missouri Studies, XIX, 1 (Columbia, Mo., 1944), pp. 133–134. For discussion, see Paul Oskar Kristeller, *The Philosophy of Marsilio Ficino,* trans. Virginia Conant (New York, 1943), p. 268.

59 As Robert J. Clements has noted, in *The Poetry of Michelangelo* (New York, 1965), pp. 75, 121, the word "velo" is used here, as in several other of the poems, in the sense of the nude male body. Cf. G 209, G 215, G 227.

60 Pico, *Commento,* II.xxiv, in Benivieni, *Opere,* fols. 37ᵛ–38ʳ, trans. Edmund G. Gardner in his edition of Stanley's *A Platonick Discourse upon Love by Pico della Mirandola* (London, 1914), p. xxiii.

61 "Comento sopra alcuni de' suoi sonetti," in Lorenzo de' Medici, *Opere,* ed. Attilio Simioni (Bari, 1913), I, 24: ". . . il principio dell'amorosa vita proceder dalla morte, perché chi vive ad amore, muore prima all'altre cose. E, se lo amore ha in sé quella perfezione che già abbiamo detto, è impossibile venire a tale perfezione se prima non si muore, quanto alle cose più imperfette."

62 Wind, *Pagan Mysteries,* p. 155.

63 Baldesar Castiglione, *The Book of the Courtier,* trans. Charles S. Singleton (Garden City, 1959), IV, [70] (p. 357). Cf. Ficino, *Commentary on Plato's "Symposium,"* p. 141: "It also often happens that the lover wishes to transform himself into the person of the loved one. This is really quite reasonable, for he wishes and tries to become God instead of man; and who would not exchange humanity for divinity?" For fundamental discussion of love as death and resurrection in the beloved, see Speech II, Chap. VIII (pp. 143 ff.).

64 For a convenient recent summary of opinion on the drawing (Casa Buonarroti, No. 51Fʳ), see Paola Barocchi, *Michelangelo e la sua scuola* (Florence, 1962), p. 251. For further discussion, see Dussler, *Zeichnungen,* p. 218; Karl A. Laux, *Michelangelos Juliusmonument* (Berlin, 1943), pp. 52–53, and Tolnay, *Michelangelo. IV,* pp. 148–149.

65 From the rendering of "Non è sempra di colpa" (G 260) by J. A. Symonds, *The Sonnets of Michelangelo* (London, 1950), p. 129.

66 On the basic sources, from Xenophon to Landino, of the Neoplatonically biased, idealistic interpretation of the myth assumed by Michelangelo, see Panofsky, *Studies,* pp. 213–216. Claude Mignault's elaborate commentary in *Omnia Andreæ Alciati V. C. Emblemata* (Antwerp, 1577), p. 63, provides a typical view: ". . . per Ganymedem ab aquila raptum, animam humanam intelligimus, quæ, vt ait Plotinus, tum condere caput intra cælum dicitur, cùm relicta quasi corporis secretione, cælestia mentis oculo contemplatur: quod sanè absque raptu quodam fieri non potest. Plato etiam in Phædone & Theæteto, cùm iubet animam à corpore segregare, non loco segregandam esse intelligit, sed monet ne corpori animus adhærescat, neque ob corporis commercium à mente

superiore fiat alienus, coneturque quantum fieri poterit, subditam sibi animæ speciem ad superiora perducere."

67 Already adduced in connection with the "Ganymede" by F. Wickhoff, "Die Antike im Bildungsgange Michelangelos," *Mitteilungen des Instituts für oesterreichische Geschichtsforschung*, III (1882), 434. Regarding the phrase, "col vostro ingegno al ciel," in the next line, note the relevant significances of the eagle, s.v. "INGENIVM VELOX," in Ioannis-Pierius Valerianus Bolzanius, *Hieroglyphica sive de Sacris Aegyptiorvm Literis Commentarii* (Basel, 1556), fol. 141ᵛ; cf. Cesare Ripa, *Iconologia* (Rome, 1603), p. 390, s.v. "Pensiero"; also the Mignault commentary on Alciati's version of the emblem reproduced on my part-title page (Leyden, 1608, p. 455): "Per alas siue pennas, vigorem ingenij & acumen intellige."

68 See *Allegoriæ, PL*, CXII, col. 975: "*Juventus, reversio ad bonum, ut in Psalmis [cii.5]*" and Nicolas de Lyra, in *Biblia*, III, fol. 238ʳ: ". . . scilicet in resurrectione futura, qua resurgent in ætate virili." Also Valerianus, *Hieroglyphica*, fol. 141ʳ, s.v. "IVVENTUS RENOVATA."

69 See Charles S. Singleton, "In Exitu Israel De Aegypto," *Seventy-eighth Annual Report of the Dante Society* (Boston, 1960), p. 21, on the Ganymede-eagle passage in *Purgatorio*, IX.23.

70 See Panofsky, *Studies*, pp. 216–217, and citations. See also, on the treatment of his bonds as one indication of the significant passivity of the figure, Baruch D. Kirschenbaum, "Reflections on Michelangelo's Drawings for Cavalieri," *Gazette des Beaux-Arts*, Series VI, No. 38 (1951; published 1960), p. 102.

71 Benivieni, *Canzoniere dell'Amor Divino* (Florence, 1500), Pt. II, Canzone II, fol. 57ʳ, quoted by Robb, in *Neoplatonism*, p. 116: "nostra mente smarrita / ben disia el vero sole: ma l'ombra piglia."

72 In the light of the undoubted fact that Michelangelo and Vittoria Colonna, who shared religious ideas, also "read each others' rhymes assiduously," it is instructive to see what the Marchioness made of G 87 in echoing it (Clements, *Poetry of Michelangelo*, p. 328):

> Squarcia 'l vel tu, Signor! Rompi quel muro
> Ch'ancor gli copre; e di quell'ombre antiche
> Del vecchio Adamo freddo, empio, nemiche
> Al divin raggio tuo caldo e securo.

Michelangelo movingly confronts in G 276 (first version, p. 444) the difficulty of rising "a l'alte e diue / belleze i buon desir da quelle electi" for one given by life itself to living by "error" and by "fire."

73 The visual symbolism clearly evokes the long conventional values of legs and feet as the "members . . . upon the earth" which Christians are enjoined to "mortify" (Col. iii.5). Some of the elaborately developed conceptual imagery and its background is discussed in John Freccero, "Dante's Firm Foot and the Journey without a Guide," *Harvard Theological Review*, LII (1959), 245–281.

Is it possible that the young Victor's gesture with his chiton has something to do with the "clothing" image in "induite novum hominem" (Eph. vii.24)? Such drawing of actional metaphors from the Old Man–New Man figures does occur in literature. (See, e.g., Robert P. Miller,

"Chaucer's Pardoner, the Scriptural Eunuch, and the Pardoner's Tale," *Speculum,* xxx (1955), 189*n*36.) As for the sketched quasi-Roman armor of the Vanquished, there can be little question, of course, of its appropriateness in a statue concerned with the *vita vetus* overcome by the New Man. But one associative ground for that propriety perhaps deserves comment. That the model for such "newness of life" is "Christ . . . raised up from the dead" (Rom. vi.4) underscores the significance of the probable links between the "Victory" and Michelangelo's series of drawings of the Resurrection (see above, n. 48). This reminds us that in many Renaissance depictions of the Resurrection familiar to the artist (e.g., Della Robbia's in the Duomo at Florence) the soldiers at the tomb, below the triumphant risen Christ and contrasted with Him, wear Roman armor.

74 I should think this more likely accounts for the Victor's joyless expression than that he is "saddened by his own triumph" (Panofsky, *Studies,* p. 218) or "wishes to forget it" (Michele Saponaro, *Michel-Angelo,* trans. C. J. Richards [London, 1951], pp. 106–107). Cf. Panofsky's own comments on the erroneous "dramatic" interpretations of the action of Michelangelo's "Moses" (*Studies,* p. 193 and n. 68). For evidences of Michelangelo's early and continuing interest in the ancient image of the body as the soul's prison, see his quotation of Petrarch's *Triumfo della morte,* ii, 34, on a sheet dated 1501 ("La morte è 'l fin d'una prigione scura" [in *Rime,* ed. Girardi, App. No. 1]); also G 106, G 197, and G 264.

In appreciating the significance of the "Victory's" intended placement on the terrestrial level, it is worth noting that when, in 1542, Michelangelo finally planned to put the "Moses," a figure of spiritual domination, on the first level, he petitioned Pope Paul to be allowed to substitute the "Leah" and "Rachel" for the almost finished two Louvre "Captives," because the latter "are unsuited to the present design, nor would they by any means be appropriate for it."—*The Letters,* ed. Ramsden, ii, 19.

75 Clements (*Poetry of Michelangelo*), who remarks that soaring ascent (and falling) is a preoccupation of Michelangelo's art, discusses the theme of the wings of the soul in the *Rime* (pp. 232–234), though not, I think, with sufficiently careful distinction among Michelangelo's variations upon it. On the Christian image of *alae spirituales,* see, e.g., Gregory, in *PL,* lxxvi, cols. 297, 898, etc.; on Landino, see n. 17 above. It will be convenient to have the famous *Phaedrus* passage before us (*The Dialogues of Plato,* trans. B. Jowett, 3d ed. [Oxford, 1892], i, 452–453):

". . . And now let us ask the reason why the soul loses her wings!

"The wing is the corporeal element which is most akin to the divine, and which by nature tends to soar aloft and carry that which gravitates downwards into the upper region, which is the habitation of the gods. The divine is beauty, wisdom, goodness, and the like; and by these the wing of the soul is nourished, and grows apace; but when fed upon evil and foulness and the opposite of good, wastes and falls away."

Ficino uses the image of "gravity" for that manifestation of "the 'preponderance' of love for the body" which leads guilty souls after death to their appropriately low "place for purification and punishment" (see Kristeller, *Philosophy of Marsilio Ficino*, pp. 391–392). We should also note here the hieroglyph of wings-countered-by-a-weight (often suspended by a bond or chain) so frequently encountered in emblematic literature from the *Hypnerotomachia* on. (The device on my part-title page is an instance.) The various values given this symbol are discussed by Mario Praz, *Studies in Seventeenth-Century Imagery*, 2d ed. (Rome, 1964), pp. 35–38, Figs. 4–7: in Sambucus it is used in emblematizing "Physicae ac Metaphysicae differentia" (*Emblemata* [Leyden, 1599], pp. 71–72), in Hadrianus Junius, "Celeritatem mora, et haec illam vicissim temperet" (*Emblemata* [Leyden, 1596], p. 38), and in Alciati, "Paupertatem summis ingeniis obesse, ne prouehantur." Later emblems develop more distinctly spiritual senses. One in the Jesuit Hermann Hugo's very popular *Pia Desideria* (Antwerp, 1624), No. 39, develops this image in Christian terms (and for Baroque taste) to express the spiritual conflict in Phil. i.23 ("Coarctor e duobus, desiderium habens dissolvi, et esse cum Christo"). This shows winged Anima striving to soar heavenward toward the figure of Divine Love, but held back by the weight of the orb to which her leg is chained (see Praz, *Seventeenth-Century Imagery*, pp. 146–147, and Fig. 62). For related images (with the chains, but without the wings), see, e.g., Jacobus à Bruck, *Emblemata moralia et bellica* (Strasburg, 1615), emblem 8, and the anonymous *Amoris Divini et Humani Effectus . . .* (Antwerp, 1626).

76 Pico della Mirandola, *Of Being and Unity* (*De ente et uno*), trans. Victor Michael Hamm (Milwaukee, 1943), pp. 33–34. Cf. Psalm liv:7, "Quis dabit mihi pennas sicut columbæ, et volabo, et requiescam."

77 The Pauline text (Col. iii.1 ff.) Neoplatonically developed by Pico is an important one for the opposition between "things above" and "things on the earth" so fundamental in Christian representation:

"If ye then be risen with Christ, seek those things which are above, where Christ sitteth on the right hand of God.

"Set your affection on things above, not on things on the earth."

The relevance of this opposition to changing Renaissance fashions in funerary monuments is amusingly remarked by John Webster in *The Duchess of Malfi*, IV.ii.156–162 (ed. John Russell Brown, The Revels Plays, Cambridge, Mass., 1964): "princes' images on their tombs do not lie, as they were wont, seeming to pray up to heaven, . . . but as their minds were wholly bent upon the world, the self-same way they seem to turn their faces."

The direction of the gaze of the Vanquished surely is as significant as what the "Moses" looks upon ("the 'splendour of the light divine'"— Panofsky, *Studies*, p. 193). In the completed Julius monument (Fig. 4) we can see the care, in terms of iconographic qualifications, exercised by Michelangelo to insure for a contrasting downward gaze a different, non-pejorative value. The "Rachel," personifying the *vita contemplativa*, prayerfully looks heavenward with the "occhi alzati" (Ripa, *Iconologia*) familiar in representations of Hope; the "Leah," typifying the *vita activa*, gazes downward, but somewhat inclines her head toward a mirror held up before her in her right hand. In this, Condivi inaccurately says, she attentively contemplates herself; but he probably is

partly right in asserting that it signifies "our actions ought to be performed considerately." He adds, after noting the garland in her left
hand, that Michelangelo was here following the dream of Leah in *Purgatorio* xxvii.97–103. However, in Dante it is her "sister" (Rachel) who,
totally preoccupied with "seeing," gazes so on her mirror; Leah, instead,
gathers with her hands an adorning garland (in Michelangelo, of
laurel) to please her at the glass. Michelangelo's Rachel has no mirror;
presumably, the looking glass held by his figure of the active life guid-
ingly reflects, as, indeed, her beauty adorned with virtuous action itself
must mirror, what the "Rachel" directly contemplates. (Michelangelo's
share in the finishing of these statues remains uncertain. Still, since the
pupil of only one of the Victor's eyes was carved, it is perhaps worth
noting that the pupils of the "Leah's" eyes have been executed, those
of the "Rachel" have not.)

For relevant secular (and Neoplatonically influenced) versions of the
opposition, see the contrasting figures of Theory and Experience on the
title page of Vicenzo Scamozzi's *L'Idea Della Architettvra Vniversale*
(Venice, 1615) and those of Theory and Practice in Ripa and in Inigo
Jones's imitations (see D. J. Gordon, "Poet and Architect: The Intellectual Setting of the Quarrel between Ben Jonson and Inigo Jones,"
JWCI, xii [1949], 167, and Plates 30, 31 b, c). Theory (concerned with
Reason and the operations of the Intellect) looks up; Practice (concerned with sensible experience only) looks down. In contrast with the
youthful figure of Theory, Practice is represented as old (as Gordon,
following Ripa, explains) "because Practice follows ancient usages, is
easily deceived, doubtful, suspicious, careless of principles: evils opposed
to the light that Theory brings."

78 See, e.g., Augustine, *De Moribus Ecclesiæ Catholicæ*, in *Opera Omnia*,
editio Parisina altera . . . (Paris, 1836), I, col. 1134:
"*Primus homo de terra, terrenus; secundus homo de cœlo, cœlestis.
Qualis terrenus, tales et terreni; qualis cœlestis, tales et cœlestes. Sicut
portavimus imaginem terreni, portemus et imaginem cœlestis* [I Cor.
xv.47–49]: hoc est, exuite veterem, et induite novum. Omne igitur offi-
cium temperantiæ, est exuere veterem hominem, et in Deo renovari;
id est, contemnere omnes corporeas illecebras, laudemque popularem,
totumque amorem ad invisibilia, et divina conferre. Unde illud sequitur
quod mirifice dictum est, *Si et exterior homo noster corrumpitur, sed
interior renovatur de die in diem* [II Cor. iv.16]."

79 Ficino, *Opera*, I, 658, 375. Pico restricts the Janus image to those celestial souls capable of managing the body without interrupting "intellet-
tuale contemplatione delle cose superiori" (*Commento*, II.xxv, in Benivieni, *Opere*, fol. 38ʳ·ᵛ). This is a Neoplatonic version of the familiar
figure, "simile à Giano" (Ripa, *Iconologia*, p. 416, s.v. Prudenza) to
represent Prudence, the one head looking forward at a mirror, a young
female, the other facing rear, concerned with "cose passate," an old
man. See Guy de Tervarent, *Attributs et symboles dans l'art profane,
1450–1600* (Geneva, 1958), cols. 406–407.

80 Ficino, *Opera*, I, 657; trans. Kristeller / Conant, *Philosophy of Marsilio
Ficino*, p. 396.

81 Ibid., p. 119; trans. ibid., p. 393.

82 Ibid., p. 345 (see also pp. 408, 627); trans. ibid., p. 364.
83 Ibid., p. 441; trans. ibid., p. 394.
84 Ibid., p. 382; trans. ibid., p. 391.
85 Ibid., pp. 382, 383; trans. ibid., p. 391.
86 Ibid., p. 681.
87 See in the poetry, e.g., G 164, G 276, and G 289. See also for further citation and discussion of the later verse, and for relevant comment on the rising wingless souls in "The Last Judgment," Charles de Tolnay, *Michelangelo. V: The Final Period* (Princeton, 1960), pp. 56–58.
88 Ficino, *Opera*, I, 680.
89 See T. W. Baldwin, *William Shakspere's Petty School* (Urbana, 1943), *passim*, and *William Shakspere's Small Latine & Lesse Greeke* (Urbana, 1944), II, 578; also Virgil K. Whitaker, *Shakespeare's Use of Learning* (San Marino, 1953), pp. 17–18.
90 See Robert P. Miller, in *Speculum*, XXX (1955), 180–199.
91 Rubens did a design for a ceiling painting in St. Charles, Antwerp (now in Vienna) in which Christ's Tempter is old; this can be seen in the Christoffel Jegher wood-engraving (proof state with corrections in Rubens' hand in Paris), reproduced in F. W. H. Hollstein, *Dutch and Flemish Etchings, Engravings, and Woodcuts* (Amsterdam, n.d.), IX, 184. This treatment of the Satanic figure had appeared in prints in the later sixteenth century, e.g. in Jérome Cock's "Temptation of Christ," reproduced in A. J. J. Delen, *Histoire de la gravure dans les anciens pays-bas et dans les provinces belges* (Paris, 1935), Plate XXIII.
92 "Inventory of ye p'ticulars appartaynyng to ye Company of ye Grocers. A.D. 1565," in *Norwich Pageants, The Grocer's Play: From a MS. in possession of Robert Fitch* (Norwich, 1856), p. 23.
93 John Bale, *A brefe Comedy or enterlude concernynge the temptacyon of our lorde* . . . (London, 1538), Tudor Facsimile Texts, 1909, sigs. D^v and Diij^v. On the implied polemical attack on "the feigned contemplative life," see T. W. Craik, *The Tudor Interlude* (Leicester, 1958), p. 88. The Satan of the Temptation similarly appears as a venerable-looking old hermit in an illustration in the manuscript of the *Mystère de la Passion*, Valenciennes, 1547 (Paris, Bibl. Nat. MS. fr. 12536). However, it should be remembered that the idea of the devil quoting scripture primarily underlies such disguises.
94 See, especially, R. Weaver, *An Enterlude called lusty Iuuentus* (London, [ca. 1550?]), Tudor Facsimile Texts, 1914, sig. [b4]^v, *A new and mery Enterlude, called the Triall of Treasure* . . . (London, 1567), Tudor Facsimile Texts, 1908, sig. [A4]^v; also W. Wager, *A very mery and Pythie Commedie, called The Longer thou Livest* . . . (London, [ca. 1568]), Tudor Facsimile Texts, 1910, sig. cij^r.
95 See John S. Weld, "Old Adam New Apparelled," SQ, VII (1956), 453–456.
96 The text used for Shakespearean references is *The Complete Works*, ed. George Lyman Kittredge (Boston, etc., 1936).
97 For a brief guide to the traditions which have been supposed involved in the characterization, see *Supplement to Henry IV, Part I: A New Variorum Edition of Shakespeare*, ed. G. Blakemore Evans, pp. 84–86, in SQ, VII (1956).

98 J. A. Bryant, Jr., "Prince Hal and the Ephesians," in *Hippolyta's View: Some Christian Aspects of Shakespeare's Plays* (Lexington, Ky., 1961), pp. 52–67, earlier published in *Sewanee Review*, LXVII (1959).

99 Jonas A. Barish, "The Turning Away of Prince Hal," *Shakespeare Studies*, I (1965), 9–17. For A. C. Bradley's classic discussion of "The Rejection of Falstaff," see *Oxford Lectures on Poetry*, 2d ed. (London, 1909), pp. 247–273.

100 Bryant, in *Hippolyta's View*, pp. 64–65.

101 See W. G. Bowling, "The Wild Prince Hal in Legend and Literature," *Washington University Studies*, XIII (1925–26), 305–334.

102 See, e.g., the "Pseudo-Elmham" life, *Thomæ de Elmham Vita & Gesta Henrici Quinti Anglorum Regis*, ed. Tho[mas] Hearne (Oxford, 1727), p. 15: "felici miraculo convertitur."

103 For discussion of the problem of the unity of the two parts, see especially Harold Jenkins, *The Structural Problem in Shakespeare's Henry IV* (London, 1956), and citations; also the *Part I Variorum Supplement*, pp. 35–55, and Irving Ribner, *The English History Play in the Age of Shakespeare* (Princeton, 1957), pp. 171 ff. The term "diptych" is used by G. K. Hunter, "*Henry IV* and the Elizabethan Two-Part Play," *RES* (n.s.), V (1954), 237; the limits of its appropriateness are discussed by Jenkins, p. 24.

104 See J. Dover Wilson, *The Fortunes of Falstaff* (Cambridge and New York, 1944), pp. 17–22; also Bernard Spivack, "Falstaff and the Psychomachia," *SQ*, VIII (1957), 449–459.

105 Robert Fabyan, *Fabyans cronycle* . . . (London, 1533 [written before 1513, first publ. 1516]), II, fol. clxxᵛ. Cf. *Historia Breuis Thomæ Walshingham, ab Edwardo primo, ad Henricum quintum* [1418] (London, 1574), p. 426; *Titi Livii Foro-Juliensis Vita Henrici Quinti, Regis Angliæ* [ca. 1437], ed. Tho[mas] Hearne (Oxford, 1716), p. 5; the "Pseudo-Elmham" *Vita* (cited above, n. 102), pp. 13–15; "The Translator of Livius," *The First English Life of King Henry the Fifth written in 1513* . . . , ed. Charles Lethbridge Kingsford (Oxford, 1911), p. 17; Robert Redmayne, "Vita Henrici Quinti" [ca. 1540], in *Memorials of Henry the Fifth*, ed. Charles Augustus Cole, Rolls Series (London, 1858), p. 11. Edward Halle (*The Vnion of the two noble and illustre famelies of Lancaster and Yorke* . . . [London, 1550], fol. iʳ) follows Fabyan (". . . determined with hymself to put on the shape of a new man"); and John Stow, in his *Chronicles* (London, 1580, p. 583) and later *Annales* (London, 1592, p. 549) copies the Translator of Livius. Holinshed (*Holinshed's Chronicles of England, Scotland, and Ireland* [London, 1808], III, 61) follows Halle and Stow but secularizes, so that Roy Battenhouse sees in his description of the conversion a reshaping of the Prince's "public image" instead of a Pauline *renovatio mentis* ("*Henry V* as Heroic Comedy," in *Essays and Studies on Shakespeare and the Elizabethan Drama in Honor of Hardin Craig*, ed. Richard Hosley [Columbia, Mo., 1962], pp. 170–171).

J. H. Walter (*King Henry V*, The Arden Edition [London, 1954], p. 9) remarks that "only Elmham's Liber Metricus has anything resembling Shakespeare's treatment" of Henry's change. "It describes the change, 'rex hominem veterem sic renovare.'" Actually, this phrase occurs in Elmham's treatment of severities toward heretics and Lollards after the start of Henry's reign; in *Memorials of Henry the Fifth*, p. 100, ll. 133–138:

> Hinc suspenduntur, tracti prius, igne cremantur
> Hæretici plures, conditione pari.
> Capta cohors Castri Veteris partita crematur;
> Rex hominem veterem sic renovare studet.
> In tellure satum lolium fit in igne crematum;
> Quisque pians gramen sit benedictus. Amen.

106 For the development, under the aegis of the *Psychomachia*, of this standard visual formula "for illustrating the victory of Christianity over its adversaries," see Adolf Katzenellenbogen, *Allegories of the Virtues and Vices*, Studies of the Warburg Institute, Vol. x (London, 1939), p. 14. On appearances of the "Image of Prostration" in the moralities, see Bernard Spivack, *Shakespeare and the Allegory of Evil* (New York, 1958), pp. 439–440.

107 C. L. Barber, *Shakespeare's Festive Comedy* (Princeton, 1959), chap. viii.

108 John Dover Wilson (*The First Part of The History of Henry IV* [Cambridge, 1946] p. 155) notes, regarding the phrase "that father ruffian" (II.iv. 500), that " 'Ruffian' was a cant word for the Devil." There are numerous similar references. See, e.g., in the same scene, ll. 249–250, and Richmond Noble, *Shakespeare's Biblical Knowledge* (London, 1935), p. 171.

109 For this function of "Monsieur Remorse" and some cogent reasons for Shakespeare's making Falstaff rather than Hal exhibit repentant moods, see Wilson, *Fortunes of Falstaff*, p. 33.

110 See John W. Shirley, "Falstaff, an Elizabethan Glutton," *PQ*, xvii (1938), 271–287.

111 From a burlesque almanac, *Vox Graculi, or Jack Dawes Prognostication*, 1623, quoted by Barber, *Shakespeare's Festive Comedy*, p. 72. See also Wilson, *Fortunes of Falstaff*, pp. 25–31.

112 In Alexander Nowell's *Catechism*, which Shakespeare probably studied in school (Whitaker, *Shakespeare's Use of Learning*, p. 20), he would have found *vetus homo* s.v. *Caro* in the "Vocabula Nostratia" following the text. See *A Catechism . . . Together with the Same Catechism Translated into English by Thomas Norton*, ed. for the Parker Society by G. E. Corrie (Cambridge, 1853), p. 99.

113 As Bryant notes (*Hippolyta's View*, p. 62) the John Oldcastle, or "Jockey," of *The Famous Victories of Henry the fifth* is not represented as old. But there is plentiful evidence that Falstaff in Shakespeare's play originally was called Oldcastle (see *Henry the Fourth, Part I: A New Variorum Edition*, ed. Samuel Burdett Hemingway [Philadelphia and London, 1936], pp. 447–456). And it is not too farfetched to suppose this name may have suggested to Shakespeare the use of the Old Man image. A grim wordplay in Elmham's *Liber Metricus* (quoted above, in note 105) emphasizes that the King's treatment of Oldcastle's party illustrates his efforts "hominem veterum . . . renovare."

114 On Falstaff's "wit of inversion" see S. L. Bethell, "The Comic Element

in Shakespeare's Histories," *Anglia*, LXXI (1952), 94–95. On the pretense of the Vices to be Virtues, see Morton W. Bloomfield, *The Seven
Deadly Sins* (East Lansing, 1952), p. 76; also Craik, *Tudor Interlude*,
pp. 87 ff., who notes (p. 60) similar comic claims made by Falstaff in
1 Henry IV, II.ii.78–79. From a different viewpoint, Derek Traversi
offers acute comment on Falstaff's pretended youth in *Shakespeare
from Richard II to Henry V* (Stanford, 1957), pp. 64–65, 124.

115 See, e.g., Ripa, *Iconologia*, p. 85 ("Consiglio"). For important sources,
see Aristotle *Nichomachean Ethics* 1143ᵇ11; Cicero *De senectute* vi.20;
Job xii.12; and Ecclesiasticus xxv.4–6: "Oh how comely is the wise-
dome of olde men, and vnderstanding and counsell to men of honour."
Bernard Spivack, "Falstaff and The Psychomachia," *SQ*, VIII (1957),
458n28, compares the earlier part of this encounter between Falstaff
and the Lord Chief Justice with that between the vice Inclination
(man's natural disposition to evil) and Sapience in *The Triall of
Treasure*, sig. Cᵛ, as an instance of Shakespeare's dependence on stock
morality motifs. Inclination certainly was represented as old; the age
of an Elder would have been appropriate for Sapience but I do not
find it specified in the text. (It is worth remarking that the Christian
hero of this interlude, Just, receives a crown as the fruit of his efforts.)
An impressive adaptation of this morality method of placing the hero
between two spiritually contrasted aged figures occurs in Marlowe's
Doctor Faustus in the scene where the Old Man urges the despairing
hero to call for divine mercy, and Mephostophilis, still in his guise as
an old Franciscan friar, offers him a dagger.

116 See *The Life of Sir John Oldcastle*, 1600, The Malone Society Reprints
(London, 1908), sig. A2ʳ.

117 Thomas Wilson, *A Christian Dictionarie* (London, 1612), p. 309; *The
Writings of John Bradford*, ed. for the Parker Society by Aubrey
Townsend (Cambridge, 1848), I, 297.

118 *The Decades of Henry Bullinger*, trans. H. I., ed. for the Parker Society
by the Rev. Thomas Harding, The Fourth Decade (Cambridge, 1851),
pp. 98–100.

119 Bryant, in *Hippolyta's View*, p. 61. For further commentary on "the
old church," see *The Second Part of Henry the Fourth: A New Variorum Edition*, ed. Matthias A. Shaaber (Philadelphia and London,
1940), p. 150.

120 See Noble, *Shakespeare's Biblical Knowledge*, p. 171.

121 *Writings of John Bradford*, I, 298.

122 John Payne's title-page border for John Downame, *The Christian Warfare*, 4th ed. (London, 1634), of which the bottom panel only is reproduced in my Figure 21, may be seen in its entirety in Samuel C.
Chew, *The Pilgrimage of Life* (New Haven and London, 1962), Fig.
74. In regard to the traditions which justify relating such an image to
these plays, it should be noted that the fusion of the Prodigal Son and
Pilgrimage of Life motives is already evidenced by St. Bernard of
Clairvaux in the twelfth century; see *PL*, CLXXXIII, cols. 757 ff.

123 Walter (*King Henry V*, Arden ed., p. 9) has noted the relevant passages: "'he, being dead unto sin . . . & being buried with Christ in his
death, maye crucifye the olde man, and utterlye abolyshe the whole

bodye of sinne, . . .'. Again, 'graunt that the olde Adam in this child may be so buryed, that the new man may be raised up in him'. And, '. . . that all carnall affections maye die in him, and that all thynges belongynge to the Spirite maye lyve and growe in him' (edn. 1560)."

124 See John Danby, *Shakespeare's Doctrine of Nature: A Study of King Lear* (London, 1949), p. 89.

125 For the other sources which Shakespeare appears to have fused in his memory with the passage in Spenser, see *The First Part of King Henry IV*, The Arden Edition, ed. A. R. Humphreys (London, 1960), pp. 201–202. That it was the combination of chivalric perfection and the idea of regeneration in Spenser's verses which made the dramatist turn to them for inspiration is stressed by Wilson, *Fortunes of Falstaff*, p. 65. Spenser's Well has been interpreted as a reference to the sacrament of baptism; see R. E. N. Dodge, "The Well of Life and the Tree of Life," *MP*, vi (1908), 194–195. But from early Christian times the eagle image, as in the *Physiologus*, was applied, with explicit reference to the Old Man, to repentance. See *Physiologus*, trans. James Carlill, in *The Epic of the Beast* (London and New York, n.d.), pp. 209–210; also Joachim Camerarius, *Symbolorvm & Emblematvm ex volatilibvs et insectis desumptorvm centvria tertia collecta* (Nuremberg, 1596), xvi, fol. 16ʳ·ᵛ. For a typical Elizabethan reference, see, e.g., Thomas Playfere, *The VVhole Sermons . . .* , 5th ed. (London, 1633), p. 12: "S. *Austin* witnesseth that the Eagle feeling his wings heauy, plungeth them in a fountaine, and so reneweth his strength: After the same sort a Christian feeling the heauy burthen of his sins, batheth himselfe in a fountaine of teares, and so washing off the old man, which is the body of sinne, is made young againe, and lusty as an Eagle." For basic discussion of the symbolism of the eagle, see Rudolf Wittkower, "Eagle and Serpent: A Study in the Migration of Symbols," *JWI*, ii (1938–39), 293–325.

126 See Barber, *Shakespeare's Festive Comedy*, pp. 207–208.

127 See W. Empson, *Some Versions of Pastoral* (Norfolk, n.d.), p. 43; also, for development of the theme in *2 Henry IV*, see Ronald Berman, "The Nature of Guilt in the Henry IV Plays," *Shakespeare Studies*, i (1965), pp. 18–28.

128 Barber, *Shakespeare's Festive Comedy*, p. 200.

129 First cited by Samuel C. Chew, *The Virtues Reconciled* (Toronto, 1947), pp. 16–17.

130 Dr. Johnson supposed Hal's reply only an excrescent repetition (see *Henry the Fourth, Part I: New Variorum*, p. 159); the speech has often been misread since. *Taken for* means "understood to be," and also "taken away in exchange for" (see Kittredge, in *Part I Variorum Supplement*, p. 24); but "taken for a joined stool" evokes the commonplace contemptuous or taunting apology for overlooking a person, "Cry you mercy, I took you for a joined stool" (see Morris Palmer Tilley, *A Dictionary of Proverbs in England in the Sixteenth and Seventeenth Centuries* [Ann Arbor, 1950], M897; cf. *King Lear*, iii.vi.55). In keeping with this, *state* refers not only to his "royal throne," but also to his "dignity" and his "rule" or "body politic" itself. A "leaden sword" is a "type of ineffectual weapon" (*OED*); a "leaden dagger" not only sug-

gests a mere "theatrical property" (Wilson) but of course a hierarchical baseness in contrast to "golden." As elsewhere in Shakespeare, the substitution of a dagger (associated with treachery and private vengeance) for a symbol of true magistracy (sword, scepter) is significant (see Chew, *Virtues Reconciled*, p. 48). The "pitiful bald crown" refers to what a syphilitic Falstaff must get in exchange for the literal *luxuria* the cushion can represent.

131 Apart from Falstaff, the King, and the Lord Chief Justice, there are Northumberland, the Archbishop of York, and Justices Shallow and Silence. In regard to certain aspects of Shallow as one sort of epitomic old man figure (Jacques' "fifth age," the justice: *As You Like It*, II.vii. 253), we must recall with Falstaff the traditional association of age and cupidity, especially in the form of avarice: "A man can no more separate age and covetousness than 'a can part young limbs and lechery" (*2 Henry IV*, I.iii.256–257). On this theme, important for English drama since *The Castle of Perseverance* (ll. 5350–5473), see, e.g., Bloomfield, *Seven Deadly Sins*, pp. 76, 92, 432; and Celeste Turner Wright, "Some Conventions regarding the Usurer in Elizabethan Literature," *SP*, XXXI (1934), 176.

132 Traversi, *Shakespeare*, pp. 165, 143; cf. Berman, in *Shakespeare Studies*, I, 25, for a reading of the Gaultree sequence similarly delimited by lack of reference to the Old Man.

133 On the relation of the New Man and adoption by God, see, e.g., *Prayers and Other Pieces of Thomas Becon*, ed. for the Parker Society by the Rev. John Ayre (Cambridge, 1844), p. 622.

134 W. J. Birch (1848) first pointed out "the curious fact" that these "'are the words Jesus is to use'" (*Second Part: New Variorum*, p. 446). My text for Scripture here is the Genevan-Tomson (*The Bible* . . . [London, 1603]), the popular version Shakespeare seems most often to have in mind (see Noble, *Shakespeare's Biblical Knowledge*, p. 58).

135 Spivack, in *SQ*, VIII, 458n28, observes that exile, imprisonment, or hanging were standard dispositions of the Vices in moralities from 1530 onwards.

136 Barish, in *Shakespeare Studies*, I, 14.

137 See A. P. Rossiter, *Angel with Horns* (London, 1961), pp. 40–64; and the essay by Battenhouse, "*Henry V* as Heroic Comedy," cited above in n. 105.

138 Barish, in *Shakespeare Studies*, I, 10 ff.

139 Danby, *Shakespeare's Doctrine*, p. 91, and context.

140 See Panofsky, *Studies*, pp. 171–176.

141 See Madeleine Doran, *Endeavors of Art* (Madison, 1954), p. 304.

142 See Kenneth Clark, *The Nude* (New York, 1959), p. 279.

143 The quotations here and in the following sentence are from Panofsky, *Studies*, pp. 176–177, and 198–199.

144 Morey, *Christian Art*, pp. 61–62.

145 See Ernst Kantorowicz, *The King's Two Bodies: A Study in Medieval Political Theology* (Princeton, 1957).

146 Cf. Barish, in *Shakespeare Studies*, I, pp. 15–16, and citations.

1 William Empson, *Some Versions of Pastoral* (New York, 1960), p. 84.
2 On the Communion aspect of Ariel's feast, see Robert G. Hunter, *Shakespeare and the Comedy of Forgiveness* (New York, 1965), pp. 227–241.
3 On the poetry of *The Tempest*, see the superb essay in Reuben Brower's *The Fields of Light* (New York, 1951).
4 Francis Fergusson, "Hamlet: The Analogy of Action," chapter iv in *The Idea of a Theater* (Garden City, 1953), p. 143.
5 Kenneth Muir, *Last Periods of Shakespeare, Racine, and Ibsen* (Detroit, 1961), p. 52.
6 David Horowitz, *Shakespeare: An Existential View* (New York, 1965), p. 87. For a contrasting version of Prospero's control over his inclination towards revenge, see Bertrand Evans, *Shakespeare's Comedies* (Oxford, 1960), pp. 333–337. For criticism which tends from other points of view to support the present analysis, see Northrop Frye, *A Natural Perspective* (New York, 1965), pp. 118–159, and David William, "*The Tempest* on the Stage," in Stratford-upon-Avon Studies, 1: *Jacobean Theater* (London, 1960), pp. 133–157.
7 Paul's ship, like Alonzo's, is bound to Italy from Asia when it is "tossed with an exceeding tempest." An angel appears before Paul, telling him that the ship's passengers "must be cast into a certaine Iland." Paul promises the passengers that "there shall not an haire fall from the head of any of you." The voyage ends as "some on boardes, and some on certaine pieces of the shippe . . . they came all safe to land."—Acts xxxvii, Geneva Version. For an illuminating demonstration of how Shakespeare expanded his sources into the dramatic form of *The Tempest*, see Phillip Brockbank, "*The Tempest:* Conventions of Art and Empire," Stratford-upon-Avon Studies, viii: *Later Shakespeare* (New York, 1967), pp. 183–201.
8 Theodore Spencer, *Shakespeare and the Nature of Man* (New York, 1961), p. 198. See also Henri Fluchère, *Shakespeare and the Elizabethans* (New York, 1956), pp. 248–249.
9 This interpretation of Prospero places him closer to Marston's Altofronto than to the self-deposed Vincentio. Vincentio insists on controlling his manipulation to the very end and produces not a redemptive drama but a self-vindication. He is finally exposed by his production. As D. R. C. Marsh suggests, "The shifting vision of the play, which has exposed the pretensions of all the characters in turn, is turned in the final scene back on the Duke, showing how even his justice is rooted in the concerns of

the self."—"The Mood of *Measure for Measure*," *SQ*, xiv (1963), 37.
For another negative view of Vincentio, see Rebecca West, *The Court and the Castle* (New Haven, 1961), pp. 44–48. Most critics, of course, equate Vincentio and Prospero. See Harold S. Wilson, "Action and Symbol in *Measure for Measure* and *The Tempest*," *SQ*, iv (1953), 375–384; G. Wilson Knight, *The Wheel of Fire* (New York, 1957), pp. 76 and 79; and Francis Fergusson, Introduction to *The Tempest* (New York, 1961), p. 14. For a contrast between Vincentio and Prospero as dramatic devices, see Bertrand Evans, *Shakespeare's Comedies* (Oxford, 1960), p. 332.

10 Leslie Fiedler, "The Defense of the Illusion and the Creation of Myth," *English Institute Essays, 1948* (New York, 1949), p. 90.

11 Fergusson, "Hamlet: The Analogy of Action," p. 138.

12 Dover Wilson, *What Happens in Hamlet* (Cambridge, Eng., 1961), p. 197.

13 H. D. F. Kitto, *Form and Meaning in Drama* (New York, 1960), p. 311.

14 Andrew J. Green, "The Cunning of the Scene," *SQ*, iv (1953), 403. For similar views on the success of Hamlet's play, see *Shakespeare*, ed. Gilbert Harrison (New York, 1952), pp. 883–884; Irving Ribner, *Patterns of Shakespearian Tragedy* (London, 1960), p. 82; and Bernard Grebanier, *The Heart of Hamlet* (New York, 1960), pp. 403–406.

15 Hunter, *Shakespeare and the Comedy of Forgiveness*, p. 235.

16 Fergusson, "Hamlet: The Analogy of Action," p. 143.

17 Since Hamlet does not carry his thinking to the point of asking himself what he would do if Claudius confessed, conjecture on the point is irrelevant. Weston Babcock has him "dash across the stage and run [Claudius] through with his rapier."—*Hamlet: A Tragedy of Errors* (Lafayette, Ind., 1961), p. 101. I prefer to think of Hamlet arresting Claudius as a regicide, later to be brought to trial—but that suggestion is as idiosyncratic as Babcock's. It is idle to speculate on what Hamlet might have done after the confession, but it is *not* idle to postulate that confession, since Hamlet himself expresses the possibility. Obviously, Claudius, as regicide, would have to pay a price beyond heart's sorrow. Henry V makes the distinction between temporal and eternal punishment in sentencing the traitors to death and at the same time hoping for their salvation (ii.ii.166–181).

18 Harold Goddard, *The Meaning of Shakespeare* (Chicago, 1950), p. 364. Anyone familiar with Goddard's essay on *Hamlet* will recognize the extent of my indebtedness to him. For a conflicting version of Claudius's conscience, see Stanley Cooperman, "Shakespeare's Anti-Hero: Hamlet and the Underground Man," *Shakespeare Studies*, i (1965), 46–48.

19 Macbeth's banquet (iii.iv) is not merely deferred but broken up; Macbeth has cut himself off permanently from the healing powers of Communion. He has "Put rancours in the vessel of [his] peace" (iii.i.67). See J. P. Dyson, "The Structural Function of the Banquet Scene in *Macbeth*," *SQ*, xiv (1963), 369–378; and my "In Deepest Consequence: *Macbeth*," *SQ*, xviii (1967), 375–388.

20 Babcock, *Hamlet: A Tragedy of Errors*, p. 99.

21 Salvador de Madariaga, *On Hamlet* (London, 1948), pp. 89–90.

22 Eleanor Prosser, *Hamlet and Revenge* (Stanford, 1967), p. 179, n. 9.

Miss Prosser's valuable study appeared after I had completed this essay, hence I have been unable to avail myself completely of her many insights.

23 Alfred Harbage, *William Shakespeare* (New York, 1963), p. 324.
24 On the question of Hamlet's untoward behavior at this point, see Madariaga, *On Hamlet*, pp. 89–90; Goddard, *Meaning of Shakespeare*, pp. 366–368; and Dover Wilson, *What Happens in Hamlet*, p. 170.
25 Goddard, *Meaning of Shakespeare*, p. 364. On the play-within as torture device, see Dover Wilson, *What Happens in Hamlet*, pp. 174–197.
26 Quoted in Maynard Mack, "The World of Hamlet," *Yale Review*, XLI (1952), 518.
27 *Hamlet*, ed. George Lyman Kittredge (Boston, 1939), p. 229.
28 Roger L. Cox, "Hamlet's Hamartia: Aristotle or St. Paul?" *Yale Review*, LVI (1966), 347–364.
29 Fiedler, "Defense of the Illusion," p. 76.
30 *Johnson*, ed. Mona Wilson (Cambridge, Mass., 1951), p. 616.
31 *Coleridge's Writings on Shakespeare's Plays*, ed. Terrence Hawkes (New York, 1959), p. 163.
32 Fredson Bowers, "Hamlet as Minister and Scourge," *PMLA*, LXX (1955), 740–749.
33 Ibid., p. 745.
34 Ibid., p. 742.
35 Cf. Dover Wilson, "The play scene is the central point of *Hamlet*. It is the climax and crisis of the whole drama."—*What Happens in Hamlet*, p. 138.
36 Fredson Bowers, "Dramatic Structure and Criticism: Plot in *Hamlet*," *SQ*, IV (1964), 209.
37 Helen Gardner, *The Business of Criticism* (Oxford, 1959), pp. 25–51.
38 Derek Traversi, *An Approach to Shakespeare* (Garden City, 1956), p. 100.
39 M. R. Ridley, "Plot and Character in the Plays," in *The Living Shakespeare*, ed. Robert Gittings (New York, 1960), p. 82.
40 J. C. Maxwell, "Shakespeare: The Middle Plays," in *The Age of Shakespeare*, ed. Boris Ford (Baltimore, 1960), p. 210. For a discussion of *Hamlet's* superiority to other Elizabethan revenge plays, see J. J. Lawlor, "The Tragic Conflict in *Hamlet*," *Review of English Studies*, I (1960), 97–113, and Kenneth Muir, *Hamlet* (New York, 1963), pp. 55–61. For discussions relating Hamlet to Elizabethan ideas on revenge, see Prosser, *Hamlet and Revenge*, pp. 3–73; J. E. Hankins, *The Character of Hamlet and Other Essays* (Chapel Hill, 1941); Fredson Bowers, *Elizabethan Revenge Tragedy* (Princeton, 1940), pp. 3–61; Harold Jenkins, "The Tragedy of Revenge in Shakespeare and Webster," *Shakespeare Survey*, XIV (1961), 45–56; Lily Bess Campbell, "Theories of Revenge in Elizabethan England," *MP*, XXVIII (1931), 281–295; and Hiram Haydn, *The Counter-Renaissance* (New York, 1950), pp. 555–598.
41 Knight, *Wheel of Fire*, p. 20; Traversi, *Approach to Shakespeare*, p. 95.
42 John Holloway, *The Story of the Night* (Lincoln, Neb., 1961), p. 30.
43 For a discussion of *Hamlet's* relationship to the first years of the seventeenth century, see Paul Jorgensen, "Hamlet and the Restless Renais-

sance," in *Shakespearean Essays*, ed. Alwin Thaler and Norman Saunders (Knoxville, Tenn., 1964), pp. 131–143.

44 On the question of ritual in *Hamlet*, see Fergusson, "Hamlet: The Analogy of Action," and the interesting intertextual comments by William W. Main in his edition of *Hamlet* (New York, 1963), particularly on p. 231. For an explicit equation of Hamlet with the archetype of the fall, see Charles R. Woodard, "The Archetype of the Fall," *CE*, xxxviii (1967), 576–580.

45 D. G. James, *The Dream of Learning* (Oxford, 1951), p. 49.

46 Fiedler, "Defense of the Illusion," p. 90.

47 Arthur Sewell, *Character and Society in Shakespeare* (Oxford, 1951), p. 57.

48 Gardner, *Business of Criticism*, p. 50.

49 Quoted in Edith Sitwell, *A Notebook on William Shakespeare* (Boston, 1961), p. 82.

50 Sitwell, *A Notebook*, p. 82.

51 Grebanier, *Heart of Hamlet*, pp. 133 ff.

52 David Daiches, "Shakespeare's Poetry," in *The Living Shakespeare*, ed. Robert Gittings (New York, 1960), pp. 60–61.

53 For other possible readings, see the Furness Variorum Edition, pp. 34–35.

54 *Essays in Literary Criticism of George Santayana*, ed. Irving Singer (New York, 1956), p. 128.

55 Arthur Johnston, "The Player's Speech in *Hamlet*," *SQ*, xiii (1962), 24.

56 Prosser, *Hamlet and Revenge*, p. 153.

57 Johnston, "Player's Speech," p. 27.

58 Ibid., p. 28.

59 Dover Wilson, *What Happens in Hamlet*, p. 263. See also Muir, *Hamlet*, pp. 46–49.

60 Karl Polanyi, "Hamlet," *The Yale Review*, xliii (1954), 350.

61 Ribner, *Patterns of Shakespearian Tragedy*, p. 82.

62 S. F. Johnson, "The Regeneration of Hamlet," *SQ*, iii (1952), 206.

63 C. S. Lewis, "Hamlet: The Prince or the Poem," *Proceedings of the British Academy*, xxxviii (London, 1942), p. 148.

64 Spencer, *Shakespeare and the Nature of Man*, p. 108.

65 John Paterson, "Hamlet," *SQ*, ii (1952), 54.

66 Bertram Joseph, *Conscience and the King* (London, 1948), p. 143.

67 Roy Walker, *The Time is Out of Joint* (London, 1948), p. 143.

68 Fergusson, "Hamlet: The Analogy of Action," p. 142.

69 H. Granville-Barker, *Prefaces to Shakespeare* (Princeton, 1952), I, 253.

70 A. C. Bradley, *Shakespearean Tragedy* (New York, 1949), p. 143.

71 L. L. Schucking, *The Meaning of Hamlet* (Oxford, 1937), p. 167.

72 T. M. Parrott, *Shakespeare* (New York, 1931), II, 403.

73 Donald A. Stauffer, *Shakespeare's World of Images* (New York, 1949), p. 126.

74 H. B. Charlton, *Shakespearian Tragedy* (Cambridge, 1948), p. 103.

75 Bradley, *Shakespearean Tragedy*, p. 122.

76 Grebanier, *Heart of Hamlet*, p. 472.

77 Quoted in Maureen McKernan, *The Amazing Crime and Trial of Leopold and Loeb* (New York, 1957), pp. 176–179.

78 Alfred Harbage, *As They Liked It* (New York, 1961), p. 33.

79 Clifford P. Lyons, "'It appears so by the story': Notes on a Narrative-Thematic Emphasis in Shakespeare," *SQ*, IX (1958), 294.

80 Robert Ornstein, *The Moral Vision of Jacobean Tragedy* (Madison, 1960), p. 235.

81 Yet one critic can talk of the "confident heartwholeness of the new Hamlet" (the Hamlet of Act v)—B. L. Reid, "The Last Act and the Action of *Hamlet*," *Yale Review*, LIV (1964), 78.

82 James, *Dream of Learning*, p. 26.

83 Walter Kaufmann, *From Shakespeare to Existentialism* (Garden City, 1960), p. 22. For an existential approach to *Hamlet*, see Thomas McFarland, *Tragic Meanings in Shakespeare* (New York, 1966), pp. 17–59.

84 Laurence Michel, "Hamlet: Superman, Subchristian," *Centennial Review*, VI (1962), 230–244.

85 Jay Halio, "Hamlet's Alternatives," *Texas Studies in Literature and Language*, VIII (1966), 179.

86 Roy Battenhouse, "Stratford-upon-Avon Studies 5: *Hamlet*," *Shakespeare Studies*, I (1965), 357.

87 John F. Danby, "The Tragedies," *The Living Shakespeare*, ed. Robert Gittings (New York, 1960), p. 123.

88 T. S. Eliot, "Shakespeare and the Stoicism of Seneca," *Selected Essays* (London, 1932).

89 Gardner, *Business of Criticism*, p. 39.

90 Cf. John P. Farrell, "Hamlet carries to the duel the role of his father" ("Hamlet's Final Role: Symbolism in the Duel Scene," *Bucknell Review*, XIV [1966], 31), and Patrick Cruttwell, "[Hamlet] has done things as we all do in wars, he would rather not have done; but he believes it to be a just war and, all in all, he has borne himself well." ("The Morality of Hamlet," *Hamlet* [London, 1963], p. 128.)

91 Ornstein, *Moral Vision of Jacobean Tragedy*, p. 235.

In preparing the final draft of this study, I have eliminated virtually all references to the major book-length studies of Jane Austen: I mean Mary Lascelles' *Jane Austen and Her Art* (London, 1939); Marvin Mudrick's *Jane Austen, Irony as Defense and Discovery* (Princeton, 1952); Andrew H. Wright's *Jane Austen's Novels, A Study in Structure,* 2nd ed. (London, 1961); Howard S. Babb's *Jane Austen's Novels, The Fabric of Dialogue* (Columbus, 1962); and A. Walton Litz's *Jane Austen, A Study of Her Artistic Development* (New York, 1965)—which, incidentally, appeared after this study was completed. By so doing, I do not mean to claim for my own work an originality it does not possess. But I assume that anyone reading a long essay on Jane Austen in a publication of this kind will be familiar enough with these earlier critics to recognize the point at which my own argument significantly approaches or diverges from theirs; more particularly, it seems to me that the time has come to call a moratorium on footnotes devoted to caviling at the evident perversities of Mudrick's elegantly sustained argument. At the same time, I have not hesitated to cite significant shorter pieces which might well be unknown to those not professionally obliged to "keep up with" Jane Austen criticism and scholarship.

1 Lionel Trilling, "Manners, Morals, and the Novel," in *The Liberal Imagination* (Garden City, 1953), p. 206.

2 Mark Schorer, "Jane Austen," printed as Introduction to each volume of the series called *The Laurel Jane Austen* (New York, 1961), p. 8.

3 Erich Auerbach, *Mimesis, the Representation of Reality in Western Literature,* trans. Willard R. Trask (Princeton, 1953), pp. 457–458.

4 There are occasional passages in Jane Austen which seem to give the lie to this rule. Perhaps the most important occurs in *Mansfield Park,* when Sir Thomas, upbraiding Fanny for her refusal to consider Henry Crawford's proposal of marriage, speaks of "that independence of spirit, which prevails so much in modern days, even in young women . . ." (318). However, such comments seem to me instances of the perennial paternal horror at the ways of the younger generation—at "what the world is coming to!"—rather than specific observations of early nineteenth-century life. See also the sections on *Emma* on pp. 162–172, above.

Page references to Jane Austen's novels, included in the body of the text and in the notes, apply to the standard R. W. Chapman edition: *The Novels of Jane Austen,* 3d ed. (London, 1933): Volume i, *Sense and Sensibility;* Volume ii, *Pride and Prejudice;* Volume iii, *Mansfield Park;*

Volume IV, *Emma;* Volume V, *Northanger Abbey* and *Persuasion;* to these were added a Volume VI, *Minor Works,* in 1954.

I assume throughout that *Sense and Sensibility* and *Pride and Prejudice* as we know them represent, on the whole, a later stage of Jane Austen's development than *Northanger Abbey:* see Chapman, *Jane Austen, Facts and Problems,* rev. ed. (Oxford, 1947), pp. 42–44, 75–81, and B. C. Southam, *Jane Austen's Literary Manuscripts* (London, 1964), pp. 52–62.

5 Elie Halévy, *A History of the English People in the Nineteenth Century:* Vol. I, *England in 1815,* trans. E. I. Watkin and D. A. Backen (New York, 1949), 424. Halévy is the source of many of the historical generalizations in this chapter.

6 J. H. Hexter, "The Myth of the Middle Class in Tudor England," *Reappraisals in History* (Evanston, Ill., 1961), pp. 74–75.

7 See, for example, A. R. Humphreys, *The Augustan World* (London, 1954), pp. 2–4.

8 Chapman, *Facts and Problems,* p. 25. On pp. 198–199, Chapman adds that "the class to which Jane Austen and her Bertrams belonged regarded the aristocracy with suspicious hostility," and further that "dukes as a class, and baronets and country persons as a class, were then remote from each other; the former class despised its inferiors, and the inferiors retorted with moral reprobation."

9 It should be noted that the *OED* gives first recorded use of "middle class" as 1812, at the moment of Jane Austen's literary flowering. The date is suggestive: the term "middle class" may well reflect a contemporary attempt to denote the very conditions that Jane Austen describes.

10 Northrop Frye, "Towards Defining an Age of Sensibility," reprinted in *Eighteenth-Century English Literature, Modern Essays in Criticism,* ed. James L. Clifford (New York, 1959), p. 316.

11 Jane Austen's treatment of the ethics of female "accomplishments" is generally more subtle and indirect; a good illustration is provided by *Emma,* where the heroine's failure to buckle down to practice at the keyboard and to complete her drawings mirrors perfectly her moral deficiencies, namely her impatience, her intolerance, and her tendency to deny the homely realities of life in favor of undisciplined imaginings (the latter often of an aristocratic cast).

12 Halévy, *England in 1815,* p. 223.

13 It should be noted that, as the values that Jane Austen chooses to underscore are varied from novel to novel, so too are the symbols she employs: while London is identified with aristocratic moral delinquency and with social dishonesty in *Sense and Sensibility,* it is to be identified with capitalistic enterprise and with individual worth (as opposed to inherited rank) in *Pride and Prejudice.* Needless to say, a city like London is what one sees in it, and if the metaphoric use to which Jane Austen puts it is constantly changing, she is always careful to adjust the reader's response to her own.

14 See B. C. Southam, *Jane Austen's Literary Manuscripts,* pp. 64–65.

15 Q. D. Leavis, "A Critical Theory of Jane Austen's Writings," *Scrutiny,* X (June 1941), 61–87.

16 Southam, *Jane Austen's Literary Manuscripts,* p. 67.

17 D. J. Greene, "Jane Austen and the Peerage," *PMLA*, LXVIII (December 1953), 1017–31. Greene's scrupulous article contains much important evidence of the extensive social relevance of Jane Austen's work.

18 Lionel Trilling, *The Opposing Self* (New York, 1955), p. 211.

19 Philip Drew, "A Significant Incident in *Pride and Prejudice*," *Nineteenth-Century Fiction*, XIII (March 1959), 356–358, points out (356–357) that Darcy's initial response to the bourgeoisie is determined by the recentness of his sister's misadventure with Wickham. "Thus when Darcy comes to Netherfield he is not surprisingly still proud of having preserved the honor of the family, sensitive to any sign of fortune-hunting, and very much on his guard against people of a lower social order."

In describing Darcy, I am obliged to hedge—to report primarily what he "seems" to be. The difficulty arises from the point of view from which he is seen and judged; it does not, I think, seriously confuse or undermine my argument.

20 Samuel Kliger, "*Pride and Prejudice* in the Eighteenth-Century Mode," *University of Toronto Quarterly*, XVI (July 1947), 357–370.

21 See R. W. Chapman, *Jane Austen, A Critical Bibliography*, 2d ed. (Oxford, 1955), p. 53, and Frederick Martin Link, "The Reputation of Jane Austen in the Twentieth Century with an Annotated Bibliography of Austen Criticism from 1811 to June, 1957," unpubl. diss. (Boston University, 1958), p. 241.

22 This illustration is mine, not Kliger's.

23 Kliger, in *Univ. of Toronto Quarterly*, XVI, 364–365.

24 Ibid., p. 367.

25 Mark Schorer, "Pride Unprejudiced," *The Kenyon Review*, XVIII (Winter, 1956), 80.

26 Schorer, in *Kenyon Review*, XVIII, 87. Much of Schorer's article is devoted to the same kind of study of parallels and counterparts as that which I am attempting in these pages, though his observations are frequently quite different from mine.

27 One attempt to do just this is Mordecai Marcus, "A Major Thematic Pattern in *Pride and Prejudice*," *Nineteenth-Century Fiction*, XVI (December 1961), 274–279.

28 See Margaret Kennedy, *Jane Austen* (London, 1950), p. 67.

29 R. W. Chapman's appendix on "Improvements," on pp. 556–560 of the volume devoted to *Mansfield Park*, provides some historical background for the numerous discussions of architecture, landscaping, and decorating in Jane Austen's novels. See also Charles Murrah, "Jane Austen's Treatment of Background and Setting," unpubl. diss. (Harvard University, 1955).

30 See Greene, *PMLA*, LXVII, 1017–31.

31 For a discussion of Jane Austen's rhetorical repertoire, see Andrew H. Wright, *Jane Austen's Novels, A Study in Structure*, 2d ed. (London, 1961), pp. 36–82. I make use in this paragraph of several of Wright's terms.

32 See, among several other studies touching upon Jane Austen's economic preoccupations, Leonard Woolf, "The Economic Determination of Jane Austen," *New Statesman and Nation*, XXIV (July 17, 1942), 39–41, and

David Daiches, "Jane Austen, Karl Marx, and the Aristocratic Dance," *American Scholar*, xvii (Summer, 1948), 289–296.

33 See Mark Schorer, "Fiction and the 'Analogical Matrix,'" reprinted in *Critiques and Essays on Modern Fiction*, ed. John W. Aldridge (New York, 1952), pp. 83–98, and Dorothy Van Ghent, *The English Novel*, pp. 99–103.

34 Margaret Kennedy, *Jane Austen*, p. 70.

35 A valuable attempt to see *Mansfield Park* through its houses is Charles Murrah, "The Background of *Mansfield Park*," *From Jane Austen to Joseph Conrad*, ed. Robert C. Rathbun and Martin Steinmann, Jr. (Minneapolis, 1958), pp. 23–34. My analysis agrees with Murrah's at several points, but emphasizes different values of Mansfield Park.

36 Erich Auerbach, "La Cour et la Ville," *Scenes from the Drama of European Literature*, trans. Ralph Manheim (New York, 1959), pp. 164–165.

37 Lionel Trilling, *The Opposing Self*, p. 218. Trilling goes on to develop his idea of acting as an "assumption of roles" and thus as the denial of the real and integral self. For Trilling, *Mansfield Park* represents Jane Austen's temporary rejection of Romantic multiplicity. I would alter his terms and say that the novel is more nearly a rejection of modernity, and thus, paradoxically, wholly Romantic; see pp. 152–153 above.

Though I announced at the outset my intention wherever possible to avoid reference to earlier book-length studies of Jane Austen, the analysis of the Mansfield theatricals in A. Walton Litz's *Jane Austen, A Study of Her Artistic Development* (New York, 1965), pp. 122 ff., frequently supports my own observations.

38 David Lodge, "A Question of Judgment: The Theatricals at Mansfield Park," *Nineteenth-Century Fiction*, xvii (December 1962), 278–279.

39 Francis Fergusson, *The Idea of a Theater* (Princeton, 1949), p. 122.

40 See Erich Auerbach, *Mimesis*, pp. 434–453, and Arnold Hauser, *The Social History of Art*, trans. Stanley Godman, iii (New York, 1958), 84–99.

41 *Jane Austen's Letters to Her Sister Cassandra and Others*, ed. R. W. Chapman, 2d ed. (London, 1952), p. 410. Hereafter cited as *Letters*.

42 Margaret Kennedy, *Jane Austen*, pp. 13–14.

43 Joseph M. Duffy, Jr., "Moral Integrity and Moral Anarchy in *Mansfield Park*," *ELH*, xxiii (March 1956), 73. Though I disagree with it at several points, Duffy's article seems to me second only to Trilling's as a guide through the difficulties of the novel.

Another important study that I have not had occasion to cite is Thomas R. Edwards' "The Difficult Beauty of *Mansfield Park*," *Nineteenth-Century Fiction*, xx (June 1965), 51–67. Though Edwards' urbane essay is always stimulating, I take serious exception to his view —occasionally put forth in earlier criticism—that Jane Austen's view of Fanny is essentially ironic. Edwards affirms that Fanny is not "sentimentally exempted from Jane Austen's ironic scrutiny, as her fondness for quoting Scott warns us," backing up his assertion with a reference to Mary Lascelles to the effect that "Jane Austen is usually amused by people who quote familiar literature." But the quotations from Scott are perhaps not all that "familiar," and the "usually" leaves much room for exceptions from what seems to me anyway a doubtful rule. That Jane Austen "keeps her distance" from Fanny, as Edwards points out, does not necessarily betoken an attitude of "ironic scrutiny," and the rhetoric used to describe Fanny's amusement over Tom's "rude remark about Dr. Grant" and her later "abysmal self-pity for having excluded herself from the play" does not seem to me to reveal the irony that Edwards discerns. Edwards' interpretation renders *Mansfield Park* much more palatable to modern audiences than does mine, but I am unable to accept it.

44 The amount of alteration that would have gone into the novel had Jane Austen lived can only be a matter of conjecture, but the revision of the final chapters suggest that it might well have been considerable.

45 Virginia Woolf, *The Common Reader* (New York, 1925), pp. 203–204.

46 The expedition to Box Hill cannot be considered an instance of leaving home, since it involves a journey of a mere seven miles and introduces Emma to no new characters.

47 For a full summary of the many attempts to find the sources for Jane Austen's imaginary locales, see Murrah, "Jane Austen's Treatment of Background and Setting," pp. 52 ff. See also George R. Bramer, "The Setting in *Emma*," *College English*, xxii (December 1960), 150–156.

48 Emma's sudden moment of awareness of her own rank is one of the most revealing in the novel. Specific questions of rank are avoided in the opening pages, and it is not until Mr. Elton's daring proposal that Emma's own position bursts upon her: "Perhaps it was not fair to expect him to feel how very much he was her inferior in talent, and all the elegancies of mind. The very want of such equality might prevent his perception of it; but he must know that in fortune and consequence she was greatly his superior. He must know that the Woodhouses had been settled for several generations at Hartfield, the younger branch of a very ancient family—and that the Eltons were nobody. The landed property of Hartfield certainly was inconsiderable, being but a sort of notch in the Donwell Abbey estate, to which all the rest of Highbury belonged; but their fortune, from other sources, was such as to make them scarcely secondary to Donwell Abbey itself, in every other kind of consequence; and the Woodhouses had long held a high place in the consideration of the neighbourhood which Mr. Elton had first entered not two years ago, to make his way as he could, without any alliances but in trade, or any thing to recommend him to notice but his situation and his civility" (136). In this paragraph we have, first of all, the most sophisticated and subtle use of Jamesian point of view in all Jane Austen's work: the details of Emma's situation are not mentioned until they assume a dramatic importance for the "central intelligence" of the tale. And we also see in this scene the importance of rank in Highbury: Emma's supremacy is not—or should not be—a factor in the story until a proposal of marriage dares to challenge it.

49 Susanne Howe, *Wilhelm Meister and His English Kinsmen* (New York, 1930), p. 1.

50 G. Armour Craig, "Jane Austen's *Emma*: The Truths and Disguises of Human Disclosure," *In Defense of Reading*, ed. Reuben A. Brower and Richard Poirier (New York, 1962), p. 239.

51 Lionel Trilling, Introduction to Riverside edition of *Emma* (Boston, 1957), p. xxii.

52 Mark Schorer, "The Humiliation of Emma Woodhouse," *Literary Review*, II (Summer, 1959), 557, deals in some detail with the many ironic parallels between Emma and Mrs. Elton.

53 Compare this passage from Jane Austen's juvenile burlesque called *Love and Freindship:* "My Father was a native of Ireland and an inhabitant of Wales; my Mother was the natural Daughter of a Scotch Peer by an italian Opera-girl—I was born in Spain and received my Education at a Convent in France. When I had reached my eighteenth Year I was recalled by my Parents to my paternal roof in Wales. Our mansion was situated in one of the most romantic parts of the Vale of Uske" (77).

54 Craig in *In Defense of Reading*, p. 238. I have suppressed one misleading sentence: "Enscombe," says Craig, "the seat of the proud Churchill family, is in a northern county where feudal haughtiness still flourishes." Here and elsewhere—as when he speaks on p. 242 of the "mysterious ladder" of rank "that reaches from the not-being of Mr. Woodhouse's coachman to the pure essence of Mrs. Churchill"—Craig appears to labor under the delusion that Frank's guardian aunt is comparable to a Darcy in birth as well as in condescension. But Mrs. Churchill is, in fact, a spiritual cousin to Mrs. Elton. Weston says of her (ironically enough, to Elton himself) that "her pride is arrogance and insolence! And what inclines one less to bear, she has no fair pretence of family or blood. She was nobody when he married her, barely the daughter of a gentleman; but ever since her being turned into a Churchill she has out-Churchill'd them all in high and mighty claims: but in herself, I assure you, she is an upstart" (310).

55 Lionel Trilling, Introduction to *Emma*, pp. xxii and xviii. The quotation is from Schiller.

56 Ibid., p. xxi.

57 Craig in *In Defense of Reading*, p. 238. As Craig's sentences suggest, Jane Austen comes closer in *Emma* than anywhere else to that Stendhalian sense of historical change that I discuss above, pp. 103–105.

58 The treatment of Robert Martin may be relevant here. Trilling (Introduction to *Emma*, pp. xii–xiii) quotes Tocqueville on the meaning of the word "gentleman" in England, and concludes that, in her contempt for the yeomanry, Emma "makes a truly serious mistake, a mistake of nothing less than national import"; she is denying the long-established English tradition of "relatively easy recruitment to the class of gentlemen," the generous process by which Martin is already called (by Mr. Knightley) a "gentleman farmer," and is clearly "on his way to being a gentleman pure and simple." But perhaps Jane Austen felt—as Washington Irving, for example, felt in Jane Austen's time—that by the first decade of the nineteenth century the old English rural ways were no longer what they had been, "the larger estates having, in late years of distress, absorbed the smaller, and, in some parts of the country, almost annihilated the small race of sturdy farmers." (The observations from *The Sketchbook* most directly applicable to Jane Austen's work are excerpted in Bradford A. Booth's edition of *Pride and Prejudice* [New

York and Burlingame, 1963], pp. 176–179.) If Jane Austen shared
Irving's impression of English social history—an impression corroborated
by such twentieth-century studies as A. S. Turberville's *English Men
and Manners in the Eighteenth Century* (New York, 1957), pp. 136–
141—then her ideal of the gentlemanly yeomanry, as personified by
Robert Martin, is also an ideal of things already past.

59 Booth, in *The Rhetoric of Fiction* (Chicago, 1961), pp. 250–253, was,
I believe, the first to develop the idea that "In *Emma* there are many
breaks in the point of view, because Emma's beclouded mind cannot
do the whole job. In *Persuasion*, where the heroine's viewpoint is faulty
only in her ignorance of Captain Wentworth's love, there are very few."
Though I argue below that the vision of Jane Austen and the reader is
much wider than that of Anne, and that our sympathies and antipathies
are more freely bestowed than hers, Booth is correct in claiming that
in *Persuasion* Jane Austen came closer than ever before to consistent
approximation of the technique later advocated by Henry James.

60 Lionel Trilling, Introduction to *Emma*, p. xxiii.

61 See R. W. Chapman's appendix on the "Chronology of *Persuasion*"
(280–282), which establishes September 14 as the date of the Elliots'
departure from Kellynch and late February as the date of Anne's reconciliation with Wentworth.

62 In *Emma* we are reminded of the early death of Emma's mother, and
one important strand of the plot hinges upon the death offstage of Mrs.
Churchill. We are also made aware of the early death of the first Mrs.
Weston, and even more sadly aware of the tragic history of Jane Fairfax'
parents (163). However, even though *Emma* is similar to *Persuasion*
in this way, Jane Austen never allows the many deaths she introduces
to affect the tone of the novel.

63 Chapman asserts that, in light of other chronological details of the novel,
the year should in fact be 1801. Appendix on the "Chronology of *Persuasion*," p. 280.

64 Joseph M. Duffy, "Structure and Idea in Jane Austen's *Persuasion*,"
Nineteenth-Century Fiction, VIII (March 1954), 272–289, notes on p.
274 that "the book's toll of dead and of victims of illness and accident
would provide a mournful set of statistics on human mortality." In this
article—the best single study of *Persuasion*—Duffy makes several of
the same points as I do in this chapter, but marshals his evidence toward
rather different conclusions.

65 Wayne C. Booth, *The Rhetoric of Fiction*, p. 253.

66 Some critics have argued that *Sanditon* is less the draft of a novel than
a diversion concocted for the pleasure of Jane Austen's intimates. But
the new breadth and depth of its concerns suggests goals higher than
those of most casual amusements: see Southam, whose discussion of
Sanditon in *Jane Austen's Literary Manuscripts*, pp. 100–135, is at once
the most complete and the most persuasive yet published. Exploring the
relevance of the resort setting much more fully than I have chosen to
do in this study, Southam emphasizes the "extent" to which "Jane
Austen's fictional scene was widening to include the day-to-day concerns
of people outside the conventional middle-class family groups, until now
the staple population of her works"; hence, inevitably, the disappearance

of the metaphor of rank as she had used it up to this point in her writing.

67 C. S. Lewis, "A Note on Jane Austen," *Essays in Criticism,* IV (October 1954), 364. It is not within my province to explore the meaning that "the great abstract nouns" might have held for Johnson, but it does seem to me curious that, when Lewis himself mentions Johnson's "countless moods," he seems to ignore the possibility that these moods had their roots in intellectual as well as psychological disturbances.

INDEX